Kinship Care
Improving Practice Through Research

*Edited by James P. Gleeson
and Creasie Finney Hairston*

CWLA Press
Washington, DC

CWLA Press is an imprint of the Child Welfare League of America. The Child Welfare League of America (CWLA), the nation's oldest and largest membership-based child welfare organization, is committed to engaging all Americans in promoting the well-being of children and protecting every child from harm.

CHILD WELFARE LEAGUE OF AMERICA, INC.
440 First Street, NW, Third Floor, Washington, DC 20001-2085
E-mail: books@cwla.org

CURRENT PRINTING (last digit)
10 9 8 7 6 5 4 3 2 1

Cover design by Sarah Hoctor

Printed in the United States of America

ISBN # 0–87868–721–1

Library of Congress Cataloging-in-Publication Data
Kinship care research : improving practice through research / edited by James P. Gleeson and Creasie Finney Hairston.
    p.   cm.
   Includes bibliographical reference.
   ISBN 0-87868-721-1 (alk. paper)
   1. Kinship care--United States.   2. Foster home care--United States.   3. Foster children--Services for--United States.   4. Foster children--United States--Family relationships.   I. Gleeson, James Patrick.   II. Hairston, Creasie Finney.
HV881.K55   1999   99-34781
362.73'3'0973--dc21   CIP

This book is dedicated to all our kin, especially:

to Linda, my life partner and my greatest source of strength;
to Tara and Kristen, our children, our pride, our hope;
and to my mother, Therese, whose love, strength, and example
as a parent and as a person are always with me.
—JPG

and

to my son and daughter, Richard and Cynthia,
and to those in my family who have taken care of me,
my children, and all our other kin.
—CFH

Contents

Preface ix

**Part I. Building Knowledge About Kinship Care
as a Child Welfare Service** 1

1. Kinship Care as a Child Welfare Service:
    What Do We Really Know? *James P. Gleeson* 3

Part II. Facilitating Permanence 35

2. Defining Best Practice in Kinship Care Through
    Research and Demonstration *Faith Johnson Bonecutter* 37

3. Who Decides? Predicting Caseworkers' Adoption and
    Guardianship Discussions with Kinship Caregivers
    James P. Gleeson 61

4. Adoption and Subsidized Guardianship as Permanency
    Options in Kinship Foster Care: Barriers and Facilitating
    Conditions *Sally J. Mason & James P. Gleeson* 85

Part III. Children, Mothers, and Fathers 115

5. The Well-Being of Children in Kinship Foster Care
    Sandra J. Altshuler 117

6. Comparing Mothers of Children in Kinship Foster Care:
    Reunification vs. Remaining in Care *Marian S. Harris* 145

7. Casework Practice with Fathers of Children in
    Kinship Foster Care *John M. O'Donnell* 167

8. Kinship Care When Parents Are Incarcerated
    Creasie Finney Hairston 189

Part IV. Kinship Caregivers 213

9. Child-Rearing Perspectives of Grandparent Caregivers
    Olga Osby 215

10. The Effect of Caregiver Preparation and Sense of Control
    on Adaptation of Kinship Caregivers *Donna D. Petras* 233

11. Caregiver Burden in Kinship Foster Care
    Rocco A. Cimmarusti 257

Part V. Conclusion **279**

12. Future Directions for Research on Kinship Care
    James P. Gleeson & Creasie Finney Hairston 281

About the Editors 315

About the Contributors 317

List of Tables

Table 2-1. Characteristics of Children 44

Table 2-2. Characteristics of Kinship Caregivers and
Kinship Homes 45

Table 2-3. Characteristics of Biological Mothers 46

Table 2-4. Permanency Planning 48

Table 2-5. Contributors to the Most Recent Service Plan 48

Table 2-6. Practice Principles and Methods 50

Table 3-1. Zero-Order Correlations Between All Independent
and Dependent Variables 75

Table 3-2. Logistic Regression Analysis of Predictors of Whether
Adoption of the Child Was Discussed with the Kinship
Caregiver 77

Table 3-3. Logistic Regression Analysis of Predictors of
Whether Private Guardianship Was Discussed with
the Kinship Caregiver 78

Table 5-1. Child Well-Being 121

Table 5-2. Clusters of Independent Variables in
Quantitative Analyses 122

Table 5-3. Means, Standard Deviations, and Zero-Order
Correlation Matrix of Well-Being and Child's
Individual Case History 125

Table 5-4. Means, Standard Deviations, and Zero-Order
Correlation Matrix of Well-Being and Mother's
Life Situation 126

Table 5-5. Means, Standard Deviations, and Zero-Order
Correlation Matrix of Well-Being and Caregiver's
Life Situation 127

Table 5-6. Means, Standard Deviations, and Zero-Order
Correlation Matrix of Well-Being and Child's Level
of Input 128

Table 5-7. Summary of Regression Analyses for Variables Explaining the Well-Being of Children in Kinship Foster Care 128

Table 6-1. Demographic Comparisons of Mothers Whose Children Returned Home and Mothers Whose Children Remain in Kinship Foster Care 153

Table 6-2. Wilcoxon-Mann-Whitney Rank Sum Test for Levels of Object Representations of Mother and Child for Mothers Whose Children Returned Home and Mothers Whose Children Remain in Kinship Foster Care 158

Table 6-3. Comparison of Severity Ratings for Addiction Severity Index Problem Areas for Mothers Whose Children Returned Home and Mothers Whose Children Remain in Kinship Foster Care 158

Table 6-4. Comparison of Composite Scores for Addiction Severity Index Problem Areas for Mothers Whose Children Returned Home and Mothers Whose Children Remain in Kinship Foster Care 159

Table 7-1. Characteristics of Fathers 172

Table 7-2. Frequency of Caseworker Contact with Fathers During Six Months Preceeding Interview 174

Table 7-3. Fathers' Involvement in Service Planning and Service Delivery 176

Table 7-4. Mean Number of Contacts Caseworkers Had with the Father and Service Involvement of the Father by Race of the Caseworker 178

Table 7-5. Zero-Order Correlations Between Caseworker Experience and Number of Contacts with Father, Service Involvement of Father, in the Last Six Months 178

Table 7-6. Mean Number of Contacts Caseworkers Had with the Father and Service Involvement of the Father by Placement of the Child with Maternal or Paternal Relatives 179

Table 7-7. Comparison of Casework Practice with Mothers and Fathers 181

Table 10-1. Characteristics of Kinship Caregivers 238

Table 10-2. Zero-Order Correlations Between Variables Included in the Analysis 244

Table 10-3. Hierarchical Multiple Regression Predicting
    Caregiver Depression 245
Table 10-4. Hierarchical Multiple Regression Predicting
    Caregiver Satisfaction 246
Table 11-1. Caregiver Characteristics 264
Table 11-2. Mean, Median, Range, and Standard Deviation
    for Caregiver Burden, Social Support, and Emotional
    Distress Measures 265
Table 11-3. Zero-Order Correlations Between Descriptive,
    Independent, and Dependent Variables 266

Preface

This book adds to the knowledge base on relatives caring for children who have been taken into the custody of the child welfare system—kinship care. It grows out of several years of research on kinship care that has been conducted in connection with the Jane Addams College of Social Work at the University of Illinois at Chicago. In September of 1997, the university held a symposium that featured a number of these studies. The symposium brought together child welfare practitioners and researchers to discuss the results of these studies and implications for practice, policy, and future research. Eight of the chapters in this book are enhanced versions of the papers presented at the symposium.

The book is divided into five parts. Part I comprises one chapter, authored by James Gleeson, that summarizes the current state of knowledge on kinship care, identifies what is known about kinship care as a child welfare service, and places the kinship care research presented in this volume in the context of the body of research that exists. Part II contains three chapters that focus on permanency planning for children in kinship care. The first of these, Chapter 2, by Faith Johnson Bonecutter, describes the development of a model of practice that is designed to facilitate permanency for children in kinship foster care, as well as four principles of best practice and the processes by which those principles were identified. In Chapter 3, James Gleeson examines factors that predict whether caseworkers discuss adoption or guardianship with kinship caregivers. The final chapter in this section, written by Sally Mason and James Gleeson, summarizes a study conducted at the request of the Illinois Department of Children and Family Services to examine permanency planning decisionmaking. Results of the study revealed specific barriers to adoption and subsidized guardianship for children in kinship care, including caseworker attitudes and preferences, characteristics of the families and children served, and characteristics of the child welfare and larger social service systems.

Part III contains four chapters and focuses on children in kinship care and their parents. Sandra Altshuler's study, reported in Chapter 5, examines the experience of children in kinship care. The study examined the well-being of children in kinship foster care through a secondary analysis of data collected during case-specific interviews with caseworkers and in-depth interviews with six children living in kinship foster care. In Chapter 6, Marian Harris summarizes a study that compared ten mothers whose children had been reunified with them after kinship care placements to ten mothers whose children remained in kinship care. Comparisons looked at measures of object relations, addiction severity, and extended family support. Qualitative data were also collected through observation and open-ended questions. Chapter 7, by John O'Donnell, examines casework practice with fathers of children in kinship care. Using data from interviews with caseworkers in two child welfare agencies, this chapter describes the extent to which fathers participated in services on behalf of their children placed in kinship foster homes because of abuse, neglect, or dependency. In Chapter 8, Creasie Finney Hairston summarizes research on kinship care when parents are incarcerated and discusses the need for further research in this area. The chapter incorporates findings of three research projects conducted by the author and the results of forums on families and the correctional system convened by the Jane Addams Center for Social Policy and Research.

Part IV contains three chapters that focus on kinship caregivers of children in the custody of the child welfare system. Chapter 9, by Olga Osby, reports the results of in-depth qualitative interviews with ten grandparent caregivers of children in the custody of the child welfare system. Results of these interviews provide a description of the perceptions of these caregivers about the experience of kinship caregiving, the reasons that they were providing this care, the systems of support that surrounded them, experiences interacting with the child welfare system, and attitudes about child rearing. In Chapter 10, Donna Petras describes a study of the relationship between caregiver preparation, sense of control, and adaptation of kinship caregivers. Rocco Cimmarusti's research, reported in Chapter 11, examines relationships between caregiver burden, social support, and emotional distress in kinship foster care. Dr. Petras and Dr. Cimmarusti incorporated structured measures of the key variables and quantitative analysis with observations and the responses of caregivers to open-ended questions.

Part V is the concluding section of the book, and it contains one chapter. This final chapter, co-authored by James Gleeson and Creasie Finney Hairston, summarizes the contributions of kinship care research presented in this volume and proposes a detailed agenda for future research in kinship care.

While all of the research reported in this volume was conducted in Chicago, the findings of these projects are placed in national perspective in the first and last chapters. Clearly, the policy environments that are unique to each state and locality influence the delivery of any child welfare service, yet there are broad policy and practice questions that cut across geographic and political boundaries. We hope that this book will be useful to child welfare caseworkers, supervisors, administrators, policymakers, and researchers. Ultimately, we hope that it benefits children and families by contributing to improved practice and enlightened policies to support this practice.

JPG & CFH
1999

Part I
Building Knowledge About Kinship Care as a Child Welfare Service

1

Kinship Care as a Child Welfare Service: What Do We Really Know?

James P. Gleeson

Traditionally, kinship care has been an informal service that family members provide for each other, without the involvement of the child welfare system [Child Welfare League of America 1994; Hegar & Scannapieco 1995; Hill 1972, 1977, 1997; Martin & Martin 1978; Scannapieco & Jackson 1996; Stack 1974; Timberlake & Chipungu 1992]. Informal kinship care has been provided on a temporary basis when parents are unable to care for children for a period of time. When parents have died or become permanently incapacitated, kin have informally adopted children, making a commitment to rear them to adulthood without the legal authority provided by formal adoption. In some cases grandparents, aunts, and uncles, or other kin share parenting responsibilities until a teen parent matures and is able to assume the major responsibility for child rearing. Informal kinship care is still overwhelmingly the most common type of kinship care.

In recent years, kinship care has also become a part of the child welfare system's array of services. Kinship care has been considered a diversion from the child welfare system (to informal kinship care), a type of family preservation or home-based service, or a type of foster care [Gleeson & Craig 1994]. Kinship foster care, also known as "formal kinship care," has attracted recent attention because the use of this service has grown so dramatically and because it is costly to the child welfare system and to tax payers. Only since the mid 1980s, has the number of children in state custody and living with relatives increased to become a sizable proportion

3

of the foster care caseload, particularly in major urban centers [Gleeson & Craig 1994; Wulczyn et al. 1997; Kusserow 1992a, 1992b]. Approximately one-third of all children in foster care in the United States are living with relatives [Harden, Clark, & Maguire 1997]. Forty to 52% of the children on child welfare systems' foster care caseloads in California, Illinois, and New York are in kinship foster care and at one time 57% of the children in out-of-home care in Illinois were living with kin [IDCFS 1995; Testa 1995, 1997; Wulczyn et al. 1997].

The use of kinship care as a child welfare service escalated without the benefit of guidance from the research and scholarly literature. It was not until the early 1990s that kinship foster care began to appear as a focus of professional journals [Thornton 1991]. In 1992, the U. S. Children's Bureau funded research and demonstration projects that focused on permanency for children in kinship care, and in 1995 the same organization began to fund training grants that focused on kinship foster care. Numerous articles and book chapters that focus on different dimensions of kinship care have now been published. In any study of foster care, it is now common practice to examine the similarities and differences between kinship foster care and nonrelated foster care. Even with this proliferation of research and writing, it is not clear what we really know about kinship care as a child welfare service.

Research on kinship care can be organized by seven categories: (1) demographics and caseload growth, (2) policy studies and debates, (3) caseload dynamics and pathways to permanence, (4) definitions and implementation of best practice, (5) child safety and well-being, (6) parents of children in kinship foster care, and (7) caregiving experiences and consequences. This chapter summarizes the professional literature in each of these areas and identifies the gaps in our knowledge that are addressed by studies reported in the remainder of this book.

Demographics and Caseload Growth

The best source of data describing national patterns and trends in children's living arrangements and households is the Current Population Survey (CPS), a large and ongoing national sample of the United States population [Harden et al. 1997]. An analysis of 12 years of CPS data revealed that the prevalence of kinship care has increased nationally to approximately 2.15 million children who lived with relatives without a parent present in 1994, slightly more than 3% of the child population [Harden et al. 1997]. It is estimated that 150,000 of these children were in the custody of the child welfare system and considered to be in formal kinship care placements. In recent years the prevalence of informal and formal kinship care has increased among African American and Latino families. African American children are more likely than other ethnic groups to live in kinship care and the gap between African Americans and all other ethnic groups widened from 1983 to 1993. While informal kinship care is more prevalent in the South and for older children (ages 6 to 17 years) living outside of metropolitan areas, formal kinship care is most common for younger children in the major urban areas of three states: New York, Illinois, and California.

Approximately two-thirds of formal and informal kinship caregivers are the children's grandparents, with great-grandparents, aunts and uncles, and older siblings also well represented [Harden et al. 1997; Berrick, Barth, & Needell 1994]. The CPS data reveal that approximately 50% of all kinship caregivers are currently unmarried. A survey of formal kinship caregivers in California revealed similar results, with 52% of the formal kinship caregivers in that sample being unmarried, compared to 24% of the nonrelated foster parents. Studies in New York City [Thornton 1991], Chicago [Gleeson et al. 1997], and Baltimore [Dubowitz et al. 1994] describe samples of formal kinship caregivers, 60% to 70% of whom were single heads of household.

Of greatest concern to policymakers has been the fact that the growth in both informal and formal kinship care has occurred primarily among families in economically disadvantaged communities, many of whom require some type of government support. Both formal and informal kinship caregiving families have substantially lower average incomes and are more likely to be receiving government assistance through SSI, school lunch programs, public housing, food stamps, social security, or disability, than families headed by parents [Harden et al. 1997]. Poverty rates have grown faster for children living with relatives compared to children living with their parents. The percentage of children living with relatives with no earned income increased from 23.8% in 1983-85 to 26.3% in 1992-94. During the same time period, the percentage of children in parent-headed families with no income increased only slightly, from 8.9% to 9.2%. Also during this time period, AFDC participation rates increased from 21.1% to 27% for kinship caregiving families, but only slightly for parent-headed families.

Several studies of the demographics of kinship foster care have revealed similar descriptions of kin caring for children in state custody [Berrick et al. 1994; Harden et al. 1997; Thornton 1991; Testa 1997]. The majority of persons involved in kinship foster care are children and families of color and the use of kinship care as a child welfare service has been predominantly in major urban areas. Compared to nonrelated foster parents, kinship caregivers are more likely to be single parents, live in publicly subsidized housing, work outside of the home, have lower incomes, and more health problems. Similar results are found in comparisons between relative and nonrelative adoptive families [Magruder 1994].

Policy Studies and Debates

Studies of states' policies on the use of kinship care as a child welfare service have revealed a lack of clarity regarding purpose and goals, considerable variation across states, and value conflicts regarding policies guiding placement of children with their relatives [Gleeson & Craig 1994; Hornby et al. 1995, 1996; Kusserow 1992a, 1992b]. While most states' policies indicate a preference for placing children with relatives, in some states placement with relatives is primarily a diversion from the child welfare system to informal kinship care. In other states such as Maryland, placement of children in state custody with relatives is viewed as a type of home-based service intended to keep families together. In most states, however, when a child who has been taken into state custody is placed with relatives, this is considered a type of foster care placement.

Financial support for relatives who provide care for children varies according to the legal formality of the caregiving arrangement. When relatives provide informal kinship care, or when they care for children in state custody but do so without pursuing licensure or approval as a foster parent, they are, in most cases, eligible to receive financial support for the care of the child through AFDC/TANF or SSI [Gleeson & Craig 1994]. When relatives are licensed or approved as foster parents, they are generally eligible to receive foster care board payments that are three to five times higher than the AFDC child-only rate in most states, and the disparity becomes greater as the number of children in care increases [IDCFS 1995; Kusserow 1992a; Testa 1993]. In 1995, Illinois put in place a third type of reimbursement for relatives who are not licensed as foster parents, but who provide care for children who are in the custody of the child welfare system. These families receive a financial subsidy at the level of the state standard of need, an amount that is greater than the AFDC/TANF payment but substantially lower than the foster care payment.

With licensure or approval as foster parents, and higher rates of reimbursement for families, the child welfare system's regulation and control of the placement increases [Hornby et al. 1995, 1996]. Some states, like New York, and at one time Illinois, made it easier for relatives to become licensed or approved as foster parents through development of approval standards specific to relatives, waiver of foster care licensing standards, and/or expedited approval processes [Gleeson 1996; Gleeson & Craig 1994; Hornby et al. 1995, 1996; Kusserow 1992a, 1992b]. These regulatory standards specific to relatives served the dual purpose of making kinship care placements easier and enabling the child welfare agency to claim federal matching funds for the placement.

While the significant growth in the numbers of kinship care placements has been well-documented, the reasons for this growth are not clear. There are at least two points of view on the role that public policies have played in the growth of kinship foster care. Testa's [1993, 1995, 1997] analysis of Illinois' policies suggests that growth of the child welfare caseload and the increased use of kinship foster care in Illinois were primarily due to the financial incentive of foster care subsidies that were three to five times higher than AFDC/TANF, and child welfare policies that were shaped by lawsuits and states' interpretations of court decisions and consent decrees. He cites Illinois' response to the *Miller v. Youakim* [1979] Supreme Court decision that required states to provide the same foster care subsidy for relatives and nonrelatives caring for children in state custody, if the placement was in compliance with all criteria for federal reimbursement. Illinois responded by providing the full foster care payment to relatives as soon as they began to care for children in the custody of the child welfare system even when federal reimbursement criteria were not met. In addition, Illinois' establishment of relatives as the first placement preference, the state's adoption of home of relative approval standards that were less stringent than foster home licensing standards, and an Illinois Appellate Court decision [*Reid v. Suter*, 1992] that discouraged diversion of kinship care cases through private guardianship awarded to relatives in probate court all encouraged the state agency to take into custody children who had been abandoned by parents and left in the care of relatives.

Gleeson's analysis concludes, on the other hand, that changes in kinship care policies in Illinois were a result of the growing demand for child welfare services rather than the cause of this growth [Gleeson 1996, 1999]. The increased demand for child welfare services, combined with a serious shortage of licensed, nonrelative foster homes, required implementation of policies that quickly created more placement resources for the children coming to the attention of the child welfare system. Relative placements provided that resource. The fact that the greatest demand for services came from seven of the most economically disadvantaged African American communities in Chicago, where rates of dire poverty, single-parent households, and drug abuse were the highest suggests that the demand for child welfare services was driven by severe needs that were not adequately addressed outside of the child welfare system.

The kinship care policy debate is largely about distinguishing the responsibilities of family and government when children come to the attention of the child welfare system. Testa [1992, 1993, 1995, 1997] argues that a substantial portion of the children entering formal kinship care might well have been cared for adequately through informal kinship care if the child welfare system had not gotten involved. He posits that the growth of kinship foster care represents an unnecessary and inappropriate incorporation of the informal system of care. While it is true that in larger cities, there appears to be an inverse relationship between formal and informal care [Harden et al. 1997], it really is not possible to determine what this relationship means. Do higher rates of formal kinship care and lower rates of informal kinship care represent inappropriate intrusion of government into family life, higher levels of need, or differing levels of societal willingness to meet the needs of the most vulnerable children and families?

It may be that the children who grow up in informal kinship care and their families are different from children and families involved in kinship foster care. Children who end up in kinship foster care may be in greater need of the support of the child welfare system to ensure safety, permanency, and well-being. Harden, Clark, and Maguire's [1997] examination of Illinois data indicates that, compared to children living with relatives in informal kinship care and supported by AFDC, children in formal kinship care were younger, were more likely to live in the Chicago area, and a higher percentage were African American. It is not known if the child, parent, and family functioning differ for those involved in formal and informal kinship care in ways that justify the need for child welfare services in one group but not the other. The research conducted to date has not been helpful in determining the level of need that children and families experience that requires intervention by the child welfare system.

A study of 60 informal kinship caregivers and their families in Philadelphia revealed that these caregivers' demographic characteristics, numbers of children cared for, reasons for providing kinship care, and service needs were similar to those of caregivers involved in formal kinship care [McLean & Thomas 1996]. These caregivers were all participating in a voluntary program providing services to informal kinship caregiving families to help them access legal services and community resources needed to provide care for the child. Since only 20% of the children cared for by these families between December 1992 and August 1995 became part of the child welfare system's caseload, the researchers suggest that providing services to support informal kinship care may reduce the need for child welfare services. However, without a control group, it is not possible to determine what percentage of children may have been taken into the custody of the child welfare system if program services were not available.

Regardless of the role public policies have played in the growth of kinship foster care, it does appear that they can be instrumental in reducing the number of children in state custody and in kinship care in particular. In Illinois, the Home of Relative Reform plan tightened eligibility requirements and provided services to families to divert children from the child welfare system and maintain them in informal kinship care. In addition, just since 1995, Illinois has implemented several policy initiatives designed to reduce the number of children in out-of-home care, including the following:

- redesign of adoption policies to speed the process of termination of parental rights and adoption,

- a juvenile court improvement project designed to eliminate delays and shorten the amount of time to achieve legal permanence,

- the subsidized guardianship IV-E waiver demonstration project designed to test whether providing financial subsidies to caregivers who assume private guardianship of a child at the same level as is provided for subsidized adoption increases the number of children who exit state custody to permanent homes, and

- Performance-based contracting, a managed care approach to shortening the length of time a case is opened, which provides financial incentives to agencies that meet specific targets for closing cases through reunification, adoption, or transfer of guardianship and sanctions to those agencies that do not.

Also, a new permanency initiative changed the state's permanency goals and shortened timelines for case reviews, termination of parental rights, and adoption, consistent with new federal policy directions and requirements of the Adoption and Safe Families Act of 1997.

There has been a marked reduction in the Illinois foster care caseload from 51,105 at the end of fiscal year 1997 to 41,800 as of December 31, 1998 [IDCFS 1999b]. The percentage of children in foster care who were placed with relatives dropped from a high of 57% in 1995 to 51% at the end of 1998. The number of completed adoptions nearly doubled in one year, from 2,229 in 1997 to 4,293 in 1998, with the majority of these adoptions by relatives [IDCFS 1999a]. Also, 744 children exited state custody to private guardianship through the subsidized guardianship waiver demonstration with most of these representing children living with relatives [IDCFS 1998]. In a focus group interview, representatives of the juvenile court and public and private child welfare agencies stated that the caseload reduction and the increased number of adoptions was a result of the combined effect of Illinois policies, which deflected significant numbers of children and families from the child welfare system and focused the efforts of child welfare practitioners and their agencies on closing cases [Gleeson et al. 1999].

Because several policy initiatives were implemented in the same time span in Illinois, it is difficult to determine the contributions that each policy may have made to reducing the child welfare caseload. However, early results of the IV-E waiver demonstration project in Illinois suggest that having access to subsidized guardianship increases the likelihood of achieving a legally permanent outcome by a small but statistically significant amount [IDCFS 1998]. This project uses an experimental design, with random assignment to experimental and control conditions. Cases assigned to the experimental condition are eligible to consider subsidized guardianship if reunification and adoption have been ruled out. Cases assigned to the control condition are not eligible for subsidized guardianship. Initial results of the evaluation of this project indicate that 4.94% more of the children assigned to the experimental condition exited the custody of the child welfare system (through reunification, adoption, or subsidized guardianship) than did children assigned to the control condition.

The initial results of Illinois' efforts to reduce the number of children in state custody and placed with relatives appear to be successful, but this should not be viewed as an indicator of improved child or family well-being.

While the child welfare system's goals of caseload reduction are being achieved, it is too early to tell what impact this has on children and families.

Caseload Dynamics and Pathways to Permanence

Discussions of permanency are rare with reference to informal kinship care. In most cases, children living with kin informally are considered to be with their families and we rarely ask if this is a permanent home. However, when federal and state funds are used to support kinship care as foster care, permanency becomes a public concern. One definition of permanency is life with a family that makes a commitment to raise the child to adulthood. However, permanency has been defined more narrowly in public policy to mean that the child exits the custody of the child welfare system through reunification with a biological parent, adoption, or transfer of legal guardianship from the child welfare system to a relative or other permanent caregiver. Therefore, when we use the term "permanency," what we really mean is that legal responsibility for the child has been transferred from the child welfare system to a family, and, in most cases, the financial burden on the child welfare system and taxpayers has decreased.

Most of what is known about pathways to permanence comes from research that uses administrative data collected in the normal course of child welfare practice and entered into computerized data systems. Research on kinship care, particularly research that depends on administrative data, is limited by the same narrow definition of permanence that is found in public policy. Permanence is most often measured by a change in case status as the child exits custody of the child welfare system through reunification, adoption, or private guardianship. Some studies also examine length of time in placement, number of placements, and reentry to the child welfare system after reunification or disrupted adoption. These case status measures are useful indicators of achievement of the child welfare system's goals that are articulated in federal and state policies but are, at best, incomplete measures of permanence from the perspective of the children and families involved.

Using the narrow definition of permanence, much of the research suggests that placing children with kin reduces their chances of being in a permanent home. Analyses of administrative data indicate that until recently, children in kinship foster care have been less likely to be adopted than children in nonrelated foster care. Children in kinship care remain in state custody longer and return home at a slower rate than children in other substitute care arrangements [Barth et al. 1994; Goerge 1990; Wulczyn & Goerge 1992; Wulczyn et al. 1997]. This longer time in custody is a problem for the child welfare system and tax payers because the longer a case remains open, the more it costs. Many people argue that this is also a problem for children and families because involvement of the child welfare system and the court makes the child's living arrangement appear temporary. Most experts agree that a child's healthy development is supported by the security of a family committed to rearing the child to adulthood and committed to that child's safety and well-being. However, the research indicates that long-term stays in foster care are not necessarily harmful to children. In fact, there are many benefits of long-term foster care for many children, especially if this long-term care is provided in one home with the same family [Altshuler & Gleeson 1999].

Using a broader definition, kinship care looks much more successful in facilitating permanency for children. For example, trends in administrative data indicate that many kinship caregivers maintain a high level of commitment to rearing and ensuring the safety of children in their care [Barth et al. 1994; Goerge 1990; Wulczyn & Goerge 1992; Wulczyn et al. 1997]. Kinship care placements tend to be more stable than placements with nonrelatives. Children placed with relatives tend to have fewer disrupted placements. Also, although children in kinship care return home at a slower rate, they are less likely to reenter the custody of the child welfare system than children who return home after foster care placements with nonrelatives [Berrick et al. 1998; Courtney & Needell 1997]. In addition, recent trends in Illinois and New York suggest that adoption by relatives may be a more likely exit from state custody than once thought [Gleeson et al. 1997; Link 1996; Testa et al. 1996].

Comparisons of relative and nonrelative caregivers in the Casey program and in the Louisiana Department of Social Services provide one possible explanation for the stability of placements in kinship care. Responses to systematic measures suggest that, compared to nonrelated foster parents, kinship caregivers perceive themselves to have higher levels of responsibility for maintaining contact between the children and their biological parents and for helping these children with their social and emotional development, including dealing with feelings of separation and loss [Le Prohn 1994; Pecora, Le Prohn, & Nasuti 1999]. Nonrelatives were more likely to attribute these responsibilities to the child welfare system and relatives were more likely to see these as their responsibilities as family members.

The achievement of permanency through reunification, adoption, or guardianship may be hampered by insufficient services. Research on kinship care practice has consistently revealed that children in kinship care and their caregivers receive fewer services and have less contact with their caseworkers than children in nonrelative foster care [Berrick et al. 1994; Dubowitz et al. 1993; Gebel 1996; Iglehart 1994]. It should not be surprising, then, that children in kinship foster care have been returning home at a slower rate and have been less likely to be adopted than children placed with nonrelatives. The permanency planning projects of the 1970s found that the caseworker's work with family members and the caregiver to facilitate permanency planning decisionmaking was predictive of both reunification and adoption [Emlen et al. 1978; Stein et al. 1978].

Differences in financial subsidies have also been identified as barriers to permanency for children in kinship foster care. The assumption has been that families are reluctant to pursue permanency goals that provide lower levels of financial support than they currently receive to care for the children while they are in the custody of the child welfare system. There is some support for this assumption, since research in California indicates that reunification rates are lower for children in kinship homes that are IV-E eligible and receive the full foster care subsidy than they are for children in kinship homes that are not IV-E eligible [Courtney et al. 1997]. When children are reunified with parents, the parents may be eligible to receive the TANF child-only rate. If the case is not IV-E eligible, there is no difference in the subsidy received by the caregiver and the parent. If the case is IV-E eligible, the family experiences a reduction in the subsidy provided to help them care for the child if the child is reunified with the parent. However, Courtney, Piliavin, and Entner Wright [1997] acknowledge that it may not be family members who are deciding that they cannot support the care of the child at the lower subsidy level. It may be the caseworker. A study contained in this volume examines this issue more closely to determine what factors predict the caseworker's decision to discuss adoption or guardianship with kinship caregivers [Gleeson, Chapter 3].

Two studies of casework practice and decisionmaking that are included in this book identify barriers to permanency planning as well as conditions that facilitate permanence [Bonecutter, Chapter 2; Mason & Gleeson, Chapter 4]. Bonecutter describes barriers to permanence that were identified during a research and demonstration project that developed and tested a model of practice for facilitating permanence for children in kinship foster care. Mason and Gleeson report the results of a qualitative study of caseworker decisionmaking related to the implementation of the subsidized guardianship IV-E waiver demonstration and adoption redesign in Illinois. They identify barriers to permanency planning, as well as conditions that appeared to facilitate permanency planning for children in kinship foster care.

Definitions and Implementation of Best Practice

Concerns have been expressed in the literature about the quality of services received by children in kinship foster care and their families. These concerns relate to the level of service provided, the appropriateness of casework practice models, and the quality of kinship homes. Research that relates to each of these quality concerns will be discussed in this section.

Although a lower level of service to children in kinship foster care has been consistently reported, some kinship caregivers are satisfied with the services they receive from their child welfare caseworkers. A survey of kinship caregivers in California revealed that children in kinship foster care were less likely than children in nonrelative foster care to receive specialized services or special service needs increments in the financial support provided [Berrick et al. 1994]. Results of this study also revealed that caregivers had high levels of satisfaction with caseworkers but desired more frequent contact with them and access to services such as child and family counseling. Wilson and Conroy [1999] report that 76% of 1,100 children randomly selected from children living in out-of-home care in Illinois from 1993 through 1996 revealed that they were "happy" to "very happy" with their caseworkers, but the authors do not describe similarities and differences in ratings by type of placement (nonrelated foster care, kinship foster care, group care). In response to a survey, child welfare caseworkers in California reported that their work with kinship care cases was more time intensive than their work with nonrelated foster care cases [Berrick et al. 1999]. However, these caseworkers reported that they needed more time than they could spend to adequately assess the adequacy and needs of families providing kinship foster care.

Beyond the level of service provided, there is growing consensus that kinship foster care requires a different model of practice than is generally implemented by child welfare caseworkers. While there are common elements in the developing practice models, there have been no rigorous evaluations of the effectiveness or efficiency of these models. The common wisdom is that the model of practice should be tailored to fit extended kinship systems, emphasizing collaboration with extended families and respect for the cultural traditions of the family [Bonecutter & Gleeson 1997a, 1997b; Jackson 1996, 1999; Link 1996; Mills & Usher 1996; Scannapieco & Hegar 1996; Testa et al. 1996; Wilhelmus 1998]. Common components of these models are extended family meetings and mediation. The mediation that is characteristic of these models is not only applied to disputes or disagreements between family members; often the disputes are between the child welfare system and the family. What is being negotiated, in many cases, is an agreement between the child welfare system and the child's extended family regarding the most appropriate permanent living arrangement for the child. Some of these models encourage the use of family group decisionmaking conferences that originated in New Zealand [Ernst 1999; Connolly 1994]. Mills and Usher's [1995, 1996] approach also incorporates a "wraparound" service plan, ensuring that families get access to community-based services to address needs that are identified in family group conferences, and is the only model to report any evaluation of outcomes. They report greater movement toward permanency for the children in their demonstration project who received wraparound services provided by social work students in field units, compared to a randomly selected comparison group of children.

There have been concerns expressed in the professional literature about the quality of care provided by kinship caregivers [Dubowitz et al. 1993; Scannapieco & Hegar 1999]. One of the concerns is related to whether kinship homes should meet licensing standards that govern nonrelated foster care [Scannapieco & Hegar 1999]. Several studies have been funded to assess quality of foster homes, including kinship foster homes, but results are not yet available [Harden et al. 1997; Hatmaker & Pratt 1997; Ryan & Weincek 1997; Wells 1997].

Another concern pertains to the lower level of financial support for many children placed with kin, either because the home is not licensed as a foster home or because the placement is otherwise ineligible for federal matching funds. While some argue that higher reimbursement rates for licensed homes reflect the higher standard of care children receive [Testa 1995], others have asked whether a two-tiered system of care exists, one that provides a considerably higher level of financial support for white children and a lower level of support for African American children [Berrick et al. 1999; Gleeson & Craig 1994; Scannapieco & Hegar 1999]. No studies have yet examined whether and in what way different reimbursement levels affect the safety, permanency, or well-being outcomes for children in kinship care.

A third concern about the quality of kinship homes relates to whether kinship caregivers should attend training that is similar or identical to the training that is required for nonrelated foster parents [Scannapieco & Hegar 1999]. There has been some effort to develop training curricula that are specifically tailored for kinship foster parents [see McFadden 1995]. To date no systematic research has been conducted that examines the impact of caregiver training or support groups on caregiver or family functioning or the achievement of safety, permanency, and well-being for the child.

Whether the focus is the quality of service provided by child welfare caseworkers or the quality of care provided in the kinship home, rigorous evaluation of effectiveness and efficiency is hampered, in many cases, by difficulties in implementing the components of the practice model in daily practice [Gleeson et al. 1995]. Bonecutter [Chapter 2] describes a research and development approach that was used to identify four practice principles in a kinship foster care permanency planning project and to develop a training curriculum for child welfare caseworkers based on these principles. This approach incorporates formative evaluation that monitors implementation of the prescribed practice methods and identifies implementation barriers and facilitating conditions. Bonecutter describes steps that can be taken to

- understand current practice,
- develop an initial definition of the practice principles and methods that are components of best practice,
- train caseworkers in the use of these principles and methods,
- field test and monitor implementation of the principles and methods, and
- refine the practice model based upon the formative evaluation.

Child Safety and Well-Being

The research that has been conducted to date suggests that, on average, kinship care placements may be the safest type of living arrangement for children in the custody of the child welfare system. Several studies have concluded that rates of substantiated child abuse and neglect while in kinship foster care are even lower than rates reported for children in traditional foster care [IDCFS 1995; Zuravin et al. 1993]. While these findings appear to be good news, they should be viewed with caution. These studies rely on reports of alleged abuse or neglect. As reported earlier, the child welfare system's contact with children in kinship care and their families and the specialized services received have been considerably less than that experienced by children in nonrelated foster care. Since child welfare caseworkers and other service providers are common reporters of suspected child maltreatment, it is not surprising that reports are more frequent in nonrelated foster care. Research that systematically examines risk as well as protective factors in kinship care is yet to be conducted.

Several studies have reported high rates of behavioral problems among children and adolescents in kinship foster care. Although their studies did not incorporate a comparison group, Dubowitz and his colleagues report that their findings suggest that the behavioral problems experienced by children and adolescents in kinship care are similar to those reported for children in nonrelative foster care [Dubowitz et al. 1993, 1994; Starr et al. 1999]. One of these studies also found that children in kinship foster care display health problems that are higher than national norms and similar to that reported for foster children and other economically disadvantaged children [Dubowitz et al. 1993, 1994]. Similarly, Berrick, Barth, and Needell [1994] found that kinship caregivers rated children in their care as displaying high rates of behavioral problems, but they noted, however, that these ratings were not as high as ratings completed by nonrelative foster parents for the foster children in their care. Berrick and her colleagues point out that the difference may reflect measurement bias, with related caregivers and nonrelated foster parents interpreting the same behaviors in quite different ways. Iglehart [1994] found that adolescents in kinship care in Los Angeles displayed similar educational and behavioral problems as children in nonrelative foster care, but were less likely to display serious mental health problems, according to their caseworkers. However, since caseworkers had less contact with children in kinship foster care, it is possible that they were less aware of problems displayed by these children than displayed by children in nonrelative foster care.

Since the studies on the well-being of children in kinship foster care that have been conducted to date are cross-sectional, when children in kinship care are described as functioning at higher levels than children in nonrelative foster care, it is not possible to determine whether differences in functioning existed when the children were taken into the custody of the child welfare system, or if living with relatives or experiencing fewer disrupted placements contributes to this higher level of functioning [Iglehart 1994]. Neither is it known if child well-being and family functioning improve, remain the same, or are damaged when a kinship care arrangement becomes legally permanent through adoption or guardianship.

There is some evidence that persons who grew up in kinship foster care function somewhat better as adults than those who spent time in nonrelative foster care. A follow-up study of adults who had lived in licensed foster homes in Baltimore as children revealed that, compared to a matched comparison group who lived with their parents, former foster children appeared to be less self-sufficient, displaying higher rates of homelessness as adults [Benedict et al. 1996; Zuravin et al. 1999]. However, those who spent time in kinship foster care were more self-sufficient than persons who had lived in nonrelative foster care.

Perceptions of children are also important indicators of the effects of kinship care. Wilson and Conroy's [1999] interviews with children in out-of-home care in Illinois revealed that 94% of the children in kinship foster care reported that they "always" felt loved, compared to 82% of children in nonrelative foster care and 46% of children in group care. Ninety-two percent of children in kinship foster care and nonrelative foster care reported that they "always" felt safe, compared to 64% of children in group care. Children's perceptions of being protected and their sense of belonging are important measures of permanence that are being incorporated into a comprehensive evaluation of the Illinois IV-E subsidized guardianship demonstration [Westat n.d.]. These and other measures of child well-being are important indicators that need to be incorporated into evaluations of success in all types of out-of-home care [Altshuler & Gleeson 1999].

Altshuler's [1996, 1998] study, summarized in Chapter 5 of this volume, examined the well-being of children in kinship foster care through a secondary analysis of data collected during a permanency planning research and demonstration project and qualitative interviews with children in kinship foster care. Her study examines whether factors that predict the well-being of children in nonrelative foster care are also relevant to kinship foster care. Altshuler's study also describes children's perspectives on the experience of kinship foster care.

Parents of Children in Kinship Foster Care

Few studies have paid any attention to the mothers of children in kinship foster care. When data about mothers are reported, the study usually focuses on their demographic characteristics and the problems that were reported in case records or in interviews with caseworkers [Gleeson et al. 1995; Gleeson et al. 1997; Scannapieco et al. 1997]. Scannapieco and her colleagues found that mothers of children in kinship foster care were more likely to be African American, married, and had fewer children than mothers of children placed in nonrelative foster care. Benedict and her colleagues reported that drug abuse was more frequently reported for mothers of children in kinship foster care compared to mothers of children in nonrelative foster care who displayed higher rates of health problems.

Gleeson, O'Donnell, and Bonecutter [1997] reported that more than 80% of the mothers of children in kinship foster care in their study were identified by caseworkers as having problems with drug or alcohol use that prevented them from adequately caring for their children, yet only 16% were receiving substance abuse treatment. Other problems that mothers experienced which were so severe that they prevented the mother from caring for their children included lack of adequate housing (30%), criminal behavior (14%), financial problems (11%), mental illness (11%), and mental retardation or developmental disabilities (8%). Caseworkers in this study were able to identify strengths for 61% of the mothers but these strengths were not described with the same specificity as were problems. The most common strengths identified were the mothers' expressions of love for their children (46%) and participation in services (24%).

One study reported in this volume did collect data directly from mothers of children in kinship care, through in-person interviews [Harris 1997;

Chapter 6]. Ten mothers whose children were reunified with them were compared to ten mothers whose children remained in kinship care on measures of substance abuse severity, object relations, and extended family support. This study also compared mothers' descriptions of their problems and strengths, reasons for the child's removal from their care, services they received, and their experience with the child welfare system.

The one study of casework practice with fathers of children in kinship foster care is included in this book [O'Donnell 1995; Chapter 7]. The study examines caseworkers' descriptions of the involvement of fathers in the assessment, case planning, and decisionmaking process. The study also compares caseworkers' involvement with fathers whose children were placed with maternal and paternal relatives.

A growing number of parents of children in the custody of the child welfare system are incarcerated and little attention has been paid to this phenomenon in the professional literature. Hairston [Chapter 8] summarizes research findings and describes research priorities based on a review of the literature on prisoners and families, three empirical studies of parents in prison that she conducted, and forums on families and the correctional system convened by the Jane Addams Center for Social Policy and Research at the Jane Addams College of Social Work, University of Illinois at Chicago.

Caregiving Experiences and Consequences

A few researchers have examined the complexity, diversity, and uniqueness of kinship care arrangements and demands on caregivers [Burton 1992; Davidson 1997; Gleeson et al. 1997; Minkler et al. 1992, 1994]. While some relatives care for one or two children, the number of children and the number of sibling groups in a single home varies considerably. Studies in California and Illinois report that the average number of children in the custody of the child welfare system living in kinship caregivers' homes is between two and four, and 29% to 35% of kin caring for related children also have their own biological children under age 18 living with them [Berrick et al. 1994; Gleeson et al. 1994]. Also, some kin care for related children through formal agreements with the child welfare system at the same time that they are rearing other related children through informal family agreements [Gleeson et al. 1997]. Siblings may be living in different homes, some with other relatives, and some in nonrelative foster care. Ensuring contact between siblings further complicates caregiving responsibilities.

Interviews with grandparents raising grandchildren primarily because of parental substance abuse describe consequences of parenting again [Burton 1992; Minkler et al. 1994, 1992]. Although it is not clear what percentage of caregivers in these studies were involved with the child welfare system and what percentage were providing informal kinship care, these studies do identify benefits and costs of caregiving identified by kinship caregivers themselves. These grandparents report high levels of satisfaction and gratification from parenting their grandchildren and at the same time report social, psychological, physical, and economic costs [Burnette 1997]. Several studies of kinship caregivers report high levels of health problems experienced by these caregivers [Berrick et al. 1994; Minkler et al. 1992] and some speculate that these health problems can often be attributed to caregiver burden [Burton 1992; Minkler et al. 1992]. The burden of caregiving is further complicated by the environment in which caregiving is undertaken. Minkler, Roe, and Price [1992] described the fear caregivers experienced when attempting to rear children in neighborhoods with high levels of violence.

Clinical observations made in therapy sessions with kinship caregivers [Crumbley & Little 1997], as well as interviews with grandparent caregivers [Minkler et al. 1994], indicate that rearing a related child has a stressful impact on members of the caregiver's nuclear and extended family who live in the same home and in other households. When grandparents or other relatives assume primary responsibility for the care of a child, relationships with other family members change. Some studies report that kinship caregivers receive inadequate levels of assistance from families and friends [Burton 1992], while others have found that kinship caregivers report high levels of social support [Minkler et al. 1994]. Even when social support is high, caregivers report that taking on the care of related children resulted in decreased contact with family and friends, interrupted adult relationships, and reduced marital satisfaction.

Some of the stress and strain experienced by kinship caregivers has been attributed to conflict with the child welfare system. Davidson [1997] reports that kinship caregivers expressed anger toward the child welfare system for providing lower levels of funding and service for children placed with relatives compared to those placed with nonrelative foster parents. They expressed frustration with the lack of information provided to them about the child welfare system, the court, and case progress. The nine kinship caregivers interviewed were not licensed as foster parents and most were not willing to pursue licensing, although higher levels of reimbursement would then be available. Some caregivers stated that they saw no reason for the licensing requirement for relatives. Others stated that their home would not meet licensing standards, and yet others said they did not have time to attend the training that was required for foster home licensing. The caregivers in Davidson's [1997] study identified service needs that included respite care to give them a break from rearing the related child, recreational opportunities and daycare for the child, and someone to spend a couple of hours a week with the child. Most of the caregivers in this study reported that the related children moved into their home with little notice in the midst of a family crisis. Three of the nine caregivers stated that they would have liked the child welfare system to have better prepared them for the arrival of these children in their home.

Studies that detail the experience and consequences of caring for related children in the custody of the child welfare system tend to rely on small samples that are not randomly selected. Therefore, findings of any one of these studies cannot be generalized to the entire population of families providing kinship care. However, the findings of these studies are remarkably similar, suggesting at least that many kinship caregivers have heavy and complicated caregiving responsibilities that extend beyond the related children in the custody of the child welfare system.

Three studies presented in this book examine in greater depth the experiences and consequences of caring for related children who are in the custody of the child welfare system [Cimmarusti, Chapter 11; Osby, Chapter 9; Petras, Chapter 10]. Both Petras [Chapter 10; 1998] and Cimmarusti [Chapter 11; 1998] tested hypothesized relationships between variables that have been supported in studies of spousal caregivers and family caregivers of the frail elderly. Petras examined the relationship between kinship caregivers' perceptions of their preparation for caregiving, their sense of control, satisfaction with caregiving, and depression. Cimmarusti examined the relationship between perceived social support, caregiver burden, and psychological distress. Osby's [Chapter 9] qualitative interviews with grandparent caregivers explored their views on parenting their grandchildren and their experience with the child welfare system, using a world view perspective.

Summary and Conclusion

Much of what is known about the use of kinship care as a child welfare service has emerged from the research on caseload growth and dynamics involving sophisticated analyses of administrative data that are collected in the normal course of providing child welfare services. The caseload dynamics research has helped us understand that children placed with relatives spend more time in state custody than children placed in foster care with nonrelatives. Analyses of administrative data also reveal that reunification of children with their parents occurs at a slower rate for children placed with kin than for children placed in nonrelated foster care, but once reunified, children who had been placed with kin are less likely to re-enter the custody of the child welfare system than other children. Also, child abuse and neglect databases indicate that kinship care may be one of the safest types of placements for children, since reports of child abuse and neglect while in kinship care are even lower than rates reported for children placed in nonrelated foster care.

Using administrative data for research purposes has tremendous advantages, because these data can be collected on all cases served by the child welfare system. On the other hand, these data do have limitations. Since administrative data are collected by caseworkers in the normal course of doing business, the amount and depth of information collected is limited. Collection of administrative data usually does not engage children, parents, caregivers, or caseworkers in an in-depth examination of specific research questions that may provide some explanation of the caseload dynamics that these data reveal.

While research that analyzes administrative data has probably had the greatest impact on our understanding of kinship care to date, others have examined case records [Scannapieco et al. 1997; Thornton 1991], compared kinship caregivers' and nonrelated foster parents' responses to mailed and phone surveys [Berrick et al. 1994; Le Prohn 1994], conducted surveys of caseworkers to assess the needs of youth in kinship care and nonrelated foster care [Iglehart 1994], conducted interviews with caseworkers [Gleeson et al. 1997; Thornton 1991] and caregivers [Minkler et al. 1992; Testa, et al. 1996; Thornton 1991], or adults who had grown up in kinship care [Benedict et al. 1996; Zuravin et al. 1999]. Also, recent studies have compared informal and formal kinship care by using national survey data [Harden et al. 1997] and by comparing demographic data collected from informal kinship caregivers served through a support program to results of studies of formal kinship care of children in the custody of the child welfare system [McLean & Thomas 1996]. One study analyzed data collected through comprehensive assessments of the health, academic, behavioral, and mental health functioning of children in kinship care in one city [Dubowitz et al. 1994, 1993]. Each of these studies has contributed to our knowledge of kinship care, many in significant ways.

As a whole, the research completed to date provides a good foundation for answering the questions that face the child welfare field about the use of kinship care as a child welfare service today and in the future. The studies that are reported in this volume complement and contribute to this growing body of research, using smaller samples, participant observation of case staffing and training sessions, secondary data analysis, and in-depth interviews with caseworkers, children, parents, and caregivers to examine important aspects of kinship care as a child welfare service. They help us develop deeper understanding of the patterns observed in administrative data, explore new topics and issues, and provide richer descriptions of the experiences of those involved in and affected by kinship foster care.

References

Altshuler, S. J. (1996). *The well-being of children in kinship foster care.* Unpublished doctoral dissertation, University of Illinois at Chicago.

Altshuler, S. J. (1998). Child well-being in kinship foster care: Similar to, or different from, non-related foster care? *Children and Youth Services Review, 20*(5), 369-388.

Altshuler, S. J., & Gleeson, J. P. (1999). Completing the evaluation triangle for the next century: What is 'child well-being' in family foster care? *Child Welfare, 78*(1), 125-147.

Barth, R. P., Courtney, M. E., Berrick, J. D., & Albert V. (1994). *From child abuse to permanency planning: Child welfare services, pathways and placements.* New York: Aldine de Gruyter.

Benedict, M. I., Zuravin, S., & Stallings, R. Y. (1996). Adult functioning of children who lived in kin versus nonrelative family foster homes. *Child Welfare, 75*(5), 529-549.

Berrick, J. D., Barth, R. P., & Needell, B. (1994). A comparison of kinship foster homes and foster family homes: Implications for kinship care as family preservation. *Children and Youth Services Review, 16,* 33-63.

Berrick, J. D., Needell, B., & Barth, R. P. (1999). Kin as a family and child welfare resource: The child welfare worker's perspective. In R. L. Hegar, & M. Scannapieco (Eds.), *Kinship foster care: Practice, policy, and research* (pp. 179-192). New York: Oxford University Press.

Berrick, J. D., Needell, B., Barth, R. P., & Jonson-Reid, M. (1998). *The tender years: Toward developmentally sensitive child welfare services for very young children.* New York: Oxford University Press.

Bonecutter, F. J., & Gleeson, J. P. (1997a). Broadening our view: Lessons from kinship foster care. *Journal of Multicultural Social Work, 5,* 99-119.

Bonecutter, F. J., & Gleeson, J. P. (1997b). *Achieving permanency for children in kinship foster care: A training manual.* Chicago: Jane Addams College of Social Work and the Jane Addams Center for Social Policy and Research, University of Illinois at Chicago.

Burnette, D. (1997). Grandparents raising grandchildren in the inner city. *Families in Society, 78*(5), 489-499.

Burton, L. M. (1992). Black grandparents rearing children of drug-addicted parents: Stressors, outcomes, and social service needs. *The Gerontologist, 32*(6), 744-751.

Child Welfare League of America. (1994). *Kinship care: A natural bridge.* Washington DC: Author.

Cimmarusti, R. A. (1998). *Caregiver burden of kinship foster care caregivers: Impact of social support on emotional distress.* Unpublished doctoral dissertation, Jane Addams College of Social Work, University of Illinois at Chicago.

Connolly, M. (1994). An act of empowerment: The Children, Young Persons and Their Families Act (1989). *British Journal of Social Work, 24,* 87-100.

Courtney, M. E., & Needell, B. (1997). Outcomes of kinship care: Lessons from California. In R. P. Barth, J. D. Berrick, & N. Gilbert (Eds), *Child welfare research review. Volume 2* (pp. 129-159). New York: Columbia University Press.

Courtney, M. E., Piliavin, I., & Entner Wright, B. R. (1997). Transitions from and returns to out-of-home care. *Social Service Review, 71*(4), 652-667.

Crumbley, J., & Little, R. (1997). *Relatives raising children: An overview of kinship care.* Washington, DC: Child Welfare League of America.

Davidson, B. (1997). Service needs of relative caregivers: A qualitative analysis. *Families in Society, 78*(5), 502-510.

Dubowitz, H., Feigelman, S., Harrington, D., Starr, R., Zuravin, S., & Sawyer, R. (1994). Children in kinship care: How do they fare? *Children and Youth Services Review, 16,* 85-106.

Dubowitz, H., Feigelman, S., & Zuravin, S. (1993). A profile of kinship care. *Child Welfare, 72,* 153-169.

Emlen, A., Lahti, J., Downs, G., McKay, A., & Downs, S. (1978). *Overcoming barriers to planning for children in foster care.* Portland, OR: Regional Research Institute for Human Services, Portland State University.

Ernst, J. W. (1999). Whanau knows best: Kinship care in New Zealand. In R. L. Hegar & M. Scannapieco (Eds.), *Kinship foster care: Practice, policy, and research* (pp. 112- 138). New York: Oxford University Press.

Gebel, T. J. (1996). Kinship care and nonrelative family foster care: A comparison of caregiver attributes and attitudes. *Child Welfare, 75*(1), 5-18.

Gleeson, J. P. (1999). Kinship care as a child welfare service: Emerging policy issues and trends. In R. L. Hegar & M. Scannapieco (Eds.), *Kinship foster care: Practice, policy, and research* (pp. 28-53). New York: Oxford University Press.

Gleeson, J. P. (1996). Kinship care as a child welfare service: The policy debate in an era of welfare reform. *Child Welfare, 75*(5), 419-449.

Gleeson, J. P., Anderson, G. R., Mason, S., Carlberg, C., Adamy, D., & Thompson, T. (1999). *Case planning for children entering state custody as infants: Final report*. Chicago: Jane Addams College of Social Work and the Jane Addams Center for Social Policy and Research, University of Illinois at Chicago.

Gleeson, J. P., Bonecutter, F. J., & Altshuler, S. J. (1995). Facilitating permanence in kinship care: The Illinois project. In G. R. Anderson & J. P. Gleeson (Eds.), *Kinship care forum* (pp. 7-24). New York: National Resource Center for Permanency Planning at the Hunter College School of Social Work.

Gleeson, J. P., & Craig, L. C. (1994). Kinship care in child welfare: An analysis of states' policies. *Children and Youth Services Review, 16*, 7-31.

Gleeson, J., O'Donnell, J., Altshuler, S., & Philbin, C. (1994). *Current practice in kinship care: Caseworker's perspectives*. Chicago: University of Illinois at Chicago, Jane Addams College of Social Work and Jane Addams Center for Social Policy and Research.

Gleeson, J. P., O'Donnell, J., & Bonecutter, F. J. (1997). Understanding the complexity of practice in kinship foster care. *Child Welfare, 76*(6), 801-826.

Goerge, R. M. (1990). The reunification process in substitute care. *Social Service Review, 64*, 422-457.

Harden, A. W., Clark, R. L., & Maguire, K. (1997). *Informal and formal kinship care: Volumes 1 and 2*. Washington, DC: U. S. Department of Health and Human Services.

Harden, B. J., Clyman, R., Walker, C. D., & Rubinetti, F. (1997). Assessing the quality of foster family care: An initiative for the integration of research and practice. In *Profiles of research grants funded by NCCAN and the Children's Bureau (FYs 1991- 1996)*. Washington, DC: National Center on Child Abuse and Neglect, U.S. Department of Health and Human Services.

Harris, M. S. (1997). *Factors that affect family reunification of African American birth mothers and their children placed in kinship care.* Unpublished doctoral dissertation, Smith College School for Social Work.

Hatmaker, C., & Pratt, C. (1997). Project REFRESH: Research and evaluation of foster children's reception into environmentally supportive homes. In *Profiles of research grants funded by NCCAN and the Children's Bureau (FYs 1991-1996).* Washington, DC: National Center on Child Abuse and Neglect, U.S. Department of Health and Human Services.

Hegar, R. L., & Scannapieco, M. (1995). From family duty to family policy: The evolution of kinship care. *Child Welfare, 74,* 200-216.

Hill, R. B. (1972). *The strengths of Black families.* New York: Emerson Hall.

Hill, R. B. (1977). *Informal adoption among Black families.* Washington DC: National Urban League Research Department.

Hill, R. B. (1997). *The strengths of African American families: Twenty-five years later.* Washington, DC: R & B Publishers.

Hornby, H., Zeller, D., & Karraker, D. (1995). *Kinship care in America: A national policy study.* Portland, ME: Edmund S. Muskie Institute of Public Affairs, University of Southern Maine.

Hornby, H., Zeller, D., & Karraker, D. (1996). Kinship care in America: What outcomes should policy seek? *Child Welfare, 75*(5), 397-418.

Illinois Department of Children and Family Services [IDCFS]. (1995, February 27). *Illinois HMR Reform Plan.* Chicago: Author.

Illinois Department of Children and Family Services [IDCFS]. (1998). *Semi-Annual Progress Report, October 1, 1997 - March 31, 1998, Illinois Subsidized Guardianship Waiver Demonstration.* Chicago: Author.

Illinois Department of Children and Family Services [IDCFS]. (1999a, January 1). Substitute care services. *Foster care brochure.* http://www.state.il.us./dcfs /FCBRO.htm.

Illinois Department of Children and Family Services [IDCFS]. (1999b). *Illinois subsidized guardianship waiver demonstration* (fact sheet), February 15, 1999.

Iglehart, A. (1994). Kinship foster care: Placement, service and outcome issues. *Children and Youth Services Review, 16,* 107-127.

Jackson, S. M. (1999). Paradigm shift: Training staff to provide services to the kinship triad. In R. L. Hegar & M. Scannapieco (Eds.), *Kinship foster care: Practice, policy, and research* (pp. 93-111). New York: Oxford University Press.

Jackson, S. M. (1996). The kinship triad: A service delivery model. *Child Welfare, 75*(5), 583-599.

Kusserow, R. P. (1992a). *Using relatives for foster care.* Washington, DC: U. S. Department of Health and Human Services, Office of the Inspector General, OEI-06-90-02390.

Kusserow, R. P. (1992b). *State practices in using relatives for foster care.* Washington, DC: U. S. Department of Health and Human Services, Office of the Inspector General, OEI-06-90-02391.

Le Prohn, N. S. (1994). The role of the kinship foster parent: A comparison of the role conceptions of relative and non-relative foster parents. *Children and Youth Services Review, 16,* 65-84.

Link, M. K. (1996). Permanency outcomes in kinship care: A study of children placed in kinship care in Erie County, New York. *Child Welfare, 75*(5), 509-528.

Magruder, J. (1994). Characteristics of relative and non-relative adoptions by California public adoption agencies. *Children and Youth Services Review, 16,* 123-131.

Martin, E. P., & Martin, J. M. (1978). *The Black extended family.* Chicago: The University of Chicago Press.

McFadden, E. J. (1995). Kinship caregivers' training and support. In G. R. Anderson & J. P. Gleeson (Eds.), *Kinship care forum* (pp. 31-33). New York: National Resource Center for Permanency Planning at the Hunter College School of Social Work.

McLean, B., & Thomas, R. (1996). Informal and formal kinship care populations: A study in contrasts. *Child Welfare, 75*(5), 489-505.

Mills, C. S., & Usher, D. (1996). A kinship care case management approach. *Child Welfare, 75*(5), 600-618.

Mills, C. S., & Usher, D. (1995). Eastern Michigan University Kinship Project. In G. R. Anderson & J. P. Gleeson (Eds.), *Kinship care forum* (pp. 25-30). New York: National Resource Center for Permanency Planning at the Hunter College School of Social Work.

Miller v. Youakim, 440 U.S. 125 (1979).

Minkler, M., Roe, K. M., & Robertson-Beckley, R. J. (1994). Raising grandchildren from crack-cocaine households: Effects on family and friendship ties of African-American women. *American Journal of Orthopsychiatry, 64*(1), 20-29.

Minkler, M., Roe, K. M., & Price, M. (1992). The physical and emotional health of grandmothers raising grandchildren in the crack cocaine epidemic. *The Gerontologist, 32*(6), 752-761.

O'Donnell, J. M. (1995). *Casework practice with fathers in kinship foster care.* Unpublished doctoral dissertation, University of Illinois at Chicago.

Pecora, P. J., Le Prohn, N. S., & Nasuti, J. J. (1999). Role perceptions of kinship and other foster parents in family foster care. In R. L. Hegar & M. Scannapieco (Eds.), *Kinship foster care: Practice, policy, and research* (pp. 155-178). New York: Oxford University Press.

Petras, D. D. (1998). *The effect of caregiver preparation and sense of control on adaptation of kinship caregivers.* Unpublished doctoral dissertation, University of Illinois at Chicago.

Reid v. Suter. (May 20, 1992). No. 89J6196, Order approving consent decree; No. 89J6196, Consent decree.

Ryan, P., & Wiencek, P. (1997). Factors related to quality of family foster care. In *Profiles of research grants funded by NCCAN and the Children's Bureau (FYs 1991-1996).* Washington, DC: National Center on Child Abuse and Neglect, U.S. Department of Health and Human Services.

Scannapieco, M., & Hegar, R. L. (1996). A nontraditional assessment framework for formal kinship homes. *Child Welfare, 75*(5), 567-582.

Scannapieco, M., & Hegar, R. L. (1999). Kinship foster care in context. In R. L. Hegar & M. Scannapieco (Eds.), *Kinship foster care: Practice, policy, and research* (pp. 1-13). New York: Oxford University Press.

Scannapieco, M., Hegar, R. L., & McAlpine, C. (1997). Kinship care and foster care: A comparison of characteristics and outcomes. *Families in Society, 78*(5), 480-488.

Scannapieco, M., & Jackson, S. (1996). Kinship care: The African American response to family preservation. *Social Work, 41*(2), 190-196.

Stack, C. (1974). *All our kin: Strategies for survival in a black community.* New York: Harper and Row.

Starr, R., Dubowitz, H., Harrington, D., & Fiegelman, S. (1999). Behavior problems of teens in kinship care: Cross informant reports. In R. L. Hegar & M. Scannapieco (Eds.), *Kinship foster care: Practice, policy, and research* (pp. 193-207). New York: Oxford University Press.

Stein, T. J., Gambrill, E. D., & Wiltse, K. T. (1978). *Children in foster homes: Achieving continuity of care.* New York: Holt Rinehart, & Winston.

Testa, M. F. (1992). Conditions of risk for substitute care. *Children and Youth Services Review, 14,* 27-36.

Testa, M. F. (1993). *Home of relative (HMR) program in Illinois: Interim report* (rev. ed.). Chicago: School of Social Service Administration, University of Chicago.

Testa, M. F. (1995). Home of relative (HMR) reform in Illinois. In G. R. Anderson & J. P. Gleeson (Eds.), *Kinship care forum* (pp. 47-57). New York: National Resource Center for Permanency Planning at the Hunter College School of Social Work.

Testa, M. F. (1997). Kinship foster care in Illinois. In R. Barth, J. D. Berrick, & N. Gilbert (Eds.), *Child welfare research review. Volume 2* (pp. 101-129). New York: Columbia University Press.

Testa, M. F., Shook, K. L., Cohen, L., & Woods, M. G. (1996). Permanency planning options for children in formal kinship care. *Child Welfare, 75*(5), 451-470.

Thornton, J. L. (1991). Permanency planning for children in kinship foster homes. *Child Welfare, 70,* 593-601.

Timberlake, E. M., & Chipungu, S. S. (1992). Grandmotherhood: Contemporary meaning among African-American middle-class grandmothers. *Social Work, 37,* 216-222.

Wells, S. (1997). Evaluating quality of out-of-home care in kinship foster families. In *Profiles of research grants funded by NCCAN and the Children's Bureau (FYs 1991-1996).* Washington, DC: National Center on Child Abuse and Neglect, U.S. Department of Health and Human Services.

Westat. (n.d.). *Children in household and youth interview,* developed for the Illinois Subsidized Guardianship IV-E Waiver Demonstration Evaluation.

Wilhelmus, M. (1998). Mediation in kinship care: Another step in the provision of culturally relevant child welfare services. *Social Work, 43*(2), 117-126.

Wilson, L., & Conroy, J. (1999). Satisfaction of children in out-of-home care. *Child Welfare, 78*(1), 53-69.

Wulczyn, F. H., & Goerge, R. M. (1992). Foster care in New York and Illinois: The challenge of rapid change. *Social Service Review, 66,* 278-294.

Wulczyn, F. H., Harden, A. W., & Goerge, R. M. (1997). *Foster care dynamics 1983-1994: An update from the multistate foster care data archive.* Chicago: The Chapin Hall Center for Children at the University of Chicago.

Zuravin, S. J., Benedict, M., & Somerfield, M. (1993). Child maltreatment in family foster care. *American Journal of Orthopsychiatry, 63,* 589-596.

Part II
Facilitating Permanence

2

Defining Best Practice in Kinship Care Through Research and Demonstration

Faith Johnson Bonecutter

The permanency planning movement of the late 1970s and early 1980s was prompted by public awareness that children were "drifting in foster care" and the foster care caseload had grown—some say to 500,000 children in care on any single day. Current knowledge suggests that estimates of the number of children in care were in error and the actual number was considerably lower [Barth et al. 1994]. Therefore, although the number of children in out-of-home care was closer to 250,000 by the early 1980s, it is not clear whether the permanency planning movement and the passage of the Adoption Assistance and Child Welfare Act of 1980 actually reduced the number of children in care. However, it is clear that the median length of stay for children in out-of-home care decreased by 46% from 1977 to 1987 [Barth et al. 1994].

The number of children in out-of-home care did grow from 1982 to 1987, but only modestly, from 262,000 on the last day of the fiscal year to approximately 300,000 [Tatara 1994]. Caseload dynamics changed again after 1987 and the number of children in out-of-home care began increasing dramatically. While the number of children entering the custody of the child welfare system increased only slightly from 1988 through 1991, a steady decline in the number of children exiting custody each year resulted in a foster care caseload that grew to 429,000.

This recent growth in child welfare caseloads, combined with the increasing use of kinship foster care, raised new questions about effective permanency planning. Once again, public attention was focused on the growth of the foster care population and the cost of providing this care. Once again, the public perceived that the number of children in foster care on any single day would soon reach half a million. Once again, there was concern about children drifting in care with little chance of living in a permanent home by returning to their parents or being adopted.

There were two major differences in the children who were drifting in care in the late 1970s and the late 1980s. The more recent cohort of children were younger and many were placed with relatives in kinship foster care. In fact, in large urban centers where caseload growth was the greatest, the majority of this growth was accommodated through placement of children with relatives [Testa 1997]. Children placed with relatives were remaining in the custody of the child welfare system longer than children in any other types of placement. They were less likely to return home or to be adopted than children placed with nonrelative foster parents. In addition, the majority of children in kinship foster care were children of color living in major urban areas [Barth et al. 1994; Goerge 1990; Testa 1992, 1993; Thornton 1991; Wulczyn & Goerge 1992].

Early studies suggested that relatives caring for children in kinship foster care were rarely willing to adopt, though willing to rear these children to adulthood [Meyer & Link 1990; Thornton 1991]. In 1992, the U. S. Children's Bureau's Adoption Opportunities Program issued a request for applications for a research and demonstration project to determine the feasibility of adoption as a permanency option for children in kinship foster care. In many ways, this pattern of federal funding is similar to the late 1970s when the U. S. Children's Bureau funded permanency planning research and demonstration projects in Oregon [Emlen et al. 1978] and California [Stein et al. 1978]. These projects developed models of practice that were found to be effective in facilitating permanency for children in nonrelative foster care through reunification and adoption. However, it was not clear whether the practice principles and methods developed through these projects were relevant for children in kinship foster care.

The Children's Bureau funded three projects to improve the permanency outcomes for children placed in kinship foster care: one in New York, one in Michigan, and one in Illinois. This chapter describes the Illinois project entitled, "Achieving Permanency for Children in Kinship Foster Care." The purpose of this project was to develop and test a practice model designed to improve the permanency outcomes for children placed in foster care with relatives.* The project used a research and development approach to accomplish the following:

- understand current child welfare practice in kinship foster care,
- develop an initial definition of the practice principles and methods that are components of best practice in kinship foster care,
- train caseworkers in the use of these principles and methods,
- field test and monitor implementation of the principles and methods, and
- refine the practice model based upon feedback received during the field test.

This approach incorporated formative evaluation techniques to identify barriers to implementation of the practice principles and methods as well as conditions that facilitate their implementation.

This chapter describes the project design, processes used to identify key components of the practice model, results of the study, and the practice principles and methods that comprise the model. The chapter ends with recommendations for designing research and demonstration projects to define principles and methods of best practice in kinship foster care and other child welfare services.

---

* Supported by grant number 90-C0-0595 from the Adoption Opportunities Office of the Administration for Children, Youth, and Families, U.S. Department of Health and Human Services, with in-kind contributions from the Jane Addams College of Social Work, Central Baptist Family Services, Lutheran Social Services of Illinois, the Jane Addams Center for Social Policy and Research, the Jane Addams Hull-House Museum, Loyola University of Chicago School of Social Work, Life Concerns, and the Assistance of the Illinois Department of Children and Family Services.

Description of the Study: The Illinois Project*

The purpose of the Illinois project was to develop and test a practice model designed to improve the "permanency outcomes" for children in kinship foster care. Permanence was defined as exiting custody of the child welfare system through adoption by relatives currently acting as foster parents, adoption by other family members, transfer of legal guardianship to a relative, adoption by nonrelatives, or safe return to biological parents when possible. The children selected for the study had been in state custody for at least one year, and were living with relatives who were approved as "relative foster parents" and received monthly foster care board subsidies to help them care for these children. Although safe reunification was the initial permanency goal, generally, the children in this study were considered unlikely to return home to their parents, since return home is most likely during the first year of care.

The Illinois project had three phases and worked with two voluntary agencies that serve children in kinship foster care in Cook County, through purchase of services contracts with the Illinois Department of Children and Family Services (IDCFS). Staff who participated in the project served kinship foster care cases exclusively. The three phases of the project will be summarized in this section.

The First Phase (1992-1993)

The purposes of the first phase of the project were to define current practice in kinship foster care, identify barriers to permanence, and identify practice principles and methods that have the likelihood of facilitating permanence for children in kinship foster care. Three research methods were used to achieve these purposes:

- In-depth interviews were conducted with 41 caseworkers regarding casework practice on behalf of 77 children in kinship foster care and their families.

---

* Results of this study are also presented in Gleeson, Bonecutter, & Altshuler [1995] and Gleeson, O'Donnell, & Bonecutter [1997].

- In-depth interviews, averaging two hours in length, were conducted with 11 supervisors regarding casework and supervisory practice in kinship foster care.

- Twelve kinship care cases were reviewed by a steering committee of persons with expertise in a wide variety of areas in social work and child welfare.

The case-specific interviews conducted with caseworkers generated an extensive database that provided a rich description of the children in kinship foster care, their caregivers, living arrangements, parents, siblings, reasons for the child welfare system's involvement, and the case planning process [see also Gleeson et al. 1995; Gleeson et al. 1997]. Interviews with supervisors provided another perspective on the complexity of kinship foster care practice and the difficulty that supervisors encounter as they assist caseworkers in learning to develop and implement permanent plans for children living with relatives (also see Gleeson & Philbin [1996]).

Results of the caseworker and supervisor interviews were analyzed and presented to steering committee members for discussion at quarterly meetings. These discussions, combined with the steering committee's in-depth review of 12 cases, led to the identification of barriers to permanence and practice principles and methods for facilitating permanence for children in kinship foster care. The ten steering committee members had expertise in a wide variety of areas. Two steering committee members were public child welfare agency administrators and four were private child welfare agency administrators. One was the author of the family preservation and family reunification curricula for Illinois. Three steering committee members were social work professors whose research focused on African American families. The principal investigator, training director, and project coordinator, who also participated in steering committee meetings, had extensive child welfare practice, research, and training experience.

Second Phase (1993-1994)

In the second phase, the practice principles and methods were incorporated into a draft training curriculum. In one of the agencies, two supervisors volunteered their teams, which included ten caseworkers, to serve as the demonstration group. The remaining four teams in that agency served as a comparison group. All of the caseworkers in the second agency and their supervisors participated as part of the demonstration group. Caseworkers in the demonstration group participated in four half-day training sessions followed by three to five half-day case consultations. Caseworkers who participated in the training were asked to implement the practice principles and methods in their daily practice and to discuss their implementation efforts during the case consultations. The training and consultation sessions were conducted by project staff in conjunction with agency supervisors heading each demonstration unit. Caseworkers in the comparison group did not participate in the training sessions or consultations and were not asked to change their casework practice with children and families.

In addition, project staff provided ongoing monthly consultation to supervisors to assist them in their efforts to facilitate caseworkers' implementation of the practice principles and methods. These consultations were also helpful in providing feedback to project staff, assisting them in refining the practice principles and methods for facilitating permanency for children in kinship foster care. Project staff also monitored the practice of caseworkers in demonstration and comparison groups through case record reviews, to determine if the practice principles and methods were more likely to be implemented in the six months following training compared to the six months preceding training. The case records of 267 children were reviewed.

Third Phase (1994-1995)

The third and final phase of the project focused on analysis of the data collected during phase two, to determine whether the practice principles and methods were implemented by caseworkers in the demonstration group and whether their practice differed from that of caseworkers in the comparison group. Cases selected from the demonstration and comparison groups were also compared to determine whether there were differences in the achievement of permanency for children served by caseworkers who were part of the demonstration group compared to those who were part of the comparison group. Also, further revisions of the training curriculum were completed during the final phase of the project.

Phase One Results: Defining Current Practice

The caseworkers employed by the participating agencies were similar in education and training to caseworkers described in a variety of national studies of child welfare practitioners, with only 12% having masters degrees and the median experience being less than two years. Eighty percent of the caseworkers were female, 54% were African American, 42% white, and 5% Latino.

Two family cases were randomly selected from each caseworker's caseload. Then, one eligible child was randomly selected from each of these families. Interviews focused on the individual children, their immediate and extended family systems, and practice with and on behalf of these children and their families. Interviews were completed on 77 cases, representing 9% of all kinship care cases in the two participating agencies at the time the sample was drawn. The interviews averaged two hours per case and were completed between March and May of 1993.

The children in the sample were predominantly African American, ranging in age from 19 months to 19 years of age, with a median age of 7 years (Table 2-1). The majority of these children entered state custody because of neglect. Only 21% of the children were known to be substance exposed at birth. However, this is likely to be an underestimate, since substance exposure was more likely to be identified for younger children and screening for substance exposure was not common practice when the older children in the sample were born. Most of the children had siblings and were living in the same kinship foster home with at least one sibling.

Many of the children also had siblings living at home with their parents, with other relatives, and in nonrelative foster care. The kinship foster homes in which these children lived had several children and adults living in them (Table 2-2). In addition to the kinship foster child's siblings, the caregivers' biological children and other children related to the caregivers

---

Table 2-1. Characteristics of Children

Race
    African American   96%
    Latino   3%
    Causasian   1%
Gender
    Female   47%
    Male   53%
Median Age   7 yr
    Youngest   19 mo
    Oldest   19 yr
Reason for State Involvement
    Neglect   82%
    Abuse   10%
    Abuse and neglect   5%
    Dependency   3%
Prenatal Substance Exposure   21%
Living with Relative When State Became Involved   25%
The Child Has Siblings
    Living in same kinship home   78%
    Living with biological mother   17%
    Living with biological father   9%
    Living with at least one other relative   40%
    Living in traditional foster care   9%

Note: First phase data (N=77)

---

were living in many of the homes. More than three-quarters of the kinship foster homes had more than five persons living in them and 55% of the children lived in kinship foster homes with at least three other children under 18 years of age.

The majority of kinship caregivers were single females, related to the biological mother. More than 60% were grandparents, 7% were great-grandparents, and 32% were either aunts, uncles, or adult siblings of the child in kinship foster care. One-quarter of the kinship caregivers received AFDC to support the care of children other than the child in kinship foster care and slightly more than one-quarter received SSI disability or retirement

Table 2-2. Characteristics of Kinship Caregivers and Kinship Homes

Marital Status/Gender

Widowed, divorced, or never married female	70%
Currently married	30%

Related to Biological Mother	80%

Relationship to Child

Grandparent	61%
Great-grandparent	7%
Aunts/uncles	21%
Siblings	11%

Number of People Living in Caregiver's Home

Two to five	22%
Five to twelve	78%

Number of Children Living in Caregiver's Home

One to three	43%
Four to six	45%
Seven to nine	11%

Income

Employed at least part-time	53%
AFDC recipient	25%
SSI disability or retirement income	26%

Low Income Housing or Rent Subsidy	27%

Note: First phase data (N=77)

income. Yet, more than half of the kinship caregivers were employed outside of the home at least part-time. Approximately 27% lived in government subsidized housing. This sample is similar to kinship caregivers described by Berrick, Barth, and Needell [1994] in California, who were more likely to be single women of color, with fewer economic resources, yet more likely to work outside of the home when compared to traditional foster parents.

Biological mothers of the children selected for the first phase of this study ranged in age from 19 to 46 years of age, with a median age of 29 years (Table 2-3). Caseworkers were asked to describe any problems that

Table 2-3. Characteristics of Biological Mothers

Race	
African American	96%
Latino	1%
Caucasian	3%
Median Age	29 yr
Youngest	19 yr
Oldest	46 yr
Problems Preventing Mothers from Caring for Child	
Substance abuse	81%
Lack of housing	30%
Criminal behavior	14%
Financial problems	11%
Mental illness	11%
Mental retardation/developmental disabilities	8%
Mothers' Strengths Identified	
Expressing/demonstrating love for child	46%
Participating in services	24%

Note: First phase data ($\underline{N}$=72). Five biological mothers were deceased. Although 80% of fathers were known, information was available on only a small percentage of these fathers.

the biological mother had that prevented her from caring for her child. In response to this open-ended question, caseworkers indicated that 81% of these mothers had substance abuse problems. Lack of housing was a problem identified for 30% of these mothers. Criminal behavior, financial problems, mental illness, and mental retardation/developmental disabilities were identified for 8-14% of the mothers. Also in response to an open-ended question, caseworkers identified the following strengths for the biological mother of the children in the sample: (1) expressing or demonstrating love for the child (46%) and (2) participating in services (24%).

Characteristics of biological fathers are not reported here because caseworkers lacked information on most fathers, although the identity of 80% of the fathers was known to the caseworker. O'Donnell [1995; Chapter 7] has examined more closely practice with these fathers, extending both the data collection and data analysis. His study revealed that caseworkers did not identify the lack of involvement of biological fathers as a problem; however, lack of involvement of biological mothers *was* identified as a problem. These findings suggest that child welfare caseworkers, like many others in society, do not expect fathers to participate in caring for their children.

Caseworkers were asked to describe the current permanency goals for the children selected for study. They were also asked to indicate whether they thought the permanency goal for the child would change within the next year and to identify the likely goal for the case at that time. The current and projected permanency goals are listed in Table 2-4. Consistent with prior research, these data suggest that caseworkers considered it likely that only 10% of children who had been in kinship foster care for at least one year would actually return home to a biological parent. However, caseworkers thought adoption by the kinship caregiver to be a likely goal for 35% of the children, a rate considerably higher than reported in earlier studies [Meyer & Link 1990; Thornton 1991].

The fact that caseworkers suggested that they were planning for the adoption of 35% of the children in this sample was initially considered to be good news. However, concerns were raised when caseworkers' responses to a different question were analyzed. Caseworkers were asked to identify persons who contributed to development of the most recent service plan. Their responses indicate that the persons most likely to be living with the decisions made on behalf of the child were least likely to be involved in these decisions (Table 2-5). The caseworker's supervisor contributed to the plan in more than two-thirds of the cases. Other formal service providers contributed in 45% of the cases. In contrast, the current caregiver contributed to the development of the most recent service plan in less than one-third of the cases. Biological mothers contributed to the plan in 21% and biological fathers in only 5% of the cases. In no case did relatives other than the current caregiver contribute to the development of the most recent service plan.

Defining Practice Principles and Methods

Results of the first phase of the project informed the development of the training curriculum [Bonecutter & Gleeson 1997]. The project steering committee helped shape and refine the training curriculum after complet-

Table 2-4. Permanency Planning

Current Permanency Goal

Return home	26%
Adoption	12%
Long-term kinship foster care	58%
Independence	4%
Private guardianship	0%

Future Permanency Goal (including projected change in 1 year)

Return home	10%
Adoption	35%
Long-term kinship foster care	47%
Nonrelative substitute care	1%
Independence	7%

Note: First phase data (N=77)

Table 2-5. Contributors to the Most Recent Service Plan

Supervisors	67%
Other Service Providers	45%
Current Caregiver	32%
Biological Mothers	21%
Biological Fathers	5%
Other Relatives	0%

Note: First phase data (N=77)

ing in-depth reviews of 12 kinship foster care cases and reviewing reports of the results of caseworker and supervisor interviews. Additionally, the reactions, responses, and input from the staff and supervisors who participated in the training shaped the revisions and modifications of the curriculum.

Findings of the first phase of the project suggested that permanency planning for children in kinship foster care was dominated by the formal social service system's service providers with little involvement of persons in the child's kinship network. Rarely did caseworkers discuss long-term plans with caregivers who intended to adopt children. For example, it was not common to discuss with the caregiver who would care for the child if the caregiver became ill or died, although several kinship caregivers had chronic health problems. Similarly, it was rare for caseworkers to discuss with kinship caregivers the ways that raising the child may become more difficult or challenging in future years, for example, when the child enters adolescence. It was extremely rare for the caseworker to involve several members of the child's kinship system in meetings to plan for the long-term care of the child.

Members of the steering committee identified the lack of involvement of the child's family or other members of the informal helping systems in planning and decisionmaking as a serious problem that they believed contributed to irrelevant and unsuccessful permanency planning. Practice principles and methods that were incorporated into the training curriculum were intended to correct the imbalance between the formal and informal systems in decisionmaking regarding the permanency, protection, and well-being of children in kinship foster care.

The practice principles and methods were clustered into four major areas: (1) a broader view of family, (2) ongoing striving for cultural competence, (3) collaboration in decisionmaking, and (4) building the case-management capacities of kinship networks to support permanent plans. Taken as a whole, these practice principles and methods were intended to assist caseworkers in using the resources of the formal child welfare system to strengthen and support, rather than replace, the informal kinship network. These practice principles and methods were also intended to help the caseworker engage members of the child's kinship system in decisionmaking on behalf of the child. They were intended to help caseworkers engage families from diverse cultural backgrounds. They were also intended to assist caseworkers in taking a long-term view of child rearing and permanency planning that extends several years beyond the child's exit from state custody. The four groupings of practice principles and methods are listed in Table 2-6 and the curriculum content related to each of these is briefly described in this section.

Table 2-6. Practice Principles and Methods

- A broad view of family
  - going beyond the child/caregiver/parent constellation
  - identifying members of the child(ren)'s kinship network
  - facilitating building or strengthening of the kinship network around the goals of protection, permanency, and well-being of the child(ren)
  - Tools: genogram, ecomap
- Ongoing striving for cultural competence
  - self-awareness
  - valuing diversity
  - knowledge of cultural strengths and vulnerabilities
  - recognition of the enduring nature of family (emotional) ties
  - knowledge and use of formal and informal systems of support
- Collaboration in decisionmaking
  - convening relevant members of the kinship network
  - engaging the kinship in a network plan that ensures the child's protection/safety and well-being
  - facilitating the family's definition of permanence
  - facilitating the family's (re)definition of relationships
  - using principles of "successful" permanency planning and family preservation projects
- Building the case management capacities of kinship networks
  - supporting permanency plans
  - building the network's skills to anticipate needs and access to services in the future and to ensure that other needs of the child(ren) and family are met

Source: Bonecutter, F. J., & Gleeson, J. P. (1997). *Achieving permanency for children in kinship foster care: A training manual.* Chicago: Jane Addams College of Social Work and the Jane Addams Center for Social Policy and Research, University of Illinois at Chicago.

A Broad View of Family

Curriculum content that focuses on this principle emphasizes that effective permanency planning requires the awareness that many children, particularly children of color, are reared not by one or two parents, but by a caregiving system of related and nonrelated kin. It stresses that parents who are trying to have their children reunited with them and kinship caregivers who may be willing to care permanently for a child need social supports to achieve these goals successfully.

Contents of the training curriculum that help caseworkers develop a broad view include two specific tools, the genogram and ecomap. The genogram, commonly know as a family tree, assists the family and the caseworker in identifying important members of the family across several generations and identifies patterns of shared caregiving in the family. The ecomap helps the family and the caseworker identify elements in the family's ecological system that currently provide support, contribute to strained relationships, and those that may be incorporated into a system of support for the family. Exercises in the training curriculum allow caseworkers to practice constructing genograms and ecomaps during role play, case staffing, and discussion of fictitious cases.

Ongoing Striving for Cultural Competence

Results of the first phase of the project suggested that many child welfare caseworkers are not aware of the cultural strengths of many families of color, which include involvement of several members of the extended family in child rearing. Curriculum content stresses that child welfare caseworkers must be able to recognize cultural values and strengths that may be different from those of the dominant society. The curriculum includes content on cultural strengths and natural helping traditions, with special emphasis on African American families. It includes exercises and stresses that cultural competence is not a goal that is achieved, but a process of striving to become increasingly self-aware, to value diversity, and to become knowledgeable about cultural strengths of families served by the child welfare system. It also includes a framework for assessing families that is strengths based and applicable to a variety of family forms.

Collaboration in Decisionmaking

Steering committee members felt strongly that effective permanency planning required collaboration in decisionmaking between members of the child's kinship system and the child welfare system and noted that this appeared to be missing in the practice of caseworkers interviewed during the first phase of the project. Interviews with supervisors revealed that most caseworkers did not have skills in convening and engaging relevant members of the child's kinship network in the development of a safe and permanent plan for the child. Therefore, the curriculum includes substantial content on convening members of the kinship network, conducting family meetings, and negotiating with families to facilitate permanency decisions. Learning activities include exercises to help caseworkers develop a strategy for convening members of the kinship network and family meeting role plays.

Building the Case Management Capacities of Kinship Networks

The steering committee expressed concerns that child welfare caseworkers were apparently not looking beyond the goal of closing a case through reunification, adoption, or transfer of guardianship. The training curriculum stresses that permanent plans that ensure protection of the child and that support the child and family's well-being require a long-term view, one that goes beyond the child's exit from state custody. Curriculum content stresses that planning for permanency requires child welfare caseworkers to support or to build the kinship network's ability to anticipate problems and needs several years into the future. The curriculum contains criteria for determining the appropriateness of permanent plans that assist the caseworker in developing a long-term view with the family. Learning activities are included that apply these criteria to case scenarios or the caseworker's own cases.

Results of the Field Test

The field test involved 267 children ranging in age from nearly 1 year to 15 years of age (median age=7 years). Unlike the first phase sample, all children in each family selected for the study who had been in state custody for at least one year and were under the age of 15 were included. Therefore, in the second phase of the study, more than one child from several families were included. The average child had three siblings in state custody. Characteristics of the children included in the second phase of the study are similar to those selected for the first phase. The children selected for this study were predominantly African American, half were female, most were placed due to neglect, and approximately 28% were already living with the current caregiver when state custody was taken. There were no differences in the characteristics of the 185 children served by caseworkers in the demonstration group and the 82 children served by caseworkers in the comparison group or in the characteristics of caseworkers who served them.

Achievement of Permanency

The results of the field test revealed no differences between the demonstration and comparison groups regarding the percentage of cases for which permanency goals were achieved through adoption, transfer of legal guardianship, or reunification with birth parents. Overall, the rates of completed adoptions were very low in both the experimental and comparison groups. The low rates of completed adoptions can be primarily attributed to the slow, bureaucratic processes for scheduling termination of parental rights and adoption hearings in juvenile court in Cook County, Illinois. However, the preliminary data analyses also reveal low rates of implementation of the practice principles and methods in the six months following training of the caseworkers in the demonstration groups. For example, caseworkers rarely reported involvement of persons in the child's kinship network, other than the current caregiver, in case planning and decisionmaking.

Implementation Problems

The failure to detect differences in the practice of caseworkers in the demonstration and comparison groups is partly attributable to caseworker turnover and mobility. Several caseworkers in the demonstration group resigned, were terminated, transferred to other programs or teams in the agency, or were promoted to supervisory positions on other teams. This staff turnover and mobility problem, typical in child welfare, nonetheless resulted in cases being transferred from caseworkers who had been trained in the practice principles to caseworkers who had not been trained.

Low rates of implementation of the practice principles and methods by caseworkers who had participated in training can also be attributed to the multiple demands placed upon caseworkers and supervisors in the child welfare system. It became clear that caseworkers who were attempting to accomplish multiple tasks and to address many policy mandates related to each of their cases were not likely to implement the practice principles and methods being tested through this project, unless these practice principles and methods were stressed by their supervisors in regular supervisory contacts.

Perhaps the most serious barrier to implementation of the practice principles and methods during the field test was turnover at the supervisory level. Supervisors were considered to be "co-trainers" in this project. Project staff met with supervisors in two to three two-hour sessions to plan the training and discuss the practice principles and methods. However, only one of the six supervisors who participated in the initial meetings remained in their positions three months following the caseworker training. As each new supervisor joined the project, project staff attempted to familiarize them with the practice principles and methods; however, these new supervisors were not in a strong position to monitor implementation of the practice principles and methods that they were just learning themselves.

The practice principles and methods were markedly different from the practice of caseworkers and the emphasis of supervisors prior to the field test. Initially, supervisors, like caseworkers, were unfamiliar with the practice principles and methods. During the monthly consultation meetings with supervisors following the staff training, it became clear that supervisors were not likely to encourage and reinforce the implementation of the practice principles and methods, unless they too were consistently encouraged to do so. After approximately one year of monthly consultation meetings, supervisors began to discuss ways in which they were reinforcing use of the practice principles and methods, for example, by using the genogram and ecomap in their supervisory sessions and encouraging caseworkers to convene meetings with several members of the child's kinship network.

Usefulness and Effectiveness

Although analysis of the data collected six months prior to and six months following training revealed no differences between the demonstration and comparison units, anecdotal data collected during case consultations and consultations with supervisors support the usefulness and potential effectiveness of the practice principles and methods identified through this project. For example, caseworkers and supervisors identified specific cases that they believed represented "successful" adoptions. These cases were characterized by involvement of several members of the child's kinship network in decisionmaking and planning.

In these apparently successful cases, family members struggled with and were able to find ways of creatively redefining family roles to creatively fit their family and larger kinship system. In some cases, both maternal and paternal relatives were involved. In some cases the biological parents willingly signed specific consents to relinquish parental rights if the current relative caregiver agreed to adopt the child. Also, caseworkers facilitated case planning with a long-term view of child rearing, asking family members to plan for the child's protection, permanence, and well-being if the caregiver became ill or died, and to consider what difficulties might emerge in attempting to care for the child as the child grew older, reached adolescence, or began to display behavioral problems.

On the other hand, caseworkers and supervisors discussed with project staff specific kinship care arrangements that disrupted as termination of parental rights was being pursued or shortly after the adoption was finalized. In these cases, there was little involvement of the members of the child's kinship system in planning and decisionmaking. It appeared also that adoption was "marketed" to the caregiver as the preferred permanency option for the child. It did not appear that the caseworker was involved in facilitating informed decisionmaking or in facilitating a long-term view of child rearing in discussions with the caregiver.

Summary and Recommendations

This chapter described the Illinois project and the methods used to develop and test a model of practice designed to facilitate permanency for children in kinship foster care. The three phases of the project, the practice principles and methods, and results of the research and demonstration project were described. While results of the project suggest that further testing is needed, anecdotal data suggest that the practice principles and methods proposed by this project are essential components of child welfare practice that have the potential for facilitating true permanence for children in kinship foster care.

The results of this project suggest that considerable support is required at all levels of the child welfare system to allow an adequate test of these principles and methods. The complicated nature of the child welfare system is itself a barrier to implementation of innovative practice principles and methods. The experience of this study also suggests that attempts to change casework practice in child welfare require a multilevel and long-term approach. In this project it was clear that the training sessions alone were not effective in teaching child welfare caseworkers practice principles and methods with which they were unfamiliar. The three to five half-days of case consultation helped. However, it appears that implementation of these practice principles with actual cases only occurred when the supervisors encouraged and reinforced their use. It also appears that supervisors required ongoing reminders and support in monthly consultation sessions with project staff following the training sessions to encourage caseworkers to implement innovative practice principles and methods.

There were a number of lessons learned from this process of building practice through research. Any effort to define and implement principles and methods of best practice requires an ongoing process of negotiation and inclusion of supervisors, caseworkers, recipients of service, and others involved in the child welfare system to continually bring research closer to practice, while simultaneously influencing practice.

Also, efforts to define and test best practice models should include steering committees made up of persons with expertise directly related to the service under study, as well as persons with expertise in broadly related fields. Given the diversity of the children and families served by the child welfare system and the complexity of needs and issues to be considered, a broad view is required to counter the tendency to take narrow perspectives or focus on single solutions. Persons reflecting the perspectives of the formal as well as the informal systems of care should be represented on steering committees. Representatives of the larger systems (such as courts, health care, and schools) that impact the lives of children and families involved in the child welfare system should also be included on steering committees.

Multiple methods to solicit feedback from caseworkers, supervisors, service recipients, and other service providers about the use of and impact of practice principles and methods should be built into the project. Consultations, focus groups, case record reviews, and other interviewing procedures might be used to identify barriers to implementation, conditions that facilitate implementation, and perceived costs and benefits of the practice model.

It is critically important to reinforce the use of the principles and methods through the supervisory and in-service training process. If not reinforced, skills will not be developed or used. Also, the high rate of turnover in the child welfare field requires ongoing training to prepare newly hired caseworkers.

Research and demonstration projects that develop and test principles and methods of best practice must be flexible to accommodate to the constant changes in policy, legal mandates, and new initiatives that emerge, which may impact methods of practice. While it can be daunting indeed to attempt to define principles and methods of best practice in an environment subject to such change, these very changes provide excellent opportunities to test out and refine the principles and methods of practice.

References

Barth, R. P., Courtney, M. E., Berrick, J. D., & Albert, V. (1994). *From child abuse to permanency planning: Child welfare services, pathways and placements*. New York: Aldine de Gruyter.

Berrick, J. D., Barth, R. P., & Needell, B. (1994). A comparison of kinship foster homes and foster family homes: Implications for kinship care as family preservation. *Children and Youth Services Review, 16*, 33-63.

Bonecutter, F. J., & Gleeson, J. P. (1997). *Achieving permanency for children in kinship foster care: A training manual*. Chicago: Jane Addams College of Social Work and the Jane Addams Center for Social Policy and Research, University of Illinois at Chicago.

Emlen, A., Lahti, J., Downs, G., McKay, A., & Downs, S. (1978). *Overcoming barriers to planning for children in foster care*. Portland, OR: Regional Research Institute for Human Services, Portland State University.

Gleeson, J. P., Bonecutter, F. J., & Altshuler, S. J. (1995). Facilitating permanence in kinship care: The Illinois project. In G. R. Anderson & J. P. Gleeson (Eds.), *Kinship care forum* (pp. 7-24). New York: National Resource Center for Permanency Planning at the Hunter College School of Social Work.

Gleeson, J. P., O'Donnell, J., & Bonecutter, F. J. (1997). Understanding the complexity of practice in kinship foster care. *Child Welfare, 76*(6), 801-826.

Gleeson J. P., & Philbin, C. (1996). Preparing caseworkers for practice in kinship foster care: The supervisor's dilemma. *The Clinical Supervisor, 14*(1), 19-34.

Goerge, R. M. (1990). The reunification process in substitute care. *Social Service Review, 64*(3), 422-457.

Meyer, B. S., & Link, M. K. (1990). *Kinship foster care: The double-edged dilemma*. Rochester, NY: Task Force on Permanency Planning for Foster Children, Inc.

O'Donnell, J. M. (1995). *Casework practice with fathers in kinship foster care*. Unpublished doctoral dissertation, University of Illinois at Chicago.

Stein, T. J., Gambrill, E. D., & Wiltse, K. T. (1978). *Children in foster homes: Achieving continuity of care*. New York: Holt Rinehart & Winston.

Tatara, T. (1994). The recent rise in the U. S. child substitute care population: An analysis of national child substitute care flow data. In R. P. Barth, J. D. Berrick, & N. Gilbert (Eds.), *Child welfare research review. Volume 1* (pp. 126-145). New York: Columbia University Press.

Testa, M. F. (1992). Conditions of risk for substitute care. *Children and Youth Services Review, 14*, 27-36.

Testa, M. F. (1993). *Home of relative (HMR) program in Illinois: Interim report* (rev. ed.). Chicago: School of Social Service Administration, University of Chicago.

Testa, M. F. (1997). Kinship foster care in Illinois. In R. Barth, J. D. Berrick, & N. Gilbert (Eds.), *Child welfare research review. Volume 2* (pp. 101-129). New York: Columbia University Press.

Thornton, J. L. (1991). Permanency planning for children in kinship foster homes. *Child Welfare, 70*(5), 593-601.

Wulczyn, F. H., & Goerge, R.M. (1992). Foster care in New York and Illinois: The challenge of rapid change. *Social Service Review, 66*(2), 278-294.

3

Who Decides? Predicting Caseworkers' Adoption and Guardianship Discussions with Kinship Caregivers*

James P. Gleeson

In recent years kinship care has been viewed as a barrier rather than a pathway to permanence for children who are the legal responsibility of the child welfare system. Although the body of research has grown considerably in the 1990s, there is much that is not yet understood about kinship care as a child welfare service and the achievement of permanence for children in kinship foster care. The existing research indicates that children who are placed with relatives remain in the custody of the child welfare system longer than children who are placed with nonrelated foster parents. What is not clear is who is involved in the case planning process and what the factors are that influence caseworkers to discuss specific potential permanent living arrangements with the child's kinship caregiver.

---

* An earlier version of this chapter was presented to the 43rd Annual Program Meeting of the Council on Social Work Education, Chicago, Illinois, March 7, 1997. The author thanks Christina Carlberg, Linda Gleeson, Sally Mason, Ted Thompson, and Lori Zimand for their comments on an earlier version of this chapter. The research was supported by grant number 90-C0-0595 from the Adoption Opportunities Office of the Administration for Children, Youth, and Families, U.S. Department of Health and Human Services, with in-kind contributions from the Jane Addams College of Social Work, Central Baptist Family Services, Lutheran Social Services of Illinois, the Jane Addams Center for Social Policy and Research, the Jane Addams Hull-House Museum, Loyola University of Chicago School of Social Work, Life Concerns, and the Assistance of the Illinois Department of Children and Family Services.

The study that is described in this chapter explored whether adoption and transfer of legal guardianship were discussed with kinship caregivers of children in state custody. The study also identified variables that predicted whether child welfare practitioners discussed each of these permanency options with kinship caregivers.

Kinship Foster Care as a Path to Permanency

Child welfare caseloads have grown markedly since 1986 [Wulczyn et al. 1997; Barth et al. 1994]. Placement rates have increased most dramatically for children of color living in the poorest inner city communities [IDCFS 1995a; Testa 1997; Wulczyn 1994]. These children are entering the child welfare system at an increasing rate and are more likely to be placed in "foster care" with relatives (kinship foster care) than their white peers [Wulczyn & Goerge 1992; Wulczyn 1994]. Children in kinship foster care return home at a slower rate than children in other forms of substitute care, and children who do not return home from kinship care have been less likely to be adopted, or otherwise escape the monitoring of the child welfare system than children placed in other types of substitute care arrangements [Courtney & Needell 1997; Wulczyn, Harden, & Goerge 1997]. The fact that children in kinship care have remained in state custody longer is puzzling because many of these children have been well cared for and have lived in stable settings with kinship caregivers willing to rear them to the age of majority [Berrick, Barth, & Needell 1994; Thornton 1991; Zuravin et al. 1993].

Various reasons have been proposed to explain the slower rates of discharge from kinship foster care. There has been speculation that parents are less likely to work hard toward reunification if children are with relatives than they would be if the children were living with nonrelatives [Meyer & Link 1990]. Prior research has suggested that caregivers are reluctant to consider adopting related children in their care because they feel that the children are "already family" and they are uncomfortable with the fact that adoption requires termination of the biological parents' rights [Berrick et al. 1994; Gleeson et al. 1997; Gleeson & Philbin 1996; Schwartz 1993;

Testa et al. 1996; Thornton 1991]. Prior research also suggests that case-workers are less likely to consider adoption to be an appropriate goal for children who are in kinship foster care than they are for children placed in nonrelative foster care [Thornton 1991].

Other factors have been identified that may influence a caseworker's decision to consider adoption of children by kinship caregivers. The fact that kinship caregivers are older, on average, than nonrelative foster parents and children living in kinship care are younger, on average, than children living in nonrelative foster care has been identified by some advocates as a problem. In Illinois, for example, the Illinois Department of Children and Family Services (IDCFS) Inspector General has raised concerns about adoption of very young children being pursued with grandparents or great-grandparents who are 60 years of age or older. The concern is that these grandparents will not live long enough to raise the children to adulthood, or their health or energy level will not support the care of young, energetic children. Therefore, both the age of the child and the age of the caregiver may influence caseworkers' decisions to discuss adoption with caregivers.

The caregiver's marital status may also influence the caseworker's decision to discuss adoption. Caseworkers may believe that two parents are better able to manage the long-term care of related children than a single adoptive parent. The size of the sibling group that the kinship caregiver takes into the home may also be a consideration. Assuming permanent child-rearing responsibilities for a large sibling group is generally considered to be more challenging than assuming care of one or two children. Also, the length of time that children reside in a relative's home is likely to influence the caseworker's decision to discuss adoption. One would assume that caseworkers would be more likely to discuss adoption with relatives when the children have been living in the caregivers' homes for longer time periods, when it appears that the children will not return to live with biological parents, and the caregivers are willing to continue to care for them.

Finally, and most importantly, one would expect that caseworkers would be more willing to discuss adoption with relative caregivers who are able to provide care for the child without the ongoing assistance of the child welfare system. When children are adopted, they exit the custody of the child welfare system and the child welfare system is no longer responsible for monitoring the case. Therefore, adoption should not be considered for caregivers who are unable to ensure the child's safety and ensure that the child's needs are met, without the child welfare system's ongoing involvement.

Discharge from the custody of the child welfare system can also be accomplished by transferring legal guardianship of the child to the kinship caregiver or another adult willing and able to rear the child to the age of majority. All of the barriers to considering adoption also apply to transfer of guardianship: age of the caregiver, age of the child, the caregiver's marital status, the size of the sibling group, the length of time the child has been living in the caregiver's home, and the caregiver's ability to care for the child without the involvement of the child welfare system. Also, there may be additional concerns. Some child welfare advocates believe that adoption is the preferred permanency goal for children who cannot return to their parents, and that nonrelative adoptive homes should be sought for children whose relatives are unwilling to adopt. These advocates argue that private guardianship does not provide the level of legal permanence that is provided by adoption because parental rights need not be terminated, in most cases parents retain visitation rights, and guardianship can be vacated by the court at the request of a parent or other interested party [Schwartz 1993]. Also, guardianship ends when the child reaches age 18 and adoption is forever. Others contend that guardianship may be the highest form of permanence possible for some children because it is the option that some families can best accept, and it is the option that best supports the ability of these families to continue their commitment to care for these children, protect them, and facilitate their healthy development.

There may also be financial barriers to caseworkers discussing private guardianship. Federal policies provide financial support to states for foster care and special needs adoption subsidies at a rate that is considerably higher than the AFDC (TANF) child-only rate. While most children living in kinship foster care meet eligibility criteria for special needs adoption subsidies, in most cases only the AFDC subsidy is available to assist kinship caregivers who provide permanent homes for children through private guardianship [Gleeson & Craig 1994]. The foster care subsidy is three to five times higher than the AFDC child-only rate in most states, and the disparity becomes greater as the number of children in care increases [IDCFS 1995a; Kusserow 1992; Testa 1993]. The disparity between the AFDC subsidy and the foster care subsidy has been described as a financial disincentive and a barrier to children returning to their parents or exiting state custody through transfer of legal guardianship to kinship caregivers. While it may be that the difference in subsidy rates acts as a financial disincentive, it is not clear how this disincentive operates and what role, if any, the child welfare practitioner plays in preventing or facilitating transfer of legal guardianship to kinship caregivers.

The assumption has been that families are reluctant to pursue permanency goals that provide lower levels of financial support than they currently receive to care for children while they are in the custody of the child welfare system. Research conducted in California seems to support this assumption, since the reunification and reentry rates in that state are lower for children in kinship foster homes that are IV-E eligible and receive the full foster care subsidy than they are for children in kinship foster homes that are not IV-E eligible and receive the AFDC child-only rate [Berrick et al. 1998; Courtney & Needell 1997; Courtney et al. 1997]. When children are reunified with parents, the parents may be eligible to receive the AFDC child-only rate. If the case is not IV-E eligible, there is no difference in the subsidy received by the caregiver and the parent. If the case is IV-E eligible, the family experiences a reduction in the subsidy provided to help them care for the child if the child is reunified with the parent. However, Courtney, Piliavin, and Entner Wright [1997] acknowledge that it may not be family members who are deciding that the family cannot support the care of the child at the lower subsidy level. It may be the caseworker. The relationship between levels of reimbursement and the achievement of permanency is not clear, however, since children who lived in kinship foster homes that received foster care payments were also less likely to be adopted, even though many of these children were eligible for the special needs adoption subsidy [Berrick et al. 1998; Courtney & Needell 1997].

Description of the Study

The study is a secondary analysis of data collected during the first phase of the "Achieving Permanency for Children in Kinship Foster Care" project [see Bonecutter, Chapter 2]. The overall purpose of the "Achieving Permanency" project was to develop and test a practice model designed to improve the permanency outcomes for children placed in foster care with relatives. During the first phase of that project, current practice in kinship care was examined and barriers to permanency were identified. The study described in this chapter looks specifically at caseworkers' discussions of adoption and transfer of guardianship with the kinship caregivers of children who had been in the custody of the child welfare system and living in the caregiver's home for at least one year. The study examined the following research questions:

- Did caseworkers discuss with kinship caregivers whether they were willing to consider adopting the child in their care who was in the legal custody of the child welfare system?

- Did caseworkers discuss with kinship caregivers whether they were willing to consider assuming private guardianship of the child in their care who was in the legal custody of the child welfare system?

- Which variables explained whether child welfare practitioners discussed adoption with kinship caregivers?

- Which variables explained whether child welfare practitioners discussed transfer of guardianship with kinship caregivers?

- Did the same variables explain whether child welfare practitioners discussed adoption and transfer of guardianship with kinship caregivers?

Data were collected through lengthy interviews with caseworkers focusing on 77 children living in kinship foster care for at least one year. The interviews were conducted from March through May of 1993. The purpose of the first phase of this project was to define practice in kinship foster care and to identify barriers to permanency as well as conditions that facilitate permanency for children in kinship foster care. Permanency was defined as living in a home with adults who make a commitment to raise the child to the age of majority, outside of the care and custody of the child welfare system. While reunification with biological parents is the preferred permanency option, when this can be accomplished swiftly and safely, reunification was not likely for the majority of children in this sample. All of the children in this study had been in the custody of the child welfare system for at least one year, and in most cases it was clear that reunification efforts had been unsuccessful. If an exit from the care and custody of the child welfare system was to be achieved prior to aging out of the system, the most likely permanency options were adoption or guardianship.

Sampling Procedures

The 77 cases were selected from the caseloads of 41 caseworkers in two voluntary child welfare agencies serving children and their families through purchase of service contracts with the Illinois Department of Children and Family Services. Cases eligible for the study were defined as children who had been in out-of-home care through the child welfare system for one or more years and who were living in a kinship foster home monitored by one of the two participating agencies at the time of data collection. At the time of the interviews, all of the children in the study were in the legal custody of the state child welfare system and lived in homes that were monitored for compliance with standards for relative foster homes. All of the kinship homes were receiving foster care payments for the children in care, which averaged $314 per month. Most of the children in the study were eligible for the special needs adoption subsidy that closely approximated the foster care payment, if the caregivers adopted the children. If caregivers assumed private guardianship of the children, they were eligible to receive the AFDC child-only subsidy of $102 per month for the first child and progressively less for each additional child.

To prevent overburdening caseworkers, no more than two cases were selected from the caseload of each caseworker. Two families were randomly selected from each caseworker's caseload. One child who met the sample selection criteria was then selected from each family to be the focus of the interview. A total of 91 cases were selected. Interviews were completed on 77 of the 91 cases, an 85% completion rate and a 9% sample of the total number of kinship foster care child cases served by the two participating agencies. One of the cases was dropped from the current study because data were not available on the two dependent variables: whether the caseworker discussed adoption and whether the caseworker discussed private guardianship with the kinship caregiver. Therefore, 76 cases were included in this study.

Data Collection

Data were collected during structured, case-specific interviews with the caseworker assigned to the case. The interviews averaged two hours in length. Most caseworkers participated in two interviews, one for each of the cases randomly selected from their caseload. The interview protocol contained 195 questions that examined case background and permanency planning status; the caseworker's knowledge of and interactions with the biological parents, the kinship caregiver, the child, and maternal and paternal relatives; case planning activities and service provision; caseworker supervision and consultation; and caseworker perceptions about the difficulty of the case. The questionnaire was developed by research staff specifically to address the purposes of the "Achieving Permanency" project and was pilot tested and revised to ensure that questions were clearly worded. Research staff met throughout the data collection period to discuss the interview process and to ensure consistency in the way that interviews were conducted. The variables that are included in the current study were selected from the rich data set that resulted from the lengthy interviews with caseworkers.

Operational Definitions of Variables in the Study

The two dependent variables in this study are dichotomous measures that indicate whether adoption and private guardianship were discussed with the kinship caregiver. Caseworkers were asked whether adoption and private guardianship of the child had been discussed with the child's kinship caregiver by the current or a previous caseworker. Each of these variables was coded "1" if the specific permanency option was discussed and "0" if it was not discussed. Caseworkers were also asked to explain their reasons if either adoption or guardianship had not been discussed with the caregiver and their responses were recorded in narrative form and later categorized.

Seven independent variables were included in this study: (1) the caregiver's age, (2) the caregiver's marital status, (3) the number of siblings living in the same relative's home with the child who was the focus of the study, (4) the child's age, (5) the number of years that the child had lived in the relative's home, (6) the caseworker's rating of the caregiver's need for assistance from the child welfare system, and (7) whether adoption planning was already underway for the child. Each of these independent variables was included in the data set and was thought to possibly influence caseworkers' decisions to discuss adoption or private guardianship with kinship caregivers. Operational definitions of each of these independent variables are listed here:

- *Caregiver's age* is a ratio level variable measured in years. This variable was included among potential predictors because there has been a debate in the field regarding the appropriateness of adoption by older caregivers, particularly when the child is young and will need the care of a parent for many years.

- *Caregiver's marital status* is measured as a dichotomy. Caregivers who were married at the time of the data collection were rated "1" and those who were never married, divorced, separated, or widowed were rated "0." Although single parent adoptions are common in the child welfare system, in the past adoption standards required that adoptive parents be married. Therefore, marital status may influence caseworkers' willingness to consider adoption to be an appropriate permanency goal. Also, being married may suggest that the caregiver has some assistance in caring for the child or financially supporting the children and this may influence caseworkers to discuss adoption or guardianship with the caregiver.

- *Number of siblings in the home* is a ratio level variable that indicates how many of the child's siblings were living in the same relative home with the child who was the focus of the interview. The number of siblings living in the same home was included in the study because it is commonly thought that caring for a larger number of children is more difficult than caring for one child. Also, policies differ on financial subsidies that accompany adoption and guardianship and these differences are related to the number of children in a sibling group.

- *The child's age* is a ratio level variable measured in months. This variable was included in the study because many believe that adoption is the preferred permanency goal for very young children and that guardianship is appropriate only for older children when both reunification and adoption have been ruled out. Also, some child advocates have expressed concerns that older caregivers should not adopt or become guardians of very young children.

- *Years living with relative* is a ratio level variable measured in years. This variable was included in the study because it is expected that the longer a child lived in the same home the more likely it is that adoption or guardianship would have been discussed with the kinship caregiver.

- *Caseworker ratings of the caregiver's need for assistance* is a three category ordinal variable, with higher ratings indicating greater need for assistance from the child welfare system (1=able to care for the child without the assistance of the child welfare system, 2=needs some assistance now or will need assistance in the future, 3=needs regular monitoring and assistance from the child welfare system).

- *Is adoption planned?* Caseworkers were asked to describe the current permanency goal for the child and the permanency goal that is projected for the case in the coming year. A dichotomous variable was constructed that indicated whether the caseworker considered the case to be headed toward adoption or not (1=adoption planned, 0=adoption not planned). This variable was included in analysis of the predictors of discussions about private guardianship with kinship caregivers. This variable was included because it makes sense that private guardianship may not be discussed with a caregiver who had already decided to adopt the child.

Data Analysis

Univariate, bivariate, and multivariate analyses were conducted to address the research questions. At the univariate level, the frequency distributions and, where appropriate, measures of central tendency and dispersion were computed for each independent variable. Also, the percentage of cases for which adoption and private guardianship were discussed with kinship caregivers was calculated. In addition, the caseworkers' narrative explanations for not discussing adoption or guardianship were content analyzed. The common reasons that caseworkers gave for not discussing adoption or guardianship were identified. At the bivariate level, zero-order correlations were reported between all independent and dependent variables included in the study. At the multivariate level, two logistic regression equations were computed to determine which of the independent variables contributed to the ability to predict whether adoption or legal guardianship was discussed with kinship caregivers. Direct logistic regression analyses were conducted, entering all predictor variables in one step. Logistic regression was used because it is the most appropriate method of multivariate analysis when the dependent variable is dichotomous [Tabachnick & Fidell 1996]. Odds ratios were calculated to estimate the likelihood that discussion of adoption and guardianship was associated with each of the predictor variables. The Wald statistic was used to determine the statistical significance of the odds ratio, controlling for all independent variables in the equation.

Results

Results of the study are presented in three sections. First, results of the univariate analysis are presented, including a description of the characteristics of children, caregivers, and kinship foster care households, caseworkers' ratings of caregivers' needs for assistance and monitoring from the child welfare system, and the percentage of cases for which adoption and private guardianship were discussed. Caseworkers' reasons for eliminating adoption or guardianship from consideration as a permanency plan for the child are also reported. Second, bivariate relationships between all independent and dependent variables are presented. Third, analyses of the relationships between predictor variables and whether adoption and guardianship were discussed are presented, describing findings of the logistic regression analyses.

Univariate Analysis

While this sample was drawn from only two child welfare agencies, the characteristics of the children, caregivers, and families are similar to the characteristics of the population of children, caregivers, and families involved in kinship foster care in Illinois at the time the study was conducted. Children in this study ranged from 19 months to 19 years of age. Their mean age was 8 years (standard deviation = 4.5 years). Ninety-six percent of the children were African American. Two children in the sample were Latino and one was Caucasian. The caregivers with whom the children were living ranged in age from 25 to 72 years, with a mean age of 49.5 years (standard deviation = 10.1 years).* More than 60% of the caregivers were grandparents and 7% were great-grandparents. Nearly 21% were aunts and uncles. The remaining 11% included older siblings and other relatives. Thirty percent of the caregivers were married and 70% were single. Caseworkers identified the primary caregiver as female for each of the 76 cases. The number of people living in the caregivers' homes ranged from two to 12 individuals and the number of children living in caregivers' homes ranged from one to nine. Nearly 80% of the children selected for this study were living in the same home with at least one sibling and one child lived in the same home with five siblings. The mean number of siblings living in the same relative's home with the child who was the focus of the interview was 1.5 (standard deviation = 1.25). On

---

* Caseworkers did not know the age of two caregivers. Rather than exclude these cases from further analysis, the mean caregiver age was substituted in these cases and all cases were included in logistic regression equations.

average, the children had been in the current kinship foster home nearly three years, with a range of one to seven years (standard deviation = 1.8 years).

Caseworkers rated 42% of the caregivers as providing good care for the child and needing no help from the child welfare system. Caseworkers rated 47% of the caregivers as needing some help on occasion or needing some help in the future to raise the child. Caseworkers indicated that 11% of caregivers required close monitoring by the child welfare system because of serious or ongoing problems in caring for the child.

Caseworkers were asked whether they or previous caseworkers had discussed adoption and guardianship with the kinship caregiver. They reported that adoption had been discussed with 82% of the children's caregivers but that guardianship had been discussed with only 51% of the caregivers. Caseworkers' responses to open-ended questions explained their reasons for not discussing adoption or guardianship and caregivers' reasons for not considering adoption or guardianship. In a few cases the permanency goal for the child was to return home to the biological parents. In others the child was considered by the caseworker to be too old to be adopted or the caregiver did not want full responsibility for the child. In some cases the caregiver was described as being unable to care for the child without the support of the child welfare system because of the child's severe behavior problems, their own advanced age, illness, or other caregiving limitations.

In the cases where caseworkers thought it was inappropriate to discuss private guardianship with the caregiver, the most common reason given was that the financial support received by the caregiver would be reduced from the foster care payment level to the AFDC level. Further exploration revealed some additional systemic barriers to pursuing transfer of guardianship as a permanency goal in Illinois. While private guardianship has always been a possible exit from the child welfare system, it had not been listed among the official permanency goals in sections of the IDCFS policy and procedures manual that relate to service planning or case review. Until recently, guardianship had rarely been discussed in training on permanency planning in Illinois. Also, a lawsuit and consent decree [*Reid v. Suter*

1992] discouraged diversion of children from the child welfare system through guardianship arrangements with relatives. In spite of these systemic barriers, transfer of legal guardianship had been explored with some kinship caregivers.

Bivariate Analysis: Relationships Between Independent and Dependent Variables

The zero-order correlations between all independent and dependent variables in the study are summarized in the correlation matrix in Table 3-1. These correlations were computed using Pearson's *r*, except when the caregiver's need for assistance was one of the variables. In the latter cases, Spearman's *rho* was used, since this statistic is the appropriate measure of association for ordinal variables.

Statistically significant correlations were observed between the caregiver's need for assistance from the child welfare system and the number of siblings that lived in the caregiver's home with the child. The larger the sibling group, the greater the need for assistance. Also, a statistically significant inverse relationship was observed between the age of the child and whether adoption was planned. The younger the child, the more likely it was that adoption was planned.

Statistically significant relationships were observed between three independent variables and whether adoption was discussed. The longer the child had lived in the relative's home, the more likely it was that adoption had been discussed with the relative caregiver. Also, the greater the caregiver's need for assistance, the less likely it was that adoption was discussed. Also, a statistically significant relationship was observed between adoption being planned and adoption having been discussed with the caregiver. When adoption was being planned by the caseworker, the caseworker was more likely to have discussed adoption with the caregiver; however, the strength of this association was modest.

Three independent variables also demonstrated statistically significant relationships with whether private guardianship had been discussed with the kinship caregiver; however, only one of these variables (length of time living in the caregiver's home) also demonstrated a statistically significant

Table 3-1. Zero-Order Correlations[a] Between All Independent and Dependent Variables

	1	2	3	4	5	6	7	8	9
1 Caregiver's age (in yrs.)	1.00								
2 Caregiver's marital status[b]	.05	1.00							
3 Number of siblings in home	.02	-.02	1.00						
4 Child's age (in months)	.03	.13	-.14	1.00					
5 Years living with relative	.18	.11	.09	.16	1.00				
6 Caregiver's need for assistance[c]	.11	-.05	.32*	.05	-.05	1.00			
7 Adoption planned[d]	-.16	-.07	-.04	-.23*	.18	-.09	1.00		
8 Was adoption discussed?[d]	.08	.02	-.02	-.09	.24*	-.24*	.28*	1.00	
9 Was guardianship discussed[d]	.00	.07	-.32*	-.06	.34*	-.18	.12	.35*	1.00

*$p \leq .05$, two-tailed.

a   Pearson's *r* computed except when caregiver's need for assistance was one of the variables. Spearman's *rho* was used in these cases since caregiver's need for assistance is an ordinal-level variable.

b   Currently married=1; Not currently married=0.

c   Able to care for the child without the assistance of the child welfare system=1; Need some assistance now or in the future=2; Serious problems, need regular monitoring=3.

d   Yes=1; No=0.

relationship with adoption discussions. The longer a child lived in the caregiver's home, the more likely it was that transfer of guardianship had been discussed with the caregiver. A statistically significant inverse relationship was observed between the size of the sibling group living in the home and whether guardianship was discussed. The more siblings living in the same relative's home with the child, the less likely it was that transfer of guardianship had been discussed with the caregiver. Also, a statistically significant, but moderate, positive relationship was observed between the discussion of adoption and the discussion of guardianship with the kinship caregiver. When adoption was discussed, it was somewhat more likely that guardianship had been discussed as well. The relationship between the caregiver's need for assistance from the child welfare system and the discussion of guardianship was not statistically significant.

Multivariate Analysis: Predicting Discussion of Adoption and Guardianship

The logistic regression analysis revealed that at the .05 level, the only significant unique predictor of whether adoption was discussed with the caregiver was the caseworker's rating of the caregiver's ability to care for the child without the monitoring of the child welfare system (Table 3-2). The odds ratio of .24 indicates a 76% reduction in the likelihood that the caseworker discussed adoption with each unit increase in the rating of the caregiver's need for assistance from the child welfare system.

In contrast, the best predictors of whether guardianship was discussed with the kinship caregiver were the number of siblings living in the same home with the child and the number of years the child had lived with the relative under state custody (Table 3-3). The larger the sibling group, the less likely it was that private guardianship was discussed. The odds ratio of .38 indicates that the likelihood that a caseworker discussed guardianship with the caregiver decreased by 62% with each additional sibling living in the same relative's home with the child. Also, the longer the child had been living in the caregiver's home under the custody of the child welfare system, the more likely it was that guardianship was discussed. The odds ratio of 2.07 indicates that each year a child lived in the same relative's home doubled the likelihood that guardianship had been discussed. This logistic regression model included a dichotomous variable that indicated whether adoption was planned for the child. This variable did not contribute to the explanation of whether guardianship was discussed with the caregiver.

Each logistic regression model was statistically reliable in distinguishing between cases for which adoption or guardianship was discussed and not discussed, compared to constant only models. Prediction success was 86% overall for discussion of adoption and 74% for discussion of guardianship. The models were least successful in predicting the cases for which adoption was not discussed (29%) and highly successful in predicting when adoption was discussed (98%); this is because adoption was discussed for most cases. Success in predicting cases in which guardianship was dis-

Table 3-2. Logistic Regression Analysis of Predictors of Whether Adoption of the Child Was Discussed with the Kinship Caregiver

	Unstandardized Logit Coefficients	*r*	Odds Ratio	Wald χ^2
Caregiver's age (in yrs.)	.04	.00	1.04	1.37
Caregiver's marital status[a]	.03	.00	1.04	.00
Number of siblings in home	.09	.00	1.10	.10
Child's age (in months)	-.01	.00	.99	.70
Years living with relative	.54	.16	1.71	3.78
Caregiver's need for assistance[b]	-1.43	-.21	.24*	5.32
Constant	1.30			.55

$\chi^2 = 13.69$, $df = 6$, $p < .05$

*$p < .05$, two-tailed.

a   Currently married=1; Not currently married=0.

b   Able to care for the child without the assistance of the child welfare system=1; Need some assistance now or in the future=2; Serious problems, need regular monitoring=3.

cussed with the caregiver was 71% and prediction of cases in which guardianship was not discussed was 76%.

Clearly this study has limitations. Generalizability of results of this study is limited by the relatively small sample size and the fact that the study was conducted in two private agencies in one city in which the rate of kinship care placements is among the highest in the country. Also, the logistic regression models used in these analyses cannot be considered complete. There are other influences not included in the current analyses that may explain why caseworkers do not discuss adoption with some caregivers. Also, the current analyses do not include all factors that influence caseworkers to discuss or not discuss guardianship with caregivers. However, the current analysis did identify differences in patterns of relationships between several variables of importance and whether the caseworker discussed adoption or guardianship with kinship caregivers.

Table 3-3. Logistic Regression Analysis of Predictors of Whether Private Guardianship Was Discussed with the Kinship Caregiver

---

	Unstandardized Logit Coefficients	r	Odds Ratio	Wald χ^2
Caregiver's age (in yrs.)	-.02	.00	.98	.47
Caregiver's marital status[a]	-.19	.00	.83	.10
Number of siblings in home	-.98	-.25	.38*	8.36
Child's age (in months)	-.01	-.12	.99	3.46
Years living with relative	.73	.28	2.07*	10.37
Caregiver's need for assistance[b]	.04	.00	1.05	.01
Adoption planned[c]	.10	.00	1.11	.03
Constant	1.44			.82

$\chi^2 = 13.69$, $df = 6$, $p < .05$

*$p \leq .05$, two-tailed.

a   Currently married=1; Not currently married=0.

b   Able to care for the child without the assistance of the child welfare system=1; Need some assistance now or in the future=2; Serious problems, need regular monitoring=3.

c   Yes=1; No=0.

Discussion

Results of this study indicate that kinship caregivers of children in the custody of the child welfare system do not always have the opportunity to consider all permanency options that may be legally available to them, even when the caseworker believes that the caregiver is able to rear the child without the assistance of the child welfare system. Caseworkers reported that they did not discuss private guardianship with some kinship caregivers because they either did not understand this permanency option or they did not believe that the caregiver could financially afford to raise the child with the AFDC child-only subsidy, which was significantly lower than the foster care payments the caregiver was receiving. The disparity between foster care payments and the AFDC subsidy increases with the size of the sibling group living with the caregiver. In this study, caseworkers' willingness to discuss private guardianship with caregivers decreased as the size of the sibling group in their care increased.

The good news appears to be that caseworkers did discuss adoption with most caregivers. When they chose not to discuss adoption, the primary reasons for doing so appeared to be that the child was to be reunified with a biological parent or it was the caseworker's assessment that the caregiver was not able to care for the child without the involvement of the child welfare system. The bad news is that discussion of transfer of guardianship was not related to the caregiver's ability to care for the child. The caregiver's ability to care for the child was the only statistically significant predictor of the likelihood that the caseworker discussed adoption with the caregiver, but this did not display a statistically significant relationship to the caseworkers' decisions to discuss transfer of guardianship. At the bivariate level, the number of siblings living with the child in the relative's home was positively correlated with the caregiver's need for assistance from the child welfare system. However, the size of the sibling group was not related to the caseworker's decision to discuss adoption, only guardianship.

The longer the child had been living in the caregiver's home, the greater the likelihood that the caseworker discussed guardianship. The likelihood of the caseworker discussing guardianship with the kinship caregiver dropped as the number of the child's siblings living with the kinship caregiver increased, however. The AFDC subsidy per child decreases as the number of children in a family increases. This is not true for foster care or adoption subsidies. In fact, foster care subsidies increase with the child's age. While it has been widely speculated that the disparity between the AFDC child-only grant and the foster care payment acted as a barrier to the child exiting state custody through transfer of legal guardianship, the assumption was that kinship caregivers made the determination that they could not rear the child with the lower subsidy. In a substantial percentage of cases in the study presented here, caregivers were not even asked to consider private guardianship.

It is likely that individual caseworkers did not independently make decisions to discuss adoption or guardianship with caregivers. Other analyses of the same data set used for this study suggest that supervisors and other formal service providers have more influence over the case planning process than do family members [Bonecutter, Chapter 2; Gleeson et al. 1997]. Therefore, while it usually is the caseworker's responsibility to discuss adoption or guardianship with kinship caregivers, it may not be the caseworker who decides whether these discussions should take place. Supervisors, case reviewers, judges and court personnel, and other professionals may influence this process.

Illinois was recently granted a federal waiver to conduct a demonstration project that tests the effectiveness of using federal matching funds to provide subsidies to kinship caregivers who assume legal guardianship of the child at the same level and using the same formula as the state uses for special needs adoption [IDCFS 1995b]. This is a good idea—one that has been recommended by several child welfare scholars and advocates for more than 15 years [Leashore 1984]. If this permanency option is made available, subsidized guardianship is likely to reduce barriers to children in kinship foster care exiting state custody. Subsidized guardianship does not require termination of parental rights, and, at least in Illinois, it provides a subsidy that is comparable to the foster care and special needs adoption subsidies [IDCFS 1995b; Schwartz 1993]. It eliminates the financial barrier to transfer of legal guardianship to the kinship caregiver. There may be other reasons that caseworkers will not discuss subsidized guardianship with kinship caregivers, however, and these reasons may not be related to the caregivers' abilities to care for children or their need for assistance from the child welfare system.

For those who do not consider subsidized guardianship a legitimate permanency option, perhaps only adoption will be discussed. On the other hand, without a requirement to rule out adoption first, there is a danger that some caseworkers who may consider adoption to be inappropriate for kin, may only discuss subsidized guardianship. Also, it is not only whether these options are discussed with caregivers and other family members, but how they are discussed, whether adequate information is provided, and whether informed choices by family members are encouraged by the child welfare system.

The central question that underlies this study is, "Who decides what permanency options are best for a child and family and what are the criteria for determining whether family members are included in this decision?" When there is an obvious need for child welfare services to ensure a child's safety and adequate care, then it is understandable if child welfare caseworkers and perhaps their supervisors, other social service providers, lawyers, and judges are unwilling to ask caregivers to consider adopting a child or assuming guardianship of the child. When the caregiver is considered to be able to care for the child without the involvement of the child welfare system, however, who decides? Should child welfare caseworkers withhold information about guardianship while discussing adoption with caregivers? Whose decision is it—the formal child welfare system or the family who will live with the decision?

Several compelling implications for future research questions emerge from this study that are important to address to provide guidance to policymakers, caseworkers, their supervisors, judges, case reviewers, and others who determine what decisions families make about their own futures. One important research question that needs to be examined is the comparative benefits of adoption and private guardianship for children in kinship foster care. Studies need to be conducted that compare the stability of living arrangements and child well-being over time for children who exit the custody of the child welfare system through adoption by relatives and transfer of guardianship to relatives. Rigorous evaluations such as the one employed in the Illinois Subsidized Guardianship Waiver Demonstration project are important to determine what benefit and costs are associated with providing a financial subsidy for private guardianship at the same level as is provided for adoption [IDCFS 1995b]. Studies that actually examine the impact of different levels of financial support on placement stability and child well-being are needed to guide both child welfare policy and practice.

Also, studies are needed that closely examine the ways that caseworkers discuss permanency options with caregivers and other family members, not just whether they discuss them. It is important to examine what decisions families make when they are honestly informed of all options available to them. It is also important to compare the short-term and long-term outcomes of decisions that fully involve families and those that are made primarily by the child welfare system. These studies will help us determine the best ways of involving families and the child welfare system in decisions that determine the future living arrangements of children in kinship foster care.

References

Barth, R. P., Courtney, M. E., Berrick, J. D., & Albert V. (1994). *From child abuse to permanency planning: Child welfare services, pathways and placements.* New York: Aldine de Gruyter.

Berrick, J. D., Barth, R. P., & Needell, B. (1994). A comparison of kinship foster homes and foster family homes: Implications for kinship care as family preservation. *Children and Youth Services Review, 16*(1/2), 33-63.

Berrick, J. D., Needell, B., Barth, R. P., & Jonson-Reid, M. (1998). *The tender years: Toward developmentally sensitive child welfare services for very young children.* New York: Oxford University Press.

Courtney, M. E., & Needell, B. (1997). Outcomes of kinship care. In J. D. Berrick, R. P. Barth, & N. Gilbert (Eds.), *Child welfare research review: Volume two.* New York: Columbia University Press: 130-149.

Courtney, M. E., Piliavin, I., & Entner Wright, B. R. (1997). Transitions from and returns to out-of-home care. *Social Service Review, 71*(4), 652-667.

Gleeson, J. P., & Craig, L. C. (1994). Kinship care in child welfare: An analysis of states' policies. *Children and Youth Services Review, 16*(1/2), 7-31.

Gleeson, J. P., O'Donnell, J., & Bonecutter, F. J. (1997). Understanding the complexity of practice in kinship foster care. *Child Welfare, 76*(6), 801-826.

Gleeson, J. P., & Philbin, C. (1996). Preparing caseworkers for practice in kinship foster care: The supervisor's dilemma. *The Clinical Supervisor, 14*(1), 19-34.

Illinois Department of Children and Family Services [IDCFS]. (1995a, February 27). *Illinois HMR Reform Plan.* Chicago: Author.

Illinois Department of Children and Family Services [IDCFS]. (1995b, July 31). Illinois Title IV-E Waiver Request. Chicago: Author.

Kusserow, R. P. (1992). *Using relatives for foster care.* Washington DC: U.S. Department of Health and Human Services, Office of the Inspector General, OEI-06-90-02390.

Leashore, B. R. (1984). Demystifying legal guardianship: An unexplored option for dependent children. *Journal of Family Law, 23*(3), 391-400.

Meyer, B. S., & Link, M. K. (1990). *Kinship foster care: The double edged dilemma.* New York: Task Force on Permanency Planning for Foster Children, Inc.

Reid v. Suter. (May 20, 1992). Order Approving Consent Decree in the Circuit Court of Cook County, Illinois, County Department, Chancery Division.

Schwartz, M. (1993). *Reinventing guardianship: Subsidized guardianship, co-guardians and child welfare.* New York: Vera Institute of Justice.

Tabachnick, B. G., & Fidell, L. S. (1996). *Using multivariate statistics* (3rd ed.). New York: Harper Collins.

Testa, M. F. (1993). *Home of relative (HMR) program in Illinois: Interim report* (rev.). Chicago: School of Social Service Administration, University of Chicago.

Testa, M. F. (1997). Kinship foster care in Illinois. In J. D. Berrick, R. P. Barth, & N. Gilbert (Eds.), *Child welfare research review: Volume two* (101-129). New York: Columbia University Press. .

Testa, M. F., Shook, K. L., Cohen, L., & Woods, M. G. (1996). Permanency planning options for children in formal kinship care. *Child Welfare, 75*(5), 451-470.

Thornton, J. L. (1991). Permanency planning for children in kinship foster homes. *Child Welfare, 70*(5), 593-601.

Wulczyn, F. (1994). Status at birth and infant placements in New York City. In R. P. Barth, J. D. Berrick, & N. Gilbert (Eds.), *Child welfare research review: Volume one* (pp. 146-184). New York: Columbia University Press.

Wulczyn, F. H., & Goerge, R. M. (1992). Foster care in New York and Illinois: The challenge of rapid change. *Social Service Review, 66*(2), 278-294.

Wulczyn, F. H., Harden, A. W., & Goerge, R. M. (1997). *Foster care dynamics 1983- 1994: An update from the multistate foster care data archive.* Chicago: The Chapin Hall Center for Children at the University of Chicago.

Zuravin, S. J., Benedict, M., & Somerfield, M. (1993). Child maltreatment in family foster care. *American Journal of Orthopsychiatry, 63(4),* 589- 596.

4

Adoption and Subsidized Guardianship as Permanency Options in Kinship Foster Care: Barriers and Facilitating Conditions

Sally J. Mason and James P. Gleeson

This chapter describes a qualitative study of permanency planning decisionmaking on behalf of children in kinship foster care, with specific attention to adoption and subsidized guardianship as permanency options. The study took place in 1997, in the midst of several initiatives in Illinois with the overall goal of facilitating permanency for children and reducing the number of children in state custody. Administrators of the Illinois Department of Children and Family Services (IDCFS) requested this study to assist them in identifying barriers to permanency planning as well as conditions that facilitate permanency, particularly for children in kinship foster care.*

This chapter begins with a history of Illinois' attempts to curtail the growth of its kinship foster care caseload and a description of the initiatives that were in place at the time this study was conducted. The purpose and methods of the study are then described, followed by a summary of the results. The chapter ends with a discussion of implications for facilitating permanence in kinship foster care.

---

* Conducted through the Innovative Training for Exemplary Practice in Kinship Foster Care project, supported by Grant Number HHS05CT5037 from the U.S. Children's Bureau and a contract with the Illinois Department of Children and Family Services.

Kinship Foster Care in Illinois

Illinois is the state with the highest percentage of children in the custody of the child welfare system who are living in kinship foster care. The number of children in "home-of-relative" placements grew most strikingly in Illinois from 7,995 in March of 1990 to 26,560 in March of 1995, an increase of 232% [Testa 1995]. During this time period the state's entire caseload of children in out-of-home care grew from fewer than 21,000 to approximately 47,000 children, and the percentage of these children living with kin increased to 57% [McDonald 1995; Testa 1993, 1995]. The growing caseload of children in out-of-home care in Illinois was not only due to increased intake of new cases. The decline in discharges from state custody observed across the country was a problem in Illinois as well, particularly among children in kinship foster care [Wulczyn et al. 1997]. Consistent with findings of studies conducted in several states, placements with relatives were less likely to disrupt and tended to last longer than nonrelative placements, but resulted in lower return home and adoption rates than observed for children in nonrelative care [Barth et al.1994; Goerge 1990; Testa 1995, 1997; Wulczyn & Goerge 1992; Thornton 1991].

The growth of the kinship foster care caseload in Illinois was problematic not only because of the numbers of children in care, but also because many of these kinship foster care placements did not meet criteria for federal matching funds. Therefore, the state was required to provide all of the funding for these cases. Federal reimbursement policies required that children be placed in foster homes that were licensed or approved by the state. Illinois had developed approval standards specifically for kinship homes, but many of these homes had not been approved and remained in a pending status for years [Testa 1997]. In addition, 17% to 45% of new kinship foster care placements that occurred between September 1989 and June 1994 involved children who had been living in the relative's home prior to IDCFS intervention [Testa 1995]. These "nonremoval" cases did not meet federal criteria for out-of-home care and therefore were not eligible for federal matching funds. Although not required by federal policy, Illinois provided the full foster care payment to relatives as soon as they began to care for children in the custody of the child welfare system, even if the case was not eligible for federal matching funds.

Some of the demand for child welfare services in Illinois during the late 1980s and the early 1990s may have been due to the lack of services for children in informal kinship care arrangements. Children placed with relatives were not eligible to receive family preservation services and there were no services in place in Illinois prior to 1995 that specifically targeted kin caring for children who had been left in their care by the parents, unless these children were taken into state custody and the placement became a kinship foster care placement. Also, an Illinois Appellate Court decision [*People v. Thornton* 1990] encouraged the state agency to take into custody children who had been abandoned by parents and left in the care of relatives.

Child welfare agencies in Illinois focused on opening new cases and attempting to approve kinship homes to increase federal reimbursements for this growing service, which distracted from permanency planning for children in kinship foster care. Also, many practitioners in private agencies and IDCFS questioned whether the permanency goals that had been developed for children in traditional nonrelated foster care were relevant for children in kinship foster care. As the kinship foster care caseload grew, IDCFS placed greater emphasis on ensuring that adoption was discussed with kinship caregivers when return home seemed unlikely. It was clear, however, that a substantial percentage of relative caregivers were willing to care for a child to the age of majority but were unwilling to adopt the child. Some of these relatives said that they did not see the importance of adoption because the child was "already family." Others did not want to be part of a process that required termination of the biological parents' rights to the child [Testa et al.1996].

Private guardianship was rarely pursued as a permanency goal, partly because of a lawsuit that discouraged diversion of children and families from the child welfare system through private guardianship [*Reid v. Suter* 1992]. Also, caseworkers were reluctant to consider private guardianship because they believed that many kinship caregivers would not be able to continue to provide care for children without the foster care board payment [Gleeson, Chapter 3]. When caseworkers did discuss this option with relative caregivers, they reported that few were willing to consider it because the only financial subsidy available was the AFDC child-only rate of $102 for the first child, less for each additional child [Gleeson et al.1997]. Continued placement in family foster care, however, was subsidized at an average rate of $314 per month per child and adoption subsidies were available that were nearly as high as the family foster care subsidy rate.

Researchers at the University of Chicago, in conjunction with the Illinois Child Welfare Advisory Committee, developed an additional permanency option for children in formal kinship care who were unable to be adopted or exit the child welfare system through private guardianship arrangements [Testa et al.1996]. This option, "Delegated Relative Authority" (DRA) was intended for children in safe, stable placements with relatives, for whom reunification, adoption, and guardianship were not possible. The child assigned to DRA status continued to be under IDCFS guardianship and was entitled to receive foster care board payments and medical services, while relatives assumed additional responsibilities for the children as delegated to them by IDCFS. DRA status reduced IDCFS intervention to the minimum required by Title IV-E of the Social Security Act. IDCFS was able to recoup federal matching dollars for children with DRA status, if the case met other Title IV-E eligibility criteria.

The DRA option was not pursued for the number of children for whom it was projected that it would be appropriate [Testa et al. 1996]. Private agencies, who were responsible for the majority of kinship foster care cases, were reluctant to use the permanency goal of DRA, in part, because purchase of service contracts reimbursed private agencies at a lower level for serving DRA cases than the rate for serving other kinship foster care cases. The lower rate was based upon the premise that DRA cases required less frequent monitoring and casework activities, therefore caseworkers should be able to serve a substantially higher number of DRA cases than other kinship foster care cases. Private agency caseworkers were not only reluctant to increase their caseloads; many argued that the majority of cases on their caseloads required ongoing monitoring to ensure that the child's needs were adequately met and those that did not require this monitoring were heading toward adoption. Also, some IDCFS and private agency staff feared that since DRA cases remained the legal responsibility of the child welfare agencies, reduced monitoring would make them vulnerable to scrutiny of the public, the media, child welfare administrators, and legislators, if a tragedy did occur to a child in DRA status.

Caseload growth continued in spite of attempts to facilitate exits from state custody and in the midst of attempts to reform the child welfare system in Illinois; reform that had been initiated in response to litigation [*B.H. v. Suter* 1991]. A cornerstone of the reform was a substantial reduction in the average caseload of IDCFS caseworkers. Although the state legislature had previously increased the IDCFS budget substantially to fund many reform initiatives, it did so with the promise that their investment would result in a reduction in the state's foster care caseload and future costs. Continued caseload growth angered state legislators who were frustrated with the results of their investments.

The Illinois Home of Relative Reform Plan

The sharp growth in kinship foster care, the overall IDCFS caseload, and the IDCFS budget led to the development of the Illinois Home of Relative (HMR) Reform Plan. This plan was announced as part of the governor's budget briefing on March 1, 1995, with an implementation date of July 1, 1995. The HMR Reform Plan was one of several initiatives that were driven primarily by the governor and general assembly's mandate to reduce the cost of child welfare services in Illinois [McDonald 1995]. These initiatives attempted to narrow the scope of the IDCFS mission, reduce the growth of out-of-home care, and reduce costs. The HMR Reform Plan was designed to save the state $44.4 million in FY 96 alone by reducing the number of nonremoval cases taken into state custody, eliminating separate home of relative approval standards, requiring relatives to meet traditional family foster home licensing standards before foster care payments could be received, and creating a reimbursement level for unlicensed relatives caring for children in state custody at the state standard of need—higher than the

AFDC child-only payment but lower than the foster care payment [IDCFS 1995a; McDonald 1995]. The HMR Reform Plan was met with a federal lawsuit and opposition from community groups because the timelines for implementation were short and a substantial number of kinship caregivers would experience a severe reduction in the monthly subsidy they received to care for related children; however, it was implemented in July of 1995 [Gleeson 1996, 1999].

Changes in the State's Adoption Assistance Policy

The same state statute that "reformed" kinship care in Illinois reduced the adoption subsidy for special needs children from a maximum payment of $1 less than the foster care payment to $25 less than the foster care payment [P.A. 89-21]. The new statute and related state regulations introduced a means test, using the adoptive family's income to determine the amount of the adoption subsidy. It eliminated cost-of-living increases and emphasized that adoption subsidies were not an entitlement, giving IDCFS greater discretion in terminating or reducing adoption subsidies in future years [Gleeson 1999].

The changes in adoption policies nearly brought adoptions to a standstill in Illinois. Kinship caregivers who were considering adoption were reluctant to continue in this direction, fearing that they may lose the adoption subsidy in the future. Caseworkers were reluctant to discuss adoption because they were also uncertain what the future might hold for caregivers who adopted. Changes in the adoption policies were reversed within one year, but damage had been done.

Development of Nonadversarial Approaches to Working with Kinship Families

In the year preceding the HMR Reform Plan, several nonadversarial approaches to working with families were being developed to facilitate both diversion and exit of children from the child welfare system. First of all, IDCFS redesigned the "front-end" of child welfare services, providing "clinical retraining" for protective services investigators and caseworkers [IDCFS 1999a]. The redesign emphasized engaging families in a collaborative relationship that focused on ensuring safety of the child without unnecessarily removing children from their families. The clinical retraining was ultimately provided to all IDCFS caseworkers and supervisors.

IDCFS also funded two programs that were developed with the assistance of the IDCFS Inspector General's Office. One of these programs operated out of a church in a neighborhood that had one of the highest child placement rates in Chicago. This church-based program conducted family-group decisionmaking meetings with extended family members of children who were in danger of being taken into state custody. Modeled after a New Zealand program [Connolly 1994; Ernst 1999], family support workers met with extended families to facilitate development of a caregiving plan that avoids taking the child into state custody. A related program, the Kinship Permanency Project, provided mediation services to extended family members considering adoption, private guardianship, or delegated relative authority as permanency options for children in state custody [IDCFS 1994]. In addition, the latter program provided mediation training for small groups of child welfare supervisors and caseworkers.

Another initiative, the Extended Family Support program, provided home-based services to children who were living with relatives and had not been taken into state custody after a child abuse or neglect investigation. These children were considered to be safe in the care of relatives who were willing to continue to care for them. The HMR Reform Plan encouraged use of these nonadversarial approaches to divert families from the child welfare system and to facilitate permanency and rapid exit from the child welfare system.

Adoption Redesign

Partly in response to the President's "Adoption 2002" Initiative and forthcoming changes in federal law (P. L. 105-89, The Adoption and Safe Families Act of 1997), and partly because of the negative reactions to changes in state adoption policies, Illinois redesigned adoption policies and procedures. Adoption redesign was one component of the state's Permanency Initiative of 1997 (P.A. 90-27 & P. A. 90-28) that would not be fully implemented until 1999. Termination of parental rights and adoption screening

procedures were streamlined. Training was conducted to help caseworkers and supervisors conduct meetings with families to discuss adoption. A
sense of urgency in facilitating permanency decisions and concurrent permanency planning were emphasized. An expedited termination of parental rights
and adoption initiative was introduced for cases of egregious harm that were
identified as cases for which reunification was not appropriate.

Adoption redesign involved IDCFS administrators and the IDCFS Inspector General's office, private agency adoption supervisors and caseworkers, judges, and other key personnel from the juvenile court. The juvenile
court was simultaneously involved in a federally funded Court Improvement Project that also helped to shape the state's Permanency Initiative.

Subsidized Guardianship Waiver Demonstration

IDCFS submitted a waiver request to the U.S. Department of Health and
Human Services, proposing a five-year demonstration project to test the
effectiveness of providing subsidized guardianship as a permanency option for children in kinship care [IDCFS 1995b]. The waiver, approved in
September of 1996, allows IDCFS to use federal matching funds to support guardianship subsidies for appropriate families randomly assigned to
the experimental condition. Although planning began immediately after
approval of the waiver application, the official implementation date of the
Subsidized Guardianship Demonstration was May 9, 1997.

Subsidized guardianship has several advantages for children in kinship
foster care, their families, and the child welfare system [Schwartz 1993].
Unlike adoption, the biological parents' rights do not need to be terminated for guardianship to be transferred. Unlike DRA, the child is no longer
in the custody of the child welfare system when guardianship is transferred. The child welfare system does not have ongoing case management
and monitoring responsibilities. Also, the way that Illinois has implemented
subsidized guardianship, the subsidy received by guardians is computed
using the same formula that is used for the special needs adoption subsidy
[IDCFS 1995b]. Therefore, families receive approximately the same financial support to assist them in rearing the child whether they provide kinship foster care, adopt, or assume guardianship of the child. In some cases,

when kinship caregivers are not licensed as foster parents, they may receive more financial support if they adopt or assume guardianship of the child than they had received as kinship foster parents.

This project uses an experimental design, with random assignment to experimental and control conditions. Cases assigned to the experimental condition are eligible to consider subsidized guardianship if the child has been in the custody of the state for two years or more, has resided with the relative caregiver for at least one year, and reunification and adoption have been ruled out. Cases assigned to the control condition are not eligible for subsidized guardianship.

Purchase of Service Redesign

In March of 1996, partly as a mechanism for reducing the caseloads of IDCFS staff and to comply with other aspects of the *B.H. v. Suter* [1991] consent decree, IDCFS implemented Purchase of Service (POS) Redesign, which expanded the definition of full case responsibility required of private agencies awarded purchase of service contracts. Prior to POS redesign, children in state custody and served by private agency personnel through purchase of service agreements also had an IDCFS case manager assigned to their case. The redesign replaced the case managers with liaisons to agencies with purchase of service contracts. All tasks previously completed by the IDCFS case managers were delegated to the private agencies.

Performance-Based Contracting

Approximately one year after implementation of POS redesign, performance-based contracting was implemented, changing the way that cases were assigned to private agencies, using a managed care approach to shortening the length of time a case is opened, and providing financial incentives to agencies that facilitate permanent placements of children through reunification, adoption, or transfer of guardianship. Through performance-based contracting, private agencies are reimbursed for a specific number of cases. To maintain the funding level, 24% of cases need to be closed each year through reunification, adoption, or transfer of guardianship. A specific number of new cases must be accepted by these agencies within specified time frames. To serve cases without increasing caseload size, an equal number of cases must be discharged from care as are accepted into care.

Performance-based contracting was also adapted as a mechanism for monitoring the performance of caseworkers in the public agency. IDCFS caseworkers were expected to produce the same case closing and permanency outcomes as expected from private agency caseworkers. Performance-based contracting was a mechanism for holding caseworkers and agencies accountable for the permanency and case closing outcomes that were soon to be demanded by the state's Permanency Initiative and the federal Adoption and Safe Families Act of 1997.

Summary

Growth in the kinship foster care caseload in Illinois increased dramatically from 1990 to 1995. Beginning in 1995, the state implemented a number of initiatives that were designed to reduce the number of children in state custody, the cost of child welfare services, and the length of time children remained in state custody, with special attention to kinship foster care. Drastic changes in the state's kinship foster care policies were followed by redesign of the adoption program and efforts to improve the juvenile court's processing of child welfare cases, development of nonadversarial approaches to working with extended families to facilitate permanence for children, a subsidized guardianship waiver demonstration project, and mechanisms for improving the accountability of child welfare caseworkers and agencies in reaching permanency planning and case closing objectives demanded by new state and federal policies. The study that is described in this chapter was conducted as these initiatives were being implemented.

Description of the Study: Purpose and Methods

The study was conducted in April, May, and June of 1997 with the state's efforts to increase adoptions underway and as the subsidized guardianship demonstration was being implemented. The purpose of the study was to

- enhance understanding of the clinical decisionmaking processes that influence permanency planning in Chicago, Illinois;
- identify barriers to pursuing adoption or subsidized guardianship as permanency goals for children who are unable to safely and swiftly return to live with their biological parents; and
- identify conditions that facilitate achievement of permanency through adoption or subsidized guardianship.

The researchers used Stein and Rzepnicki's [1984] definition of clinical decisions as those decisions that are influenced by caseworker judgment. Therefore, the collection of case information, assessment of information, determination of how information is to be used, and choices made based upon the caseworker's assessment are considered components of clinical decisionmaking. Clinical decisionmaking is influenced by characteristics of the caseworker, by characteristics of the families and children served, and by characteristics of the child welfare system.

The study was qualitative, with caseworkers, supervisors, and administrators in private and public agencies as participants. Data were collected in the following ways and from the following sources:

- One of the researchers participated in four subsidized guardianship waiver demonstration planning meetings with the IDCFS Director of Research and staff from an IDCFS regional office. Contents of these meetings were recorded in field notes.

- Both researchers were participant observers of a total of four case staffings in an IDCFS regional office. The case staffings were conducted with the expressed purpose of facilitating movement of cases toward permanency outcomes as quickly as possible. The roles of the researchers as participant-observers, examining the way that permanency planning decisions were made, were explained to participants prior to each staffing. Contents of these meetings and observations made by the researchers were recorded in field notes.

- One of the researchers participated as a training facilitator with the IDCFS Inspector General Office's Family Meeting Training, which was offered five times in IDCFS regional offices. The training was conducted to prepare child welfare practitioners and their supervisors to facilitate permanency planning decisionmaking with kinship families. A component of this training was a workshop conducted by one of the researchers that focused on permanency planning philosophy. This workshop included audience participation in exercises that encouraged sharing of views on permanency planning for children in kinship foster care, barriers to permanency, and conditions that facilitate permanency for these children. Participants' responses to these exercises were recorded on newsprint. The content of discussions and other observations were recorded in field notes.

• Informal discussions were conducted by one of the researchers with administrative, supervisory, and casework staff of private agencies to identify training that caseworkers needed to facilitate permanency planning, particularly the rapid achievement of permanency and case closure that was required by performance based contracting. The key points that emerged from these discussions were recorded in field notes.

• One of the researchers examined caseworkers' responses to open-ended questions regarding 30 Chicago kinship foster care cases that were part of a study on case planning for children entering state custody as infants.* The open-ended questions asked caseworkers to identify barriers to permanency and conditions that facilitated permanency planning for children who entered state custody as infants and were in their second, third, or fourth year in custody. The 30 cases were those for which data collection had been completed, including an initial in-depth face-to-face interview with the caseworker and six and 12-month follow-up phone interviews. The interviews had been conducted by research assistants who attempted to record

* How Decisions to Change the Case Plan Goal Are Initiated, supported by grant number 90CW1095 from the U.S. Department of Health and Human Services, Administration on Children and Families with additional in-kind contributions from the Jane Addams College of Social Work and the Jane Addams Center for Social Policy and Research at the University of Illinois at Chicago and the National Resource Center for Permanency Planning at the Hunter College School of Social Work, City University of New York.

the responses of caseworkers verbatim in writing as the interviews were being conducted.

Field notes and completed interview questionnaires were reviewed to identify themes that related to permanency planning barriers and facilitating conditions. The researchers were particularly interested in those cases for which reunification had been ruled out and adoption or subsidized guardianship were the most likely exits that could be achieved, if the child would exit state custody in the near future.

Results

Results of this study are organized by two subsections: 1) conditions that appear to facilitate permanency planning, and 2) apparent barriers to permanency. The findings reported in each section are the most salient, having been observed repeatedly and in more than one of the data sources listed above.

Conditions That Appear to Facilitate Permanency Planning

Across all five sources of data, IDCFS staff and private agency staff recognized the leadership that IDCFS was demonstrating and the renewed focus on permanency planning by IDCFS and the Juvenile Court. Some units within IDCFS and some private agencies had a head start in this renewed permanency planning effort. For example, supervisors and key staff from one IDCFS regional office who were involved in planning meetings for the Subsidized Guardianship Initiative proudly showed the researchers statistics that reported impressive numbers of children moving toward and completing adoptions, in both relative and nonrelative homes. These staff persons were not enthusiastic supporters of subsidized guardianship as a permanency option, but were clearly strong adoption advocates. A few selected private agencies were identified by IDCFS and private agency staff alike as successful in completing adoptions for a high percentage of cases they served.

Various administrative staff in both IDCFS and private agencies had been working for a year or more to improve their staff's permanency planning efforts. In discussions with the researchers and during training sessions, these administrators and managers demonstrated a high level of commitment to permanency and were strong advocates for permanency within IDCFS and private agencies. They combined a sense of urgency in moving cases through the system with a commitment to family empowerment by engaging families in decisionmaking. The administrators had been trained in nonadversarial approaches to working with families and were skillful in engaging families in permanency planning and decisionmaking. These administrators, in turn, were educating and supporting caseworkers and supervisors in these approaches.

During case staffings, caseworkers reported that some relative caregivers also had a permanency planning orientation and knew the time frames under which the system was supposed to work. These caregivers tended to be newer to the child welfare system, having been oriented to the child welfare system by caseworkers who themselves displayed a commitment to permanency planning and time-limited involvement of the child welfare system in the lives of families. These caregivers were more open to adoption or guardianship earlier in the placement than those who had been caring for children in state custody for a prolonged period of time.

Performance-based contracting was identified by caseworkers, supervisors, and administrators alike as a mechanism that was placing additional pressure on them, but one that clearly was effective in focusing efforts on planning for permanency with families. The Court Improvement Project was also identified as a positive effort toward reducing the backlog in the court and some of the delays in processing cases. Subsidized guardianship was recognized as a new and creative permanency option that many caseworkers and supervisors believed was appropriate for a considerable portion of the kinship foster care caseload.

Apparent Barriers to Permanency

As might be expected, the challenges outweighed the successes at this early point in the renewed permanency effort and there were more barriers to permanency identified than facilitating conditions. These barriers are organized around the following themes: family dynamics, caseworker bias, caseworker knowledge and skills, underutilization of nonadversarial approaches to permanency planning, insufficient or inadequate services and resources, the culture of the child welfare system, the legal system, difficulty focusing caseworker efforts, and procedural barriers.

Family Dynamics

In case staffings and caseworker interviews from the case planning study, caseworkers identified the biological parents' ambivalence, characterized by sporadic participation in services, as a major barrier to permanency. Some parents say they want to be reunified with their children but do not engage in services—or stay involved just enough to prevent the goal from being changed from "return home" to "adoption" or "guardianship." According to these caseworkers, substance abuse plays a special role in prolonging the permanency process because recovery is a slow process with a high probability of relapse. During periods of drug use, parents may be inconsistent in completing tasks specified in their service plans. Parents who are absent during their child's first year or two in state custody may enter their child's life again when their recovery efforts are more successful and relapse is less likely. Although these parents may be sincere and may be successful in their efforts to regain custody, their delayed participation in the child welfare service plan often adds years to the child's tenure in the child welfare system.

All sources of the data confirmed that, in many kinship foster care cases, especially when parental substance abuse was a factor, the related caregivers and other family members continued to hope that the biological parents would "get their act together" and one day be able to care for the child. Rather than take over for the parents, which would represent "giving up," they supported the parents' repeated attempts for reunification. Caseworkers reported that relatives often resent IDCFS intruding into their informal care arrangements and forcing them to make a decision about the child's permanent living arrangement before they are ready.

During case staffings, caseworkers and supervisors indicated that many kinship caregivers view the child welfare system as a potential source of help, even if they do not currently utilize their caseworker or the available services. The responsibility of making a placement permanent was balanced with the "fear of the unknown" and the loss of the safety net provided by the child welfare system. Caregivers had learned that abused or neglected children may have difficulties at different stages through their development. They foresaw that adolescence, for example, might be a stormy period and, though they were having few problems now, they wanted the support and resources of the child welfare system should problems arise.

As children get older, their preferences are considered in the permanency plan. Caseworkers related that many older children do not want to be adopted. For some, adoption represents a permanent break from their parents; they think that adoption precludes ever seeing their biological parents again. During a case staffing, one caseworker described an adolescent's anger when the caseworker asked him why he did not want to be adopted. The teenager said he did not want to talk about it. The caseworker speculated that in this instance, and in others, the children may have heard for so long that they are "unadoptable" that they perceive themselves as such. For others, the change in status may seem unnecessary or uncomfortable after so many years as a "foster child."

Caseworker Bias

Caseworker bias clearly remained a major influence in permanency planning, even within those organizational units that had made significant progress toward achievement of permanency outcomes for children. Different biases were identified across all sources of data. Some caseworkers stated that the caregiver should not be "pressured" to adopt the child or to consider guardianship. Others stated that legal permanence does not have to be the answer for all children. In the case planning study and during staffings, caseworkers stated that legal permanence was not as important as finding a family that provides stability and meets the child's needs. Several caseworkers stated that it should not be necessary to remove a child because a relative is unwilling to adopt, even if it means that the child remains in state custody. In other cases, the caseworker was committed to one permanency option over others. For example, during case staffings and training sessions, the researchers heard about cases that were clearly moving toward adoption, had passed legal screening* with a very good chance of termination of parental rights, and had kinship caregivers who were ready to adopt—but the caseworker continued to advocate for reunification.

In case staffings and training sessions, the researchers also observed caseworkers who were unable or unwilling to discuss subsidized guardianship because they did not consider it to be permanent. Other caseworkers stated that they were not comfortable discussing adoption with related caregivers or presented adoption in a negative way to caregivers because the caseworker believed that guardianship was a more appropriate permanency option for children living with relatives.

In some cases, the greatest barrier to permanency was the caseworker's discomfort in working with biological parents. Several caseworkers in case staffings stated that the work is easier if biological parents are not involved. Some used passive language to describe their efforts to work with biological parents. For example, several caseworkers reported that they did not have contact with biological parents because these parents "did not make themselves available for services." When describing permanency planning, a number of caseworkers indicated that the process begins after waiting a year and a half or more for the biological parents to do what is necessary to have the child returned to them. An approach that waits for parents to take action creates needless delays and decreases the chances that children will return home quickly or that they will be freed for adoption.

In the case planning study, several caseworkers stated a bias against providing financial support to caregivers of related children. In staffings, caseworkers described foster care as a business that used to be about giving love and nurturing a child but now has lost its focus. They claimed that child welfare has become too focused on the financial supports provided to caregivers and that more attention needs to be paid to the children in care than to the financial support paid to people who care for

---

* In Chicago, cases must first pass legal screening to ensure that all necessary steps have been completed to schedule a termination of parental rights hearing.

them. Caseworkers' biases about financial support may hamper effective discussions of permanency in two ways. On one hand, caseworkers may misperceive the motives of caregivers and overemphasize financial concerns, failing to address other relevant concerns that need to be addressed to facilitate the family's decisionmaking. On the other hand, caseworkers may present financial discussions in a negative light, discouraging family members from asking the important financial questions that need to be addressed to determine whether they are able to care for the child without the regular involvement of the child welfare system.

Caseworker Knowledge and Skills

In the case planning study, during family meeting training, and during case staffings, caseworkers described their discussions with family members about permanency options. Some of these discussions were extended, thorough, in-depth, and occurred over several meetings. Others were single, brief discussions, accepting the caregiver and child's initial reactions to inquiries about adoption or guardianship. In some cases, the brief single discussions may be explained by heavy workloads and insufficient time to devote to individual cases. In other cases, caseworkers lacked skills in engaging caregivers and children in discussions about adoption or guardianship. They sometimes lacked understanding of the process children and families go through in considering major decisions and major changes that both adoption and guardianship represent. Caseworkers often lacked understanding of the caseworker's role in helping children and adults process these decisions.

Private agency administrators, supervisors, and caseworkers identified the need to train caseworkers to conduct family meetings and to have discussions with families about the need for permanency in a child's life. They indicated that specific training was needed to prepare caseworkers to help families weigh the advantages and disadvantages of adoption and guardianship as permanency options to be pursued if the child cannot safely and swiftly return to live with a parent. They indicated that, in recent years, child welfare training had focused heavily on policies and procedures and less on casework knowledge and skills related to working with children and families.

Underutilization of Nonadversarial Approaches to Permanency Planning

Although Illinois had initiated several projects designed to facilitate family decisionmaking and nonadversarial approaches to permanency planning, many caseworkers did not know about these services, did not think of them, or did not know how to access them for families. During a staffing, one caseworker discussed a case that appeared appropriate for mediation services through the Inspector General's Kinship Permanency Project. When asked if the case had been referred to the Kinship Permanency Project for mediation services, the caseworker stated that he was not aware of the service but thought that it would be a good service for this family. The supervisor was not present but several other caseworkers indicated that they were not aware of the Kinship Permanency Project. Another caseworker indicated that he had heard something about the service but did not know how to access it. Many caseworkers who attended family meeting training were also unfamiliar with mediation services provided through the Kinship Permanency Project.

In the case planning study, caseworkers were asked questions about how adoption was discussed with biological parents. Several caseworkers reported initiating these discussions with statements such as, "If you continue not to comply with services, then we will need to talk with the caregiver about adopting the child." Sometimes the caseworkers identified the court as the decisionmaker, saying, "If you do not get it together the court may decide that your child should be adopted." These approaches tend to create an adversarial relationship with the parent, leading to ambivalence and conflict that can extend a child's time in care.

Insufficient or Inadequate Services and Resources

Caseworkers and supervisors during case staffings and family meeting training revealed cases that they had difficulty closing because the caregiver was not willing to care for the child without the assistance of IDCFS or a private agency. In these cases, the caregivers indicated that they were fearful that they would need help in controlling the child's behavior or the behavior of the child's parent. In some of these cases, kinship caregivers who had raised other children through the teen years stated that they did not want to be left raising the child alone if the child became involved with gangs or began to display serious behavioral problems. According to caseworkers, these families were facing a crisis of commitment; apparently they were reserving the option of returning the child to IDCFS or a private agency if the child's behavior became too difficult.

In discussions with private agency caseworkers and supervisors, case staffings with IDCFS staff and supervisors, and Subsidized Guardianship project planning meetings, access to community-based services was identified as a barrier to children exiting the custody of the child welfare system. They indicated that families lacked awareness of the type of community-based services that might be helpful and accessible to them after the child exits state custody. Many caseworkers claimed that they had difficulty accessing community-based services for these families. When asked if these families could receive services through the Local Area Network of Services (LANS) that is supposed to coordinate community-based services and make them accessible to families in each of the state's planning areas, the researchers were met with laughter or tirades about the failure of LANS to work effectively to provide services to children and families. It was the view of caseworkers, supervisors, and administrators who participated in this study that services were particularly difficult to access for children and families who had at one time been involved with the child welfare system—or who were at risk of involvement with the child welfare system. Apparently, community-based service providers operated with the assumption that families once involved with the public child welfare system should continue to be served by that system indefinitely–or that the child welfare system should at least fund the services that these families may need now and in the future.

Caseworkers also stated that there was a shortage of services necessary to facilitate permanency for children. Substance abuse treatment for biological parents was identified as one of the most needed services. Parents who finally decided to participate in substance abuse treatment tended to be placed on waiting lists. By the time services were available, they had lost the motivation to participate in the treatment. Additional services are needed to reduce waiting lists and support implementation of service plans.

The Culture of the Child Welfare System

Approaching families with a sense of urgency and discussing the need for permanency was perceived by caseworkers and kinship caregivers as a major shift in the culture of the child welfare system in Illinois. This finding was consistent across all five data sources. When children had been in state custody for several years, neither caregivers or caseworkers were clear why it was important or necessary for the child welfare system to be out of the family's life. Caseworkers reported that kinship caregivers who have been involved with the child welfare system for many years had said, "What is wrong with the way things are now?" Some caseworkers and supervisors in both IDCFS and private agencies had asked the same question from their perspective. There appeared to be a widespread perception that emphasizing rapid exits of children from state custody was a major shift in child welfare philosophy, policy, and practice.

According to caseworkers and supervisors, many kinship caregivers want to maintain their current relationship with the child welfare system. They reported that although kinship caregivers develop mistrust for the system as the rules keep changing, at least they have a specific caseworker whom they can contact to help them rectify any problem they are experiencing. Several caseworkers stated that relative caregivers were fearful that they would have nobody to go to for help, once adoption was finalized or guardianship completed. Currently, if these caregivers do not receive their monthly foster care check, they contact the caseworker to report the problem. According to caseworkers and supervisors, many caregivers believe that the child welfare system is more responsive to caseworkers then it is to families. Others suggested that relative caregivers feared that future policy changes would eliminate the subsidy or change the level of subsidy—and they would be helpless to do anything about the change, if the child was no longer in state custody.

The Legal System

The court system and its delays were identified as major barriers to permanency in all data sources. Although caseworkers said that the Court Improvement Project was having some effect on moving cases a little more swiftly toward permanency, they also claimed that the many players in the court system gave contradictory messages to caseworkers about the permanency plans each of them would "allow" or "approve." The judges, permanency hearing officers, guardians ad litem, public defenders, and state's attorneys were perceived by caseworkers as giving conflicting messages. In addition to knowing state child welfare policies, caseworkers reported that they also needed to know the idiosyncratic rules and biases of each of the persons in juvenile court who could influence the permanent plan. For example, in family meeting training several caseworkers reported that they were told that families receiving public assistance would not be approved as adoptive parents, because their source of income was unstable. Yet, there is nothing in the state's adoption policies that would prevent a person receiving AFDC from adopting a child.

Private agency and IDCFS caseworkers, supervisors, and administrators described several situations in which permanency hearing officers would not approve subsidized guardianship as a permanency goal. The cases being reviewed were not part of the control group and they met all eligibility criteria for subsidized guardianship; the caseworkers had every indication that subsidized guardianship should be considered. Several caseworkers and supervisors reported that one permanency hearing officer stated that young children should be adopted and indicated that she would not approve a permanency plan of subsidized guardianship for very young children.

Generally, caseworkers across all data sources reported that the court system moved too slowly. Continuances were the greatest contributor to the problem but court procedures in general offered numerous opportunities for problems to develop along the way, e.g., petitions not filed, files not completed, or siblings on different court calendars. Conversely, with some cases, caseworkers were concerned that the court system moved too quickly. They perceived that court personnel did not understand the families. If cases were not individualized then decisions could be made based entirely on protocol, rather than the special circumstances of a family. Some of the lack of individualization could have been attributable to the high turnover of lawyers. Without a grasp of the family's history in the system, attorneys cannot be effective advocates. Attorneys could, of course, be provided the necessary information on a case but that process takes additional time.

Caseworkers were not clear who made decisions regarding permanency—the guardian ad litem, the permanency hearing officer, the judge, or the administrative case reviewer. They were also confused about differences between hearings conducted by hearing officers and those conducted by judges. In addition, some caseworkers did not understand the court system of calendars used to assign cases to specific judges and courtrooms, especially the difference between general calendars and those that were dedicated to termination of parental rights hearings. Caseworkers reported missing court dates because of confusion about the calendars.

Difficulties Focusing Caseworker Efforts

Caseworkers, across all data sources, reported that facilitating permanency required more time and energy than they were able to devote to families. They reported that the family situations were complex and they had too many cases to give families the attention they deserved. IDCFS caseworkers were especially frustrated, stating that the promised reduction to 20-25 cases had not occurred. The caseworkers indicated that this frustration sometimes leads to high caseworker turnover. In turn, the high rate of change in caseworkers contributes to a lack of continuity in services to families. Each new caseworker assigned to the case starts over in many respects, learning about the case and building relationships with family members. Newly assigned caseworkers often begin the case planning process again. Rather than building on the previous work done, caseworkers often give the parents "one more chance," extending the child's stay in the system for months.

Caseworkers expressed frustration at the number of competing initiatives that fragmented them—the renewed focus on permanency, purchase of service redesign, the Subsidized Guardianship Waiver Demonstration project, Adoption Redesign, performance-based contracting, and clinical retraining. In addition, IDCFS and several private child welfare agencies were participating in Council on Accreditation site visits, in response to a new requirement by IDCFS that all child welfare agencies must be accredited. These accreditation visits and the preparation that precedes them also consumed caseworkers' time and energy. Several caseworkers indicated that they expected permanency planning efforts to be easier in a year, when the renewed focus on permanency had become part of the fabric of the child welfare system and was the expectation of all key players in the system. Until then, caseworkers expected to be overwhelmed with introducing the topic of permanency and a sense of urgency in achieving permanency to so many families at one time.

Procedures

During staffings, training sessions, and in the case planning interviews, caseworkers commonly described the case planning process as a series of procedural steps required by the child welfare and legal system. These procedural steps did not appear to be connected to permanency planning for and with the family. Many caseworkers did not view the permanency goal listed in the client service plan as indicative of the direction the case was heading. For example, long-term placement with a relative caregiver was commonly selected as an interim goal when adoption or guardianship were the goals that were the most likely to provide permanency on a case. Permanency goals were not viewed as goals that the caseworker and family were actively pursuing on behalf of the child; rather caseworkers searched for the goal they were allowed to document given IDCFS procedures and feedback from their supervisors, administrative case reviewers, hearing officers, attorneys, and judges.

Some of the specific procedures that were identified as time-consuming included (1) accessing approval through IDCFS for payment for specialized services; (2) diligent searches for parents; (3) case documentation, especially completion of packets required to screen cases for termination of parental rights hearings; and (4) interstate adoptions that require knowledge of other states' reporting regulations and considerable time communicating with officials in other states.

Subsidies were described as crucial to obtaining permanency for many children and the process of accessing subsidies lengthened the stays for many children in state custody, especially very young children. Caseworkers interviewed for the case planning study indicated that Illinois' policy that children must be at least 3 years old to qualify for the special needs adoption subsidy caused delays in the adoption process. If the child was in a good home and financial assistance was necessary for the family to adopt, caseworkers oftentimes suggested that caregivers wait until the child was 3 years old and subsidy-eligible to start adoption proceedings. During case staffings, several caseworkers described their decision to delay the adoption process until the child is 3 years old as if it were a common practice.

Implications

Results of this study suggest five major implications for implementing changes in the child welfare system to facilitate permanency, particularly for children in kinship foster care. These implications are related to (1) the value of strong leadership, (2) the need for training, (3) the need for casework supervision, (4) support for supervisors, and (5) development of community-based supports and services. Each of these will be briefly discussed.

Value of Strong Leadership

All sources of data in this study confirm that IDCFS demonstrated strong leadership in the renewed pursuit of permanency for children in state custody, and that this leadership had gotten the attention of child welfare caseworkers, supervisors, and administrators, as well as judges, lawyers, and other court personnel. At the time this study was conducted, it was clear that this leadership would have to continue, with ongoing, major investments of time and effort to develop a common vision among the key people involved in the child welfare system. Many caseworkers and their supervisors experienced the simultaneous introduction of multiple initiatives in Illinois' child welfare system as disjointed, disconnected, individual efforts to address various disparate goals. Relatively few caseworkers and supervisors appeared to understand that these multiple initiatives were all connected to a common goal of achieving permanency for children, particularly those in kinship foster care. The fact that caseworkers experienced mixed messages from key players in IDCFS, private agencies, and the court system, clearly indicates that strong, visionary leadership is needed not only with the introduction of initiatives to facilitate permanence, but well into the implementation process. Strong leadership is needed to build a common vision of permanency throughout the child welfare and juvenile court systems and to build strong commitments toward realizing this vision.

Need for Training

Training is an essential component of any innovation. Training caseworkers and their supervisors is essential, but it clearly is not sufficient. Training to support major efforts to improve permanency for children in kinship foster care should include representatives of all facets of the child welfare and juvenile court systems. Joint training for caseworkers, supervisors, case reviewers, administrators, attorneys, judges, and hearing officers is recommended to reduce the amount of conflicting information that caseworkers described in this study. Joint training is important to support development of a common vision regarding the importance of permanency and the best ways of achieving permanency.

Ongoing training is also needed for caseworkers and supervisors on several topics that are essential to facilitating permanency planning with families of children in kinship foster care. Some of the ongoing training needs identified in this study include the following:

- understanding family decisionmaking regarding adoption and guardianship;
- nonadversarial approaches in engaging extended families in the case planning process and facilitating decisionmaking with families;
- discussing adoption and guardianship with parents, relative caregivers, other extended family members, and children; and
- working with families affected by substance abuse.

It is important that training be available to caseworkers and supervisors in all agencies responsible for kinship foster care services. It is important that the training include opportunities for caseworkers and supervisors to practice interventions through role play and for caseworkers to receive feedback on their performance in these practice simulations. Practicing these interventions increases skills, increases comfort with using the interventions, and increases the likelihood that these interventions will be implemented in actual practice.

Need for Caseworker Supervision

Any effort to change child welfare practice to facilitate permanency requires the intimate involvement of casework supervisors. Supervisors must provide structured supervision on a regular basis to systematically review the progress of each case toward permanency. Strong supervision is necessary to focus caseworkers on permanency for each child on their caseload. Clinical supervision is essential to support the transfer of skills learned in training sessions to actual practice. Supervision may take the form of on-the-job training with the supervisor participating with the caseworker in meetings with families. As supervisors demonstrate new skills for caseworkers, they can also enhance their knowledge of the case and sharpen their clinical skills. Supervisors must also provide impromptu case consultations, seizing opportunities to reinforce principles of permanency planning and helping caseworkers apply these principles to individual cases. Strong supervision is needed to help caseworkers learn to discuss all permanency options with families and facilitate family decisionmaking. In addition, supervisors must be aware of all specialized services that may be needed by families and how these services are accessed. Supervisors also need to help caseworkers identify cases that are appropriate for specialized services and to assist caseworkers in linking these families to the needed services.

Support for Supervisors

Supervisors also need support as they provide on-the-job training and consultation to caseworkers. Many supervisors need to reconceptualize their roles, combining educational and supportive supervision with the administrative role. Ongoing training in clinical supervision and facilitating permanency planning is recommended for supervisors. Results of this study indicated that providing specialized clinical training for supervisors in mediation and conducting family meetings has a positive payoff. Those supervisors who participated in this type of specialized training became strong advocates for permanency for children in kinship foster care—and strong advocates for the systemic changes that are necessary to support a major shift in the functioning of the child welfare system.

Development of Community-Based Supports and Services

Results of this study indicate that some children remain in the custody of the child welfare system because kinship caregivers fear that the family will only have access to needed services if the child remains in state custody. In some cases, problems and service needs were immediate and obvious. In other cases caregivers feared that problems and service needs may emerge in the future and that these needs would not be adequately addressed unless the child welfare system remained involved.

A comprehensive system of community-based services is needed to support extended families who provide kinship care, and access to these services should not require the child welfare system's legal authority or funding. It is important that these services be available to support families at risk of involvement with the child welfare system as well as those who exit the child welfare system. While the child welfare system should provide family preservation, family reunification, adoption preservation, and guardianship preservation services, these services are short term and transitional A comprehensive system of supportive services for families is much broader than the role of the child welfare system. This broader network of services should be available to all families, particularly informal kinship caregiving families who desire support and services that will allow them to successfully rear children without the ongoing involvement of the child welfare system.

References

Barth, R. P., Courtney, M.E., Berrick, J. D., & Albert V. (1994). *From child abuse to permanency planning: Child welfare services, pathways and placements.* New York: Aldine de Gruyter.

B.H. v. Suter, No. 88 C 5599 (N.D. Ill. 1991).

Connolly, M. (1994). An act of empowerment: The Children, Young Persons and Their Families Act (1989). *British Journal of Social Work. 24*, 87-100.

Ernst, J. W. (1999). Whanau knows best: Kinship care in New Zealand. In R. L. Hegar & M. Scannapieco (Eds.), *Kinship foster care: Practice, policy, and research* (pp. 112- 138). New York: Oxford University Press.

Gleeson, J. P. (1996). Kinship care as a child welfare service: The policy debate in an era of welfare reform. *Child Welfare, 75*(5), 419-449.

Gleeson, J. P. (1999). Kinship care as a child welfare service: Emerging policy issues and trends. In R. L. Hegar & M. Scannapieco (Eds.), *Kinship foster care: Practice, policy, and research* (pp. 28-53). New York: Oxford University Press.

Gleeson, J. P., O'Donnell, J., & Bonecutter, F. J. (1997). Understanding the complexity of practice in kinship foster care. *Child Welfare, 76*(6), 801-826.

Goerge, R. M. (1990). The reunification process in substitute care. *Social Service Review, 64*, 422-457.

Illinois Department of Children and Family Services [IDCFS]. (1994, September 1). *Kinship permanency planning project*. Springfield: Author.

Illinois Department of Children and Family Services [IDCFS]. (1995a, February 27). *Illinois HMR Reform Plan*. Springfield: Author.

Illinois Department of Children and Family Services [IDCFS]. (1995b, July 31). *Illinois Title IV-E Waiver Request*. Springfield: Author.

Illinois Department of Children and Family Services [IDCFS]. (1999a, January 20). *Substitute care services. Foster care brochure*. Available on-line at http://www.state.il.us./dcfs /FCBRO.htm.

Illinois Department of Children and Family Services [IDCFS]. (1999b, February 15). *Illinois subsidized guardianship waiver demonstration*. Fact sheet.

McDonald, J. (1995, June 14). Written correspondence to the child welfare community regarding FY96 budget appropriations.

P. A. 89-21. (1995). Illinois Rev. Statutes, June 6.

P. A. 90-27. (1997). Illinois Rev. Statutes, January 1.

P. A. 89-21. (1997). Illinois Rev. Statutes, January 1.

People v. Thornton, Illinois Appellate Court (1990).

Reid v. Suter. (1992, May 20). No. 89 J 6195, No 89 J 6196, *Order Approving Consent Decree; Consent Decree*.

Schwartz, M. (1993). *Reinventing guardianship: Subsidized guardianship, co-guardians and child welfare*. New York: Vera Institute of Justice.

Stein, T. J., & Rzepnicki, T. L. (1984). *Decision making in child welfare services: Intake and planning*. Boston: Kluwer-Nijhoff.

Testa, M. F. (1993). *Home of relative (HMR) program in Illinois: Interim report* (rev.). Chicago: School of Social Service Administration, University of Chicago.

Testa, M. F. (1995). Home of relative (HMR) reform in Illinois. In G. R. Anderson & J. P. Gleeson (Eds.), *Kinship care forum* (pp. 47-57). New York: National Resource Center for Permanency Planning at the Hunter College School of Social Work.

Testa, M. F. (1997). Kinship foster care in Illinois. In R. Barth, J. D. Berrick, & N. Gilbert (Eds.), *Child welfare research review–volume two* (pp. 101-129). New York: Columbia University Press.

Testa, M. F., Shook, K. L., Cohen, L., & Woods, M. G. (1996). Permanency planning options for children in formal kinship care. *Child Welfare, 75*(5), 451-470.

Thornton, J. L. (1991). Permanency planning for children in kinship foster homes. *Child Welfare, 70*, 593-601.

Wulczyn, F. H., & Goerge, R. M. (1992). Foster care in New York and Illinois: The challenge of rapid change. *Social Service Review, 66*, 278-294.

Wulczyn, F. H., Harden, A. W., & Goerge, R. M. (1997). *Foster care dynamics 1983-1994: An update from the multistate foster care data archive*. Chicago: The Chapin Hall Center for Children at the University of Chicago.

Part III
Children, Mothers, and Fathers

5

The Well-Being of Children in Kinship Foster Care

Sandra J. Altshuler

The child welfare system's historic practice of placing abused and neglected children with licensed nonrelated foster parents has been accompanied by concerns about the well-being of these children who are removed from their biological families and placed with strangers. Substantial research has been conducted on the well-being of these children [Altshuler & Gleeson 1999]. Child welfare texts and training materials have incorporated practice wisdom and theoretical writings to help caseworkers understand the experiences of children removed from their parents' homes and placed in nonrelative foster homes [see for example, Kadushin & Martin 1988; McFadden 1985]. In contrast, little is known about abused and neglected children placed with relatives. Although the child welfare system has relied heavily on relatives to care for children taken into state custody in recent years, less attention has been paid to the needs of these children.

There are two primary reasons for the limited attention to the experience and well-being of children in kinship foster care. First, many assume that children placed with relatives do not experience the same level of separation trauma normally associated with foster care because they remain within their extended family; however, this assumption has not been empirically tested. Second, the well-being of children in all forms of out-of-home care has recently been overshadowed by concerns about the dramatic growth in child welfare caseloads that coincided with the increased use of kinship foster care. The permanency planning movement of the

1970s and its resurgence in the late 1990s placed great emphasis on reducing this caseload through reunification or adoption. Permanency planning proponents have argued that child well-being is inextricably tied to being a member of a family headed by at least one adult who makes a commitment to raise the child to adulthood [Goldstein et al. 1973, 1979]. They have argued that children should be moved from the temporary status of foster care to a permanent legal status in as short a time period as possible. While the achievement of permanent legal status may be associated with child well-being, the two concepts are not interchangeable. Research on the well-being of children in out-of-home care has diminished in recent years compared to research that uses changes in case status and length of time in care as proxy measures for child well-being.

Some researchers have expressed concerns about how children in kinship foster care are faring [Dubowitz et al. 1994]. There is concern that the advantages of living with family may be offset by inadequate services, exposure to other family risk factors, and prolonged involvement with the child welfare system. Comparative research has revealed that children in kinship foster care, their families, and their caregivers receive fewer services and contacts with caseworkers than children in nonrelated foster care [Berrick et al. 1994; Dubowitz et al. 1994; Thornton 1991]. Kinship caregivers tend to have lower incomes, yet are more likely to work outside of the home, be single female heads of households, be less educated, and live in lower cost housing than foster parents in nonrelated foster care [Berrick et al. 1994; Dubowitz et al. 1993; Le Prohn 1994].

Case status measures present a mixed picture. Children in kinship foster care have been less likely to return home or be adopted and tend to remain in care longer, although they also experience fewer placements and are less likely to reenter out-of-home care than children in nonrelated foster care [Barth et al. 1994; Goerge 1990; Link 1996; Thornton 1991; Wulczyn & Goerge 1992]. When indicators of child well-being are measured directly, it appears that the average child in kinship foster care is functioning better than the average child in nonrelated foster care on measures of behavioral [Berrick et. al 1994; Glisson 1996; Iglehart 1994;

Landsverk et al. 1996; Starr et al. 1999], emotional [Iglehart 1994; Landsverk et al. 1996], and academic [Berrick et al. 1994; Goerge et al. 1992] functioning. However, the average child in kinship foster care is functioning at a significantly lower level in all of these areas than children in the general population. Little is known about factors that predict child well-being for children in kinship foster care.

The well-being of children in nonrelated foster care has been studied extensively using measures of resiliency & coping [Thorpe 1974, 1980; Weinstein 1960], physical health [Halfon et al. 1992a; Kavaler & Swire 1983; Simms 1991], mental health, including behavioral problems [Fanshel & Shinn 1978; Halfon et al. 1992b; Hulsey & White 1989; Klee & Halfon 1987; McIntyre & Keesler 1986; Pardeck 1983; Rock et al. 1988; Runyan & Gould 1985a; Thompson & Fuhr 1992], and school functioning [Canning 1974; Fanshel & Shinn 1978; Fox & Arcuri 1980; Goerge et al. 1992; Heath et al. 1994; Runyan & Gould 1985b]. These studies suggest that the well-being of children in nonrelated foster care is related to the child's case history, the parents' life situation, and the caregiver's life situation. Other studies have noted that children who were asked about their own well-being indicated that having input into care decisions would have a positive impact [Allison & Johnson 1981; Festinger 1983; Gardner 1987; Gil & Bogart 1982; Kufeldt 1981, 1984; Marsh et al. 1985; Page & Clark 1977; Rest & Watson 1984; Triseliotis 1980].

This study was designed to investigate whether variables that explain the well-being of children in nonrelated foster care also explain the well-being of children in kinship foster care and to examine the experience and perception of children in kinship foster care. This was accomplished in two ways. First, a secondary analysis of quantitative data tested the hypotheses that child well-being is associated with (1) the child's individual case history, (2) the parent's life situation, (3) the caregiver's life situation, and (4) the level of input children in kinship foster care have into the decisionmaking process. Second, a qualitative analysis of in-depth interviews with children addressed their perceptions of their experiences in kinship foster care.

Methodology

Quantitative Methodology

A secondary analysis was undertaken of data collected during the first phase of a federally funded research and demonstration project, "Achieving Permanency for Children in Kinship Foster Care."* Caseworkers in two Chicago-based voluntary child welfare agencies were interviewed regarding 77 randomly selected children placed in kinship foster care for at least one year. The interview protocol was designed to elicit information describing current casework practices, barriers to permanency, and conditions which facilitate permanency in kinship foster care. The interviews lasted an average of 115 minutes and covered 195 fixed-alternative and open-ended questions. Sixty-two of the 77 children were included in the current study; 15 were excluded because they were too young to be attending school and they were not enrolled in preschool programs.

The dependent variable, "child well-being," was measured by combining the caseworkers' ratings of the child's mental health and school functioning. Caseworkers' ratings of the child's physical health were excluded from the scale due to a lack of variance in health ratings, with 89% of the children rated as having good physical health. The child well-being scale had a range of values from "2" to "6," where "2" signified that the child's well-being is good, and "6" signified that the child's well-being is poor (see Table 5-1). Internal consistency of this scale had a Cronbach's *Alpha* reliability index of .64 (including the health ratings would have reduced the Cronbach's *Alpha* to .54). Although a Cronbach's *Alpha* of .70 is normally required to demonstrate adequate internal consistency of a scale, .64 is

* Supported in part by Grant No. 90-CO-0595, awarded to Dr. James P. Gleeson, from the Adoption Opportunities Office of the Administration for Children, Youth, and Families, U.S. Department of Health and Human Services, with in-kind contributions from the Jane Addams College of Social Work, Central Baptist Family Services, Lutheran Social Services of Illinois, the Jane Addams Center for Social Policy and Research, the Jane Addams Hull House Museum, Loyola University of Chicago School of Social Work, Life Concerns, and the Assistance of the Illinois Department of Children and Family Services.

Table 5-1. Child Well-Being[a]

Level of well-being (2=No problem indicated; 6=Serious problems indicated in all areas)[b]	Number	Percent
Two	24	38.7
Three	17	27.4
Four	13	21.0
Five	8	12.9
Six	0	0.0

a   N=62.
b   Scale created from the summing of caseworkers' ratings of child's mental health and school functioning

considered to be sufficient when the scale consists of only two variables [Cronbach 1951; Nunnally 1978]. The distribution of well-being scores is skewed, with nearly 39% of the sample rated as displaying no problems and no children rated as displaying serious problems in all areas.

Table 5-2 identifies the independent variables in this study, clustered into the areas of the child's individual case history, the biological mother's life situation, and the caregiver's life situation. A scale was created for the final independent variable, the level of input the child has into the decisionmaking process, measured by whether the child provided input in each of five opportunities during the casework process. Originally, this study was designed to include variables from the biological father's life situation. Due to the high percentages of missing data from the lack of knowledge caseworkers had regarding biological fathers, no variables from the biological father's life situation could be included.

This study employed a three-tiered process of data analysis. Univariate analyses of the variables included measures of central tendency and dispersion to determine the normalcy of the distribution of each variable, and to analyze missing data, outliers, and non-normal parameters of each variable. Variables with data missing from more than 20% of the cases were excluded from further analysis, due to the inherent instability of statistical analyses performed with low numbers [Hinkle et al. 1988; Walsh 1990].

Table 5-2. Clusters of Independent Variables in Quantitative Analyses

- Child's Individual Case History
  - Age
  - Gender
  - Number of re-placements into care
  - Prenatal drug exposure
  - Placed with sibling (if any)
  - Placed due to abuse

- Mother's Life Situation
  - Educational status
  - Marital status
  - Economic status
  - Employment status
  - Housing status
  - Problems that prevent them from caring for child (including substance abuse)
  - Receiving services (other than case management) for identified problems
  - Strengths

- Caregiver's Life Situation
  - Age
  - Educational status
  - Marital status
  - Economic status
  - Employment status
  - Housing status
  - Ability to provide care for the child
  - Problems that prevent them from caring for the child
  - Receiving services (other than case management) for identified problems
  - Number of people living in their home
  - Number of children living in their home
  - Relationship with birth parents

- Scale of Involvement of Children in Decisionmaking Process
  - Provided information for updated assessment/progress report
  - Caseworker addressed child's understanding of, and reaction to, place-ment, in that assessment/progress report
  - Caseworker discussed then-most recent service plan with the child
  - Caseworker incorporated information provide by child into that service plan
  - Child's attendance at then-most recent Administrative Case Review

Bivariate analyses were undertaken between the independent variables and the dependent variable to assess the degree of association among these variables. The independent variables that displayed statistically significant relationships with the dependent variable in the bivariate analyses were included in the multivariate analysis. Multiple regression was then used to test each of the four hypotheses and to identify the variables that predict the well-being of children in kinship foster care.

Qualitative Methodology

In-depth, open-ended interviews were conducted with six African American children who were in the legal custody of the state child welfare system and living in kinship foster care. The six children were selected, based on purposive sampling, from the random sample of cases examined in the quantitative analysis, described above. Caseworkers were asked to identify all children on their caseloads who were "verbal enough to be storytellers" [Diekelmann 1994], and unlikely to be harmed by the interview process. The general purpose of the interview was to elicit the children's perspectives of their lived experience in kinship foster care and the aspects of this experience that contributed to their well-being.

This inquiry was guided by a hermeneutic phenomenological approach to research. One goal of this approach, which has been described elsewhere [Benner 1994; Diekelmann 1995; Leonard 1994; Packer 1982; Plager 1994], has been defined as a "description of the meaning of an experience from the perspective of those who have had that experience" [Cohen & Omery 1994, p. 148]. Another goal is to identify the culturally grounded, shared meanings or commonalities in human conditions through hermeneutics, which is the interpretation of stories or texts [Benner 1994]. The product of a hermeneutical phenomenological analysis is a culturally grounded interpretation by the researcher of specific human practices, identified through participants' descriptions of their lived experiences [Benner 1994].

The children, three boys and three girls, ranged in age from 10 to 15 years old. The interviews averaged one hour in length. The researcher interviewed five children at their homes and one child at the agency office. Informed consent was obtained from the state legal guardian, and informed permission was obtained from the children and their caregivers. All the children received a surprise gift for participation in the interview (the average price of which was $13), based on suggestions from their caseworkers and caregivers.

The interview protocol for this study was developed by this researcher, based on other qualitative instruments used in child welfare research [Fanshel & Shinn 1978; Gil & Bogart 1982; McKeon 1993], and on a phenomenological approach to qualitative interviewing [Benner 1994; Diekelmann 1995]. The interview protocol was designed to have the children describe their extended family systems and their kinship foster care experiences to highlight aspects of their experiences that contribute to their well-being. At the beginning of the interview, each child was asked to help the interviewer construct a genogram depicting the child's extended family. Construction of the genogram proved to be an effective way of engaging children in the interview process.

The researcher audiotaped and then transcribed all of the interviews. These data were then used to develop descriptions of the experiences of children in kinship care. The shared, culturally bound meanings can be described as themes or patterns that emerge from the texts [Diekelmann et al. 1989]. Themes were developed by the researcher through revising and recoding the data, as part of an iterative process in phenomenological research of going from the whole of the text to its parts and back to the whole again.

To achieve "bias control," a method of ensuring rigor in interpretive phenomenology [Diekelmann 1995], interview texts were evaluated by other phenomenological researchers. For assurance of cultural sensitivity, the final interpretation for this study was evaluated by two African American researchers, one of whom is familiar with hermeneutic phenomenology; the other is an informal kinship caregiver.

Findings Based on Quantitative Analysis

None of the six variables from the child's individual case history were significantly associated with well-being (see Table 5-3). Two variables from the mother's life situation were correlated with child well-being: higher

Table 5-3. Means, Standard Deviations, and Zero-Order Correlation Matrix of Well-Being and Child's Individual Case History

VARS[a]	Mean	S.D.	1	2	3	4	5	6	7
1	3.08	1.06	1.000						
2	113.29	50.37	.206	1.000					
3	1.56	.50	.067	-.016	1.000				
4	1.40	.78	.159	.005	-.173*	1.000			
5	.46	.50	.085	.123	.012	-.031	1.000		
6	1.83	.38	.144	.513***	.010	-.017	.170	.1000	
7	.81	.40	-.156	-.366***	.146	-.220**	-.035	-.245	1.000

* $p \leq .10$ (two-tailed)
** $p \leq .05$ (two-tailed)
*** $p \leq .01$ (two-tailed)
a Variable names and value labels of variables:
  1 Child Well-Being (2=No problems indicated; 6=Serious problems indicated in all areas)
  2 Child Age (in months)
  3 Child Gender (1=Female; 2=Male)
  4 Number of placements child experience since last removal
  5 Siblings placed in same home with child (0=Siblings not placed elsewhere; 1=Siblings placed elsewhere)
  6 Child exposed to drugs prenatally (1=Yes; 2=No)
  7 Child placed due to abuse (0=Yes; 1=No)

levels of child well-being were significantly associated with the child's mother being unmarried and not have housing problems (see Table 5-4).

Child well-being was inversely associated with caregivers having identified problems and displaying poorer ability to provide care for the child (see Table 5-5). These two variables, caregiver's ability to care for the child and caregiver's problems, were also highly correlated with each other. The final independent variable, the level of child's input into the decisionmaking process, was not significantly correlated with child well-being (see Table 5-6).

Table 5-7 shows the results from the multiple regression model that incorporated the independent variables significantly associated with child well-being in the bivariate analyses. Child's age was entered first to control

Table 5-4. Means, Standard Deviations, and Zero-Order Correlation Matrix of Well-Being and Mother's Life Situation

Variables[a]	Mean	S.D.	1	2	3	4	5	6
1	3.08	1.06	1.000					
2	2.63	.68	-.274**	1.000				
3	.29	.46	.250*	.172	1.000			
4	.78	.42	-.135	.233*	.164	1.000		
5	.39	.49	-.110	-.079	-.135	-.325**	1.000	
6	.74	.44	-.054	.137	-.082	-.013	.456***	1.000

* $p \le .10$ (two-tailed)
** $p \le .05$ (two-tailed)
*** $p \le .01$ (two-tailed)
a   Variable names and value labels of variables:
   1   Child Well-Being
   2   Mother's marital status (1=Married; 2=Widowed/divorced/separated; 3=Never married
   3   Housing identified as a problem for mothers (0=No; 1=Yes)
   4   Mother has substance abuse problem (0=No; 1=Yes)
   5   Mother is receiving services for problems (0=No; 1=Yes)
   6   Mother has identified strengths (0=No; 1=Yes)

for wide variation of age. Child's age explained only 3% of variance in well-being, and was not statistically significant at the .05 level. Adding the mother's marital status and problems with housing to the equation explained 17.6% of the variance in child well-being. Caregiver's ability to care for the child and caregiver's problems in caring for the child were added in the final step of the analysis, increasing the explained variance in child well-being to 28.6%. In the final step of the regression analysis, mother's marital status, mother's problems with housing, and caregiver's problems caring for the child displayed statistically significant relationships with child well-being at the .01 level, controlling for all variables in the equation.

The caregiver's ability to care for the child did not display a statistically significant relationship with child well-being in the final step, probably because of the strong bivariate correlation between the caregiver's ability

Table 5-5. Means, Standard Deviations, and Zero-Order Correlation Matrix of Well-Being and Caregiver's Life Situation

V[a]	M	SD	1	2	3	4	5	6	7	8	9	10	11	12	13	14	15
1	3.08	1.06	1.000														
2	49.48	9.74	.090	1.000													
3	3.49	1.25	.001	-.332*	1.000												
4	1.81	.67	-.115	-.206	-.002	1.000											
5	.43	.50	.152	.188	-.312**	.055	1.000										
6	.64	.48	-.135	-.090	.239*	-.371**	-.526**	1.000									
7	1.60	.56	.139	.032	.222*	-.343**	-.200	-.245*	1.000								
8	.21	.41	.146	-.042	-.061	.134	.277**	-.365**	-.343**	1.000							
9	1.95	1.06	.242**	.195	.375	.055	.009	-.067	-.006	.017	1.000						
10	.48	.50	.294**	.218*	-.020	.136	-.052	.056	.006	.000	.718***	1.000					
11	.27	.45	-.013	-.112	-.129	.070	.204	-.066	-.140	-.010	.303**	.273**	1.000				
12	5.71	2.15	.039	-.008	-.260**	.006	.141	-.155	-.003	-.001	.144	.086	.100	1.000			
13	3.74	1.97	.049	-.078	-.247*	.122	.191	-.316**	-.096	.068	.135	-.004	.099	.931**	1.00		
14	2.33	.63	.125	-.206	.204	-.056	.093	-.078	.092	.085	.166	.009	.086	-.170	-.200	1.00	
15	2.77	.58	-.045	-.094	.068	.089	.031	-.142	-.160	.053	.073	.095	.238*	-.048	.035	.377***	1.000

* $p \leq .10$ (two-tailed)

** $p \leq .05$ (two-tailed)

a Variable names and value labels of variables: (1) Child well-being; (2) Caregiver's age; (3) Caregiver's level of education; (4) Caregivers marial status (1=married, 2=widowed/divorced/separated, 3=never married); (5) Caregiver's receipt of government funding (0=no, 1=yes); (6) Caregiver's employment status (0=not employed, 1=employed); (7) Caregiver's housing status; (8) Caregiver's receipt of government help in housing (0=no, 1=yes); (9) Caregiver's ability to provide care (1=good overall, 2=occasional problem, 3=serious ongoing problems); (10) Caregiver has identified problems (0=no, 1=yes); (11) Caregiver is receiving services for problems (0=no, 1=yes); (12) Number of people living in caregiver's home; (13) Number of children living in caregiver's home; (14) Caregiver's relationship with birth mother (1-very good, 2=average, 3=poor); (15) Caregiver's relationship with birth father (1=very good, 2=average, 3=poor).

Table 5-6. Means, Standard Deviations, and Zero-Order Correlation Matrix of Well-Being and Child's Level of Input

Variables	Mean	S.D.	Input	Well-Being
Input	1.66	1.24	1.000	
Well-Being	3.08	1.06	-.0926(ns)	1.000

Table 5-7. Summary of Regression Analyses for Variables Explaining the Well-Being of Children in Kinship Foster Care

Variables	B	SE B	ß
Step 1 (Child)			
Child's age	.0047	.0028	.2227*
Adjusted R^2=0.0320; F=2.816*			
Step 2 (Mother)			
Child's Age	.0034	.0026	.1630
Marital Status	-.5002	.1858	-.3364***
Problems with Housing	.7014	.2800	.3133***
Adjusted R^2=0.176; F=4.9182***			
F_{change}=9.3814***			
Step 3 (Caregiver)			
Child's Age	.0047	.0025	.2236*
Marital Status	-.5600	.1754	-.3767***
Problems with Housing	.5732	.2663	.2560***
Ability to Provide Care for Child	-.3048	.2610	-.2287
Problems in Caring for the Child	1.1035	.4095	.5328***
Adjusted R^2=0.286; F=5.4181***			
F_{change}=10.510***			

*	$p \leq .10$
**	$p \leq .05$
***	$p \leq .01$

to provide care for the child and the caregiver's problems in caring for the child. These two variables apparently measured the same basic construct.

Results of the regression analysis indicate that the children in this sample whose mothers were married and had housing problems were rated by their caseworkers as having lower levels of well-being compared to their peers whose mothers were not married and had adequate housing. The mother's marital status and housing problems maintained their influence on child well-being even when the caseworkers' ratings of whether the caregiver had problems caring for the child were added to the equation. Children living with caregivers who were identified as having problems caring for the child were also rated as having lower levels of well-being compare to children living with caregivers who were not identified as having these problems.

Findings Based on Qualitative Analysis

This analysis begins with a brief discussion of the impact of using genograms as an introductory engagement tool. Constitutive patterns that emerged across all the texts are then explicated using selected excerpts from the various stories the children shared. This section concludes with the children's suggestions to caseworkers for improving the well-being of other children placed into kinship foster care.

Genogram Development

The process of genogram development was a powerful tool for engagement and learning. The children's knowledge of their family system was fairly extensive, although they often knew more about, and had more frequent contact with, the side of the family with whom they were living. Comments made by the children indicated that these contacts were established after they began living with their relatives. They contributed to children's well-being by giving them a sense of family ties and connectedness that had been previously lacking. As Jeremiah,* age 11, said, "All of these people are related to me? Wow, I've never looked at it like that before!"

The process of genogram development also provided an opportunity for the children and the researcher to become engaged in a nonthreatening manner. After developing their genograms, the children talked freely without distraction for an average of an hour.

Constitutive Patterns

Starting Anew, Pondering Return

The point at which the children were removed from their homes was experienced by the children as a breakdown in family functioning. How the children experienced this breakdown varied considerably and was based upon their understanding of why they were placed into care. The children who were removed due to physical abuse identified clearly why they had been removed; those removed due to neglect had vaguer understanding of the reasons for their removal. The children expressed both relief and sadness at the change, but all of them acknowledged the necessity of the removal. For example, Tyesha, age 14, was removed from her mother's care when she was 9 years old. They had been living in a homeless shelter, and a shelter worker called the state's protective services after observing Tyesha being physically abused by her mother. Tyesha explained why her Aunt Eloise's home was a good place for her when she stated, "I knew that my auntie really cared for us, and she could, she had a house." For a child living in a homeless shelter, the stability of a home offers opportunities for changes in her life.

The children were fairly guarded about describing how breakdown was experienced. For example, Ebony, a 10-year-old, explained that she was removed from her mother's care "because she had, was doin' a lot of stuff to us that was mean." Similarly, Angela, a 15-year-old, explained her removal from her mother's care "because my Mama's boyfriend had her strung out on drugs." In contrast, the children warmly described their first night's experiences at their caregiver's home and how "breakdown" could ultimately result in a positive experience. Tyesha's description was representative of all the children's stories:

> It was fun. [Auntie Eloise] picked us up, she took us to
> McDonalds, then she drove us home, and Darnell and

---

* Fictitious names are used to protect confidentiality.

> Shantay and Avisha [other relatives] were here, and we sat up, and you know, we talked, we watched TV. We cleaned up the attic, which is now mine all by myself, now that Darnell and Shantay have moved out.... Well we were trying to clean up the attic, but the first night we had to sleep with Auntie, for the first week, until we could clean it up.

Experiencing Being Loved, Being Cared About

This pattern covered a variety of themes that emerged from the data, all of which appeared to contribute to the children's sense of well-being, through such tangible outcomes as academic improvement, peer development and support, and extended family involvement. Two subthemes covered by this pattern include the "Practices of Disciplining" and "Experiencing Stability."

The children discussed the changes in discipline practices they experienced, including increases in rules and expectations, but they seemed to view these changes as opportunities to take control of their own behavior. For example, Angela described how increased discipline affected her behavior:

> Yeah, there's rules here. You have to do your chores, you have to be in at your curfew, you have to do your homework, you have to go to school, basic rules, you know, stuff like that... They discipline us. They don't hit us, they just yell so loud... you know, they make you feel so bad... You're like, "Oh God, I am never doing that again. I just want quiet." But we don't really do much to make them unhappy. We try to keep them happy.

Experiencing stability in their new homes also contributes to the children's well-being. Some of the changes Tyesha experienced since moving in with her aunt include the ability to maintain friendships, rather than just establishing acquaintances and then moving on, as she had to do when living with her mother in shelters, and grade improvements from D's and F's, to A's and B's. During the interview, Tyesha proudly proclaimed that she was going to be valedictorian of her high school class. Similarly,

Ebony, a 10-year-old, discussed her happiness that she is finally learning to read. As a fourth grader, she had been a nonreader until this year.

Expressions of loving and caring by caregivers and extended family all contribute to the sense of well-being. The children provided many examples of when their families intervened for them, which helped them to see and experience how loved they really were.

Experiencing the Many Acts of Kindness

The practices of loving and caring are exemplified by the many acts of kindness offered to children in successful kinship foster care placements. These acts of kindness appear to contribute to the children's well-being. Angela's story, for example, illustrates this constitutive pattern. Her grandparents' practices of loving are extended toward Angela in numerous ways; so numerous in fact, that when she was asked to discuss a time that exemplifies life in kinship foster care, she was unable to describe any one time. Rather, she explained the many acts of kindness that her grandparents extend to her, that are actually indescribable:

> Hmm, like, they just out there for us, tell us they love us. Like, they go shopping, they take us out to eat, they buy us stuff, do stuff like that, you know, we sit and we talk, and we argue. They're just so cool... I love my grandparents. It's like, a million and one times I can tell you that I can remember, cuz I'm sure, I know, that they made me feel good about me. They compliment us all the time, you know, "You're so good, we love you." They want to go places with you and all that. They're cool.

Similarly, Tyesha retrieved her photo album and spent the next half hour proudly sharing the many faces of the practices of caring and loving that she had experienced since moving in with her aunt.

Creating a Future of Possibilities

The children discussed their visions for the future, created by the many acts of loving and caring they now experience. Tyesha sees herself as valedictorian of her high school class and plans to attend Harvard Law School;

Ebony now sees herself as a reader; Angela plans to go to the Air Force and then become a psychologist. The contrast between Angela's life when living with an abusive relative and with her grandparents is striking:

> I was barely clothed, I barely ate, cuz my nerves were shot. Because she would physically and mentally abuse me, and since it was their house, you know, I was like, scared of her. Scared of her... cuz I didn't get no clothes, didn't get no shoes, and if I ate the last little bit, I'd be yelled at. Her son used to always pick with me, and pick fights and stuff with me, and you know, I was just scared of him, my nerves were shot, and all this other kind of stuff. And I had the same coat, the same winter coat for three years, the sleeves were way up here on me, and my hair wouldn't grow. I was so skinny and all this other kind of stuff. My face was always long, I just looked sad.

Contrasted to the "after" picture:

> If I was to go to college, I would like to live on the campus, because I don't want to go to one of those schools in [this state]. So, I was going to live on campus and, you know, my major, is going to be computer technology. My minor, I changed my minor, it was going to be law. But I changed it to psychology, because a lot of people come to me with their problems.

The children now believe they have the freedom to create their own futures, a freedom that contributes to their well-being.

Experiencing Dialogue, Practicing Input

Most of the children were not asked for input during the initial placement process. For example, Levon had to initiate a discussion with his aunt regarding his future:

> Levon: I asked her, I said, like I think it was a week later when we first got there, I asked [my auntie], "Well, what's

gonna happen next?" And she said, they might put us up
for adoption. I said, "Who gonna get us?" She said she'll try.

Interviewer: So, you mean they might put you up for adoption and someone else would get you?

L: That's what I had thought.

I: Did you ask [your caseworker] about that?

L: Well, he said that, when I asked him, he told me they
wasn't gonna get me... I wasn't gonna go up for adoption.

I: Oh, at all? What would you like to do?

L: I'd like to stay with my auntie.

When Levon initiated an interest in his future, he was told that he may
be adopted by strangers or not adopted at all. His input had not been
solicited. In contrast, some of the children are now more routinely invited
to offer input into their lives and offered examples of those experiences.
Angela said, "My grandparents ask me, 'Do you think we treat you good
enough? Do you think, you know, that things could be better?' I'm like,
'Everything is cool with me,' you know." Tyesha noted that this process is
important for her well-being, when she said, "It's good that [adults] talk to
you because, most of the time, when they don't talk to you... it'll just scar
you."

Advice to Caseworkers

The children were invited to provide advice to caseworkers. All the children wanted to ensure that other children in similar situations receive the
same benefits that they had received. The children were all quite positive
about their caseworkers. Levon was clear and concise about what caseworkers need to do: "Help kids to stay with their parents. Try to help their
parents get off the drugs. That's about it."

Tyesha's priority was for providing nurturance for children in care:

Those kids who are scared to get affection cuz they have
never been shown affection, they should, you know, their

social workers should really nurture them. I mean, it really makes you feel good that they can come and tell you that they care about you, and you can [tell they care], just in their actions... especially when you have kids where your parents that are abusing you or neglecting you. I mean, those hurt. When they pick you up and take you to a place that's really safe for you, I mean, that just shows you that someone has actually cared about you. You know, I know it's hard for them to spend, like, a lot of time with you, but they should try to spend as much time as they possibly can.

Jeremiah's priority focused on the needs of the children for the future:

Who was it that took Baby Richard away from his adopted parents? Now that was stupid... They weren't thinking in the kid's best interests, they were thinking in the father's best interest. But, who's more important, the past or the future? I mean, kids are the future, you have to take care of the future, or there will be no future.

Discussion

There are four major limitations of this study that suggest caution in interpretion of the findings. The limitations include insensitive measurement, lack of statistical power, sampling, and design. The quantitative component of this study was a secondary analysis of data not collected specifically to test the hypotheses of this study. Measures were not sufficiently sensitive to reflect accurately the continuum of experience on key variables. The measure of child well-being was particularly problematic, resulting in a skewed and truncated distribution. More sensitive measures of the child's health status, and behavioral, emotional, and academic functioning are needed to represent the continuous and multidimensional nature of child well-being.

Some variables, like whether the mother has a substance abuse problem, were dichotomous measures that did not differentiate severity. More than 80% of the mothers in this sample were identified as having a substance abuse problem that interfered with their ability to care for their children. Although this study did not find a relationship between child well-being and the mother's substance abuse problem, it may be related to the degree of severity of this problem, not just its existence. In addition, some important variables were not part of the original data. Others, like the father's life situation, had to be excluded from the analysis because of the high degree of missing data.

Statistical power was limited because of the small sample size and the skewed, uneven distribution of many of the variables. The small sample size, purposive sampling for the qualitative interviews, and data gathered from only two agencies in Chicago limit the generalizability of the findings of this study as well. In addition, the study would have been strengthened through inclusion of a comparison group of children in nonrelated foster care. Despite these limitations, the study can identify areas for future research and implications for both child welfare policy and practice.

Results of the quantitative component of this study suggest that the well-being of a child in kinship foster care may be associated with the adequacy of the mother's housing and her marital status. Further research is needed to replicate and explicate these findings. At this point, one can only speculate about the meaning of the observed relationships. For example, it may be that children feel more secure and worry less about their mothers when the mother has stable housing. Lack of adequate housing may be associated with severity of substance abuse, mental health, and economic problems. Children who experienced periods of homelessness while living with their parents may be aware of the dangers of living on the street and may be worried about their mothers' safety. Children removed from mothers who have housing problems may have experienced more severe neglect prior to being taken into the custody of the child welfare system and this early trauma may have long-lasting negative effects. It may be that they continue to have contact with their mother at the caregiver's home. If the mother is functioning well, it is likely that the child's contact with the mother will benefit the child. If the mother is severely disturbed or drug dependent, this contact may negatively affect the child.

Since children are less likely to be removed from two-parent families than single-parent families, the inverse relationship between the mother's marital status and child well-being may suggest that the two-parent families from which children were removed experienced more serious problems, such as severe spousal abuse, that affected the children. It may also be that the observed relationships between the mother's situation and the child's well-being is an indication of the importance of the child's relationship with the mother, even for children who are placed with relatives. From a practice perspective, these data suggest that attending to the mother-child relationship is as important for children in kinship foster care as it is for children in other types of out-of-home care. Had variables that measured the father's life situation been included, the importance of the relationship between the father's life situation and child well-being may have been observed as well. In child welfare practice, caseworkers may want to focus efforts on mothers' partners, ensuring stable housing, and including fathers in permanency planning and casework activities.

It is not surprising that lower levels of well-being were associated with caregivers who had been identified by caseworkers as experiencing problems that affected their ability to care for the children. Further research is needed to understand the types of problems experienced by these caregivers and whether casework or policy interventions can alleviate these problems in such a way that child well-being is enhanced. Are these problems related to caregiver preparation or competence, social support needs, caregiver burden, family relationship issues, or caring for a child with special needs? If so, can these problems be lessened through increased contact with the caseworker, participation in caregiver support groups, family conferencing, family counseling, or other support services? Are the problems related to needs for financial support, legal services, or assistance with the school system?

The qualitative component of this study suggests that the well-being of the children interviewed was based, in part, upon the many acts of loving and caring offered by their caregivers, the increased involvement in their extended family system, and the increased opportunities for dialogue and input. The importance of their first night's experience indicates that the children's experience in kinship foster care should not be overlooked. Removal from the parent and placement with a relative may be extremely traumatic for some children. For the children interviewed in this study, the many acts of kindness that they experienced in their relatives' home helped them adjust to the new living arrangements and apparently enhanced their well-being. These children were able to envision a bright future of possibilities that may not have been possible without the experience of the many acts of kindness that they experienced in kinship foster care.

Constructing a genogram with the children in this study proved to be an effective way of engaging them in the interview process. Caseworkers may want to consider using tools like genograms for engagement and to increase their knowledge and understanding of children's perspectives of their extended family systems, and their place in them.

This study reminds policymakers and researchers of the importance of measuring child well-being in more refined and direct ways, rather than using proxy measures, when determining effects of policies on children in care. Even with the rough measures used in this study, variance in the well-being of children was detected and relationships with some explanatory variables were observed.

This research study provides directions for future research. Replication of the study with a larger sample size, more precise measures of variables, and multiple sources of information would strengthen the generalizability of the findings. A longitudinal study that follows children through their "careers" in kinship foster care with precise measurement of well-being would inform practice and policy in child welfare. A qualitative study that interviews younger children, and a wider range of children, can offer a broader perspective of their views. Similarly, interviewing children in a variety of "care" programs, including family preservation, nonrelated foster care, residential and group home care, as well as kinship foster care, can provide insight into the various needs of different groups. Interviewing members of the child's environment, including parents, caregivers, teachers, and siblings, and involving them in evaluation of the findings would improve the validation of the results.

References

Allison, J., & Johnson, J. (1981). *Say hi to Julie (A commentary from children in care in Alberta)*. Calgary, Alberta: Who Cares?, Alberta: A Society for Young People in Care.

Altshuler, S. S., & Gleeson, J. P. (1999). Completing the evaluation triangle for the next century: Measuring child "well-being" in family foster care. *Child Welfare, 78*(1), 125-145.

Barth, R. P., Courtney, M., Berrick, J. D., & Albert, V. (1994). *From child abuse to permanency planning: Child welfare services pathways and placements*. New York: Aldyne de Gruyter.

Benner, P. (1994). The tradition and skill of interpretive phenomenology in studying health, illness, and caring practices. In Benner, P. (Ed.), *Interpretive phenomenology: Embodiment, caring, and ethics in health and illness* (pp. 99-128). California: Sage Publications.

Berrick, J. D., Barth, R. P., & Needell, B. (1994). A comparison of kinship foster homes and foster family homes: Implications for kinship foster care as family preservation. *Children and Youth Services Review, 16*, 33-63.

Canning, R. (1974). School experiences of foster children. *Child Welfare, 53*, 582-586.

Cohen, M. Z., & Omery, A. (1994). Schools of phenomenology: Implications for research. In J. M. Morse (Ed.), *Critical issues in qualitative research methods*. Beverly Hills, CA: Sage Publications.

Cronbach, L. (1951). Coefficient alpha and the internal structure of tests. *Psychometrika, 16*, 297-334.

Diekelmann, N. L. (1994). Personal communication with author.

Diekelmann, N. L. (1995). *Heideggerian hermeneutics: Stages of interpretation*. Unpublished manuscript.

Diekelmann, N. L., Allen, D. G., & Tanner, C. (1989). The NLN criteria for appraisal of baccalaureate programs: A critical hermeneutic analysis. *National League of Nursing*, (Pub. No. 15-2253), 3-34.

Dubowitz, H., Feigelman, S., Harrington, D., Starr, R., Zuravin, S., & Sawyer, R. (1994). Children in kinship care: How do they fare? *Children and Youth Services Review, 16*, 85-106.

Dubowitz, H., Feigelman, S., & Zuravin, S. (1993). A profile of kinship care. *Child Welfare, 72,* 153-69.

Fanshel, D., & Shinn, E. B. (1978). *Children in foster care.* New York: Columbia University Press.

Festinger, T. (1983). *No one ever asked us... a postscript to foster care.* New York: Columbia University Press.

Fox, M., & Arcuri, K. (1980). Cognitive and academic functioning in foster children. *Child Welfare, 59,* 491-496.

Gardner, R. (1987). Children's participation in care decisions. *Adoption and Fostering, 11,* 12-14.

Gil, E., & Bogart, K. (1982). Foster children speak out: A study of children's perceptions of foster care. *Children Today, 11,* 7-9.

Glisson, C. (1996). Judicial and service decisions for children entering state custody: The limited role of mental health. *Social Service Review,* 257-281.

Goerge, R. M. (1990). The reunification process in substitute care. *Social Service Review, 64,* 422-457.

Goerge, R. M., VanVoorhis, J., Grant, S., Casey, K., & Robinson, M. (1992). Special-education experiences of foster children: An empirical study. *Child Welfare, 71,* 419- 437.

Goldstein, J., Freud, A., & Solnit A. J. (1973). *Beyond the best interests of the child.* New York: Free Press.

Goldstein, J., Freud, A., & Solnit A. J. (1979). *Before the best interests of the child.* New York: Free Press.

Halfon, N., Berkowitz, G., & Klee, L. (1992a). Children in foster care in California: An examination of Medicaid reimbursed health services utilization. *Pediatrics, 89,* 1230- 1237.

Halfon, N., Berkowitz, G., & Klee, L. (1992b). Mental health service utilization by children in foster care in California. *Pediatrics, 89,* 1238-1244.

Heath, A. F., Colton, M. J., & Aldgate, J. (1994). Failure to escape: A longitudinal study of foster children's educational attainment. *British Journal of Social Work, 24,* 241-260.

Hinkle, D. E., Wiersma, W., & Jurs, S. G. (1988). *Applied statistics for the behavioral sciences.* Boston: Houghton Mifflin Company.

Hulsey, T. C., & White, R. (1989). Family characteristics and measures of behavior in foster and nonfoster children. *American Journal of Orthopsychiatry, 59,* 502-509.

Iglehart, A. (1994). Kinship foster care: Placement, service and outcome issues. *Children and Youth Services Review, 16,* 107-122.

Kadushin, A., & Martin, J. A. (1988). *Child welfare services* (4th ed.). New York: Macmillan

Kavaler, F., & Swire, M. R. (1983). *Foster-child health care.* Lexington, MA: D.C. Heath & Co.

Klee, L., & Halfon, N. (1987). Mental health care for foster children in California. *Child Abuse and Neglect, 11,* 63-74.

Kufeldt, K. (1984). Listening to children—who cares? *British Journal of Social Work, 14,* 257-264.

Kufeldt, K. (1981). *Temporary foster care: theoretical perspectives and participants' perceptions.* Unpublished doctoral dissertation. University of Calgary, Calgary, Canada.

Landsverk, J., Davis, I., Ganger, W., Newton, R., & Johnson, I. (1996). Impact of child psychosocial functioning on reunification from out-of-home placement. *Children and Youth Services Review, 18,* 447-462.

Leonard, V. W. (1994). A Heideggerian phenomenological perspective on the concept of person. In P. Benner (Ed.), *Interpretive phenomenology: Embodiment, caring, and ethics in health and illness.* (pp. 43-64). Beverly Hills, CA: Sage Publications.

Link, M. K. (1996). Permanency outcomes in kinship care: A study of children placed in kinship care in Erie County, New York. *Child Welfare, 75,* 509-528.

Le Prohn, N. (1994). The role of the kinship foster parent: A comparison of the role conceptions of relative and non-relative foster parents. *Children and Youth Services Review, 16,* 65-84.

Marsh, P., Fisher, M., & Phillips. D. (1985). Negotiating child care: The experiences of workers and clients. *Adoption and Fostering, 9*(3), 11-17.

McFadden, E. J. (1985). Practice in foster care. In J. Laird & A. Hartman (Eds.), *A handbook of child welfare: Context, knowledge, and practice.* (pp. 585-616). New York: The Free Press.

McIntyre, A. E., & Keesler, T. Y. (1986). Psychological disorders among foster children. *Journal of Clinical Child Psychology, 15,* 297-303.

McKeon, A. M. (1993). *Kinship foster care: The child's perspective.* Unpublished master's thesis, Smith College, Northampton, MA.

Nunnally, J. C. (1978). *Psychometric theory* (2nd ed.). New York: McGraw-Hill.

Packer, M. J. (1982). Hermeneutic inquiry in the study of human conduct. *American Psychologist, 40,* 1081-1093.

Page, R. & Clark, G. A. (1977). *Who cares? Young people in care speak out.* London: National Children's Bureau.

Pardeck, J. T. (1983). An empirical analysis of behavioral and emotional problems of foster children as related to re-placement in care. *Child Abuse and Neglect, 7,* 75-78.

Plager, K. A. (1994). Hermeneutic phenomenology: A methodology for family health and health promotion study in nursing. In P. Benner (Ed.), *Interpretive phenomenology: Embodiment, caring, and ethics in health and illness.* Beverly Hills, CA: Sage Publications.

Rest, E. R., & Watson, K. W. (1984). Growing up in foster care. *Child Welfare, 63,* 291- 308.

Rock, S. L., Flanzer, S. M., Bradley, R. H., & Pardeck, J.T. (1988). Frequency of maladaptive behavior in foster children. *Early Child Development and Care, 30,* 133- 139.

Runyan, D. K., & Gould, C. L. (1985a). Foster care for child maltreatment: Impact on delinquent behavior. *Pediatrics, 75,* 562-568.

Runyan, D. K., & Gould, C. L. (1985b). Foster care for child maltreatment. II. Impact on school performance. *Pediatrics, 76,* 841-47.

Simms, M. D. (1991). Foster children and the foster care system. Part II: Impact on the child. *Current Problems in Pediatrics, 21,* 345-369.

Starr, R. S., Dubowitz, H., Harrington, D., & Fiegelman, S. (1999). Behavior problems of teens in kinship care: Cross-informant reports. In R. L. Hegar & M. Scannapieco (Eds.), *Kinship foster care: Policy, practice, and research* (pp. 193-207). New York: Oxford University Press.

Thompson, A. H., & Fuhr, D. (1992). Emotional disturbance in fifty children in the care of a child welfare system. *Journal of Social Service Research, 15,* 95-112.

Thornton, J. L. (1991). Permanency planning for children in kinship foster homes. *Child Welfare, 70,* 593-601.

Thorpe, R. (1974). Mum and Mrs. So & So. *Social Work Today, 4,* 691-695.

Thorpe, R. (1980). The experiences of children and parents living apart. In J. Triseliotis (Ed.), *New developments in foster care and adoption* (pp. 85-100). London: Routledge & Kegan Paul.

Triseliotis, J. (1980). Growing up in foster care and after. In J. Triseliotis (Ed.), *New developments in foster care and adoption* (pp. 131-163). London: Routledge & Kegan Paul.

Walsh, A. (1990). *Statistics for the social sciences with computer applications.* New York: Harper & Row.

Weinstein, E. A. (1960). *The self-image of the foster child.* New York: Russell Sage Foundation.

Wulczyn, F. H., & Goerge, R. M. (1992). Foster care in New York and Illinois: The challenge of rapid change. *Social Service Review, 66,* 278-294.

6

Comparing Mothers of Children in Kinship Foster Care: Reunification vs. Remaining in Care

Marian S. Harris

Early criticisms of kinship foster care alleged that children in these placements remained in the custody of the child welfare system longer than children placed with nonrelated foster parents, and were less likely to be reunified with their parents or to be adopted [see for example Berrick & Barth 1994]. More recent analyses reveal a more complex picture, suggesting that children placed with kin do exit care at a slower rate, but when they are reunified with parents, they are less likely to reenter the custody of the child welfare system [Courtney & Needell 1997; Wulczyn et al. 1997].

A combination of factors appear to complicate efforts toward reunification after kinship care. It appears that reunification and reentering custody of the child welfare system after kinship foster care may be associated with race, poverty, substance abuse, and length of time in custody in some way. First, African American children have the highest rates of placement in kinship foster care, remain in care longer, and are less likely to return home than other children [Barth et al. 1994; Goerge 1990; Wulczyn & Goerge 1992]. Second, analysis of the foster care database in California revealed that children placed in kinship homes that were eligible to receive federal IV-E foster care payments were less likely to return to their parents and more likely to reenter care if reunified, than children placed in kinship homes that were not eligible for foster care payments [Berrick et al. 1998]. Since IV-E eligibility is partially dependent upon the parent's eligibility for TANF, it may be that poverty contributed to reentry.

It may also be that providing foster care payments to kin made them more willing to care for children [Berrick et al. 1998]. It is also possible that child welfare caseworkers are more willing to remove children from very poor parents and place them with relatives who can be provided foster care payments [Courtney et al. 1997; Gleeson, Chapter 4]. Third, the majority of children in kinship care entered the custody of the child welfare system because of neglect. Reunification is less likely for children entering care because of neglect compared to those placed because of abuse [Barth 1997]. Neglect is often associated with poverty and parental substance abuse, which further delays efforts toward reunification [Berrick et al. 1998]. Fourth, it is not known whether placement with kin or longer stays in care contribute most to lower reentry rates, since very short stays in foster care are associated with higher reentry rates [Barth 1997].

Current understanding of reunification and reentry after kinship foster care has been informed primarily by analyses of administrative data. Administrative data provide a good picture of the patterns of reunification and reentry but do not explain why these patterns occur. The study reported in this chapter attempts to contribute to current knowledge about reunification by comparing data collected from a small sample of mothers, ten whose children were reunified with them after kinship foster care and ten whose children remained in kinship foster care. The study examines similarities and differences in their demographic characteristics, descriptions of their involvement with the child welfare system, problems they experience that affect their ability to care for their children, and strengths that help them care for their children. In addition, these mothers were compared on measures of three constructs: object relations, substance abuse severity, and extended family support. These constructs were selected for study because it is likely that each is relevant to family reunification.

Object Relations, Substance Abuse Severity, and Extended Family Support

The high rates of neglect that characterize the reasons that children enter kinship foster care suggest that further understanding is needed of factors that inhibit parents' abilities to nurture and protect their children. According to Fairbairn's [1952] theory of object relations, psychic structure emanates from the experience each person has with her or his primary objects. Many mothers have attributed their problems as parents to their negative experiences with their own parents during their childhood. Similarities and differences in perceptions that mothers of reunified children and those who remain in kinship foster care have of their relationships with their own mothers may provide insight that would be helpful in fashioning interventions to strengthen the nurturing capacities of mothers of children in kinship foster care.

Substance abuse has also been identified as a barrier to family reunification [Berrick et al. 1998; Gleeson et al. 1994; Gleeson et al. 1997]. Some suggest that mothers may feel less compelled to participate in substance abuse treatment and to work toward reunification when their children are placed with relatives than they would if their children were placed in traditional foster care with nonrelated foster parents [Meyer & Link 1990]. However, the relationship between severity of substance abuse problems and reunification has not been systematically examined.

Extended family support has been identified as an important part of African American life [Hale 1982; Hill 1972, 1997; Martin & Martin 1978; McAdoo 1978; Stack 1974; Wilson 1984]. While some have suggested that placement of children with relatives would result in rapid reunification because of the support that extended families provide [Hill 1977], this has not been the case, but the reasons are not clear. It may be that reunification after kinship foster care is associated with the quality of extended family support.

Methodology

Data were collected through lengthy interviews with 20 African American mothers at a single point in time between December 1995 and March 1996. The sample of mothers was recruited with the help of three private, nonprofit social service agencies in Chicago that had served the families through purchase of service contracts with the Illinois Department of Children and

Family Services (IDCFS). This sample represents only one ethnic group and was chosen because of the over-representation of African American children in kinship foster care. To be eligible for this study, these mothers had to have at least one child who was taken into IDCFS custody between 1990 and 1993 and placed in kinship foster care. When the mother had more than one child who met this criteria, questions were focused primarily on the youngest child.

The size of the sample was limited by difficulties in gaining access to these mothers. In many cases the agencies had not been able to locate the mothers or to engage them in services. Human subjects protections prevented the researcher from contacting mothers until they were contacted by the agency staff and consented to being contacted. Some mothers refused to participate in interviews after they were contacted by the researcher or the researcher was unable to make contact with them after repeated attempts. Others agreed to be interviewed but repeatedly failed to show up for scheduled interviews. Six of the women were interviewed in their own homes, 13 were interviewed in agency offices, and one was interviewed in a substance abuse treatment facility.

Instrumentation

The interview protocol contained a mix of close- and open-ended questions, including 22 questions developed by the investigator for this study to collect demographic information and descriptions of the mothers' perceptions about the removal and return of children to the their care, their caregiving strengths, problems that affect caregiving ability, and services received. The protocol also included existing measures of object relations, substance abuse severity, and extended family support.

Object relations were conceptualized as the relationships with important people in a person's life, the internal representations of these people, and their relevance for psychic functioning [Greenberg & Mitchell 1983]. Object relations were operationally defined by the mental representations revealed by study participants in their descriptions of their mother and child, as rated on the Concept of the Object Scale continuum [Blatt et al. 1976a]. The Concept of the Object Scale is a projective instrument for rating the cognitive aspects of an individual's inner object relations. Blatt, Brenneis, Schimek, and Glick [1976a, 1976b] designed the scale to assess representational models from a developmental/object relations perspective.

Each respondent was told she would be given five minutes to describe her mother and five minutes to describe her child [Blatt & Lerner 1983]. Descriptions were audiotaped and typed verbatim by the investigator. The descriptions were rated on a nine-point scale anchored at odd values, which represent five conceptual levels based on developmental psychoanalytic theory and cognitive developmental constructs from Piaget and Werner [Blatt et al. 1981]. An analysis of how the study participants view themselves as well as significant others can be made from the spontaneous descriptions derived during the interviews. According to the rating procedures for the Blatt Scale, a single-level score is assigned to a subject's entire description of the self or other such as a parental figure. Higher scores on the Blatt Scale indicate capacity for self-other differentiation and the development of mature character formation. Lower scores represent less maturity and limited ability for self-other differentiation.

While validity of the Blatt Scale has not been reported, prior studies have demonstrated inter-rater reliability greater than 90% [Fishler et al. 1990]. In this study, four experienced, psychodynamically trained social workers who had not participated in the interviews participated as raters, using the Concept of Object Scale. Each transcribed description of mother and child was rated by two raters. Inter-rater agreement ranged from 70% to 90% based on initial ratings. Disagreements were then discussed by the two raters and reconciled with a rating that both raters agreed upon.

Substance abuse problem severity was operationally defined by the mother's responses to the Addiction Severity Index (ASI) in seven areas commonly affected when substance abuse is a problem: physical health, employment and support systems, drug use, alcohol use, legal status, family and social relationships, and psychopathology [McLellan et al. 1980]. The ASI portion of the interviews lasted approximately 45 minutes. This structured interview includes questions in language that may prompt persons who abuse substances to remember details they might otherwise forget.

The ASI provides two types of profiles: a problem severity profile and composite scores [McLellan et al. 1980]. Problem severity scores are clinician ratings of each of the seven problem areas on a ten-point scale. Higher ratings indicate greater need for treatment. The severity ratings in this study were assigned by the investigator.

ASI composite scores are derived with the participation of the person being interviewed. The investigator read each question aloud to the study participants and recorded verbal responses on the instrument. The mothers were asked to rate the extent to which each of the seven areas had been a problem for them, using a five-point scale. These ratings were used to compute the composite scores. Since the ASI relies on self-reports and clinical judgments, some concerns have been raised about the validity of the scale. However, several studies have demonstrated good reliability and adequate discriminant validity [McLellan et al. 1980, 1981, 1983].

Extended family support was conceptually defined as a system of mutual aid involving interchanging roles, jobs, family functions, and economic resources by members of a family's extended kinship network [McAdoo 1977, 1980; Stack 1974]. Extended family support was operationally defined as the type of help exchange patterns that a subject delineated in response to eight questions and one scale selected from McAdoo's [1977] Scales and Protocols for Assessing Extended Family Support of Single Black Mothers, with some modifications. The principal investigator read the questions to the mothers, who provided written responses to the eight questions and the scale. The eight questions were a mix of open-ended and fixed choice items, asking study participants to indicate the following:

- whether they have relatives who are important to them,
- how many relatives they feel close to,
- most important sources of help from family,
- their rating of the degree to which their families go out of their ways to help them,
- their feelings about their families coming to their aid in hard times,
- whether the level of help given by relatives had changed since involvement of the child welfare system,

- their feelings about relatives caring for their children, and
- three of the most positive things about their families.

The scale (Help Exchange Patterns: Help Received) is a chart that was used by study participants to describe and delineate types and frequency of extended family support, including child care, financial help, emotional support, repairs and chores, clothes and furniture, activities and social events, and other ways that the respondent specifies. While there is no information available on the reliablity or validity of McAdoo's questionnaire or any of its individual scales or items, these items and the entire interview protocol used in this study were pilot tested with a small sample of five African American women. Pilot testing suggested that the items were clear and understandable to these participants.

Data Analysis

Demographic data were compared for study participants whose children remained in kinship care and those whose children had been returned to their care. The mothers' descriptions of the removal of their children from their care, their involvement with the child welfare system, their problems, and their strengths were content analyzed. The themes that emerged in the narrative responses of mothers whose children had been returned to their care were compared to themes that emerged from the responses of mothers whose children remained in kinship care.

Mothers' responses to the Blatt scale were scored on a nine-point ordinal scale. The 20 ratings of the responses to the representations of mother and the representations of child were then ranked. Mean ranks were computed for each representation separately for mothers whose children had returned home and those whose children remained in care. The Wilcoxon Rank Sum was used to test the statistical significance of the observed differences in the mean rankings of these two groups.

The Addiction Severity Index produced severity ratings (made by the investigator) as well as composite scores (which incorporated the mothers' ratings) for each of seven subscales in the problem severity areas (physical health, employment and support systems, drug use, alcohol use, legal status, family and social relationships, and psychopathology). Each of these scores are interval level. *T*-Tests for Independent Samples were used to compare the severity ratings as well as the composite scores of study participants whose children remained in care with those whose children had been reunified with them.

The responses to four of the questions from the revised Scales for Measuring Extended Family Support of Single Black Mothers were analyzed using the statistical test appropriate to the level of data for each question. The remaining four questions produced narrative responses that were analyzed using content analysis. The Help Exchange Pattern: Help Received Scale produced nominal and narrative data. Whether study participants received help in each of the seven areas was indicated by a *yes* or *no* response. Responses of mothers who had their children returned were compared to the responses of mothers whose children had not been returned using the *Chi* Square Test for Independent Samples. Study participants were also asked to indicate the exact relationship of the person giving them each type of help. The narrative responses to these questions were content analyzed. These responses were compared between the two groups of mothers.

Major Findings

Demographic Profile

Mothers whose children returned home and those whose children remained in kinship foster care were similar in age, education, and religious preference (see Table 6-1). The age range for those study participants whose children had been returned to their care was 23-35 with a mean of 29.2. Mothers whose children had not been returned were only slightly younger, ranging in age from 19 to 33, with a mean of 28.6. Educational levels were nearly identical with five mothers whose children returned home and six mothers whose children remained in care reporting that they did not finish high school. Eight of the ten mothers in each group identified their religious preference as Protestant.

Table 6-1. Demographic Comparisons of Mothers Whose Children Returned Home and Mothers Whose Children Remain in Kinship Foster Care

Variable	Child Returned Home	Child Remains in Kinship Foster Care
Age		
Mean	29.2	28.6
Range	23-35 years	19-33 years
Marital Status		
Married	3	1
Never married	6	8
Separated	1	0
Divorced	0	1
Level of Education		
Some high school	5	6
High school diploma	2	2
Some college	3	2
Source of Income		
Employment	5	1
Public aid	5	5
SSI/Social Security	0	2
Family	0	1
Other	0	1
Religious Preference		
Protestant	8	8
Catholic	2	0
Other	0	2
Income		
Median	$11,124	$5,388
Range	$3,960-$44,122	0-$16,212

While three mothers whose children had been returned to their care indicated they were married, only one mother whose children remained in care was married. The two groups of women differed most dramatically in their income and employment. Mothers whose children had been returned home had higher incomes and were more likely to be employed. The annual income range was $3,960 to $44,122 with a median of $11,124 for these mother, whereas mothers whose children had not been returned to their care reported incomes ranging from $0 to $16,212 with a median of $5,388.

Involvement with IDCFS

The length of time families had been involved with IDCFS was considerably longer for those mothers whose children had not been returned to their care when compared with those mothers whose children had been returned to their care. The length of time involved with IDCFS ranged from three to ten years with a mean of 4.7 for those mothers whose children remained in kinship care. However, the length of time involved with IDCFS ranged from two to four years with a mean of 2.8 for those mothers whose children had been reunified with them. The length of time required for family reunification ranged from two to five years with an average of three years and four months.

The mothers in both groups provided similar answers to a question regarding why their children were removed from their homes. In both groups, half of the mothers stated that the reason for the child's removal was neglect. Two mothers in each group were unable to indicate a reason for the child's removal and one in each group stated that the child's removal was related to the mother's substance abuse. One mother in each group identified risk of harm as the reason for removal. One mother whose child had been returned to her care identified physical abuse as the reason for the child's removal. A mother whose child remained in care stated that the child was removed because her other children were in IDCFS custody.

When asked to answer a question regarding why their children had been returned to their care, nine of the study participants indicated they had completed service requirements and one indicated that risk of harm to the child had been eliminated. Mothers whose children had not been returned were asked to explain why their children had not been returned to their care. Two mothers indicated that their children had been adopted. Two mothers blamed the failure to return the children on their own parenting inabilities. One indicated the child had not returned because she was unable to explain the injuries that led to the child welfare system's involvement. One mother blamed the courts and another blamed the child's continued placement on influences of the caregiver. One mother said that her child has not returned home because of her continued substance abuse and another mother blamed her own noncooperativeness. One mother indicated she did not know why her child had not returned to live with her.

Services Received

There were variations in the answers from both groups to the question asked regarding services received since their children were placed in kinship care. Three mothers whose children had been returned to their care reported receiving no services. Four said they received case management services, one received drug counseling, one received parenting education, and one received family therapy. Four mothers whose children remained in kinship care said they had received no services. One reported receiving family therapy, one received individual therapy, one received baby clothing and supplies, one received drug counseling, and one received case management.

Mothers' Problems and Strengths

The two groups varied in their response to the question regarding any problems that may affect their ability to care for their children. Seven mothers whose children had been returned to their care reported no problems. Two mothers in the reunification group who described problems that may affect their ability to care for their children stated the following:

> I use to have a temper but going to counseling really has showed me how to keep it under control.

> She has bonded with my sister and cries every time Aunt ____ leaves.

One mother in the reunification group indicated that the only problem she and her family had was adjusting to the inappropriate involvement of the child welfare system in her life in the first place. She described the removal of her child as a mistake.

> I will describe the problem as a very big mistake. Only my child was removed because of DCFS wouldn't investigate thoroughly into the case before removing the child from home away from her mother.

Five mothers whose children remained in kinship foster care claimed that they had no problems, while five described problems that may affect their ability to care for their children. These respondents described their problems in the following way:

> Past history of substance abuse—drugs.

> Don't have a job.

> Drinking alcohol.

> In the past yes, my drug addiction was my biggest problem. It interfered with a lot of things that were important to me.

All of the respondents in the group whose children had been returned to their care described strengths in regard to caring for their child. Seven mothers whose children remained in kinship care also described strengths in regard to caring for their children and three replied, "None," when asked to describe their strengths. Two of the mothers whose children returned described their strengths in the following manner:

> Love her, take care of her, talk with her and be there for her at all times.

> I have learned how to show my feelings with another and to accept the fact that I now have four children and I love them very much.

Two mothers whose children remained in kinship care described their strengths as follows:

My strengths are numerous. I believe that a mother is not a mother because she gives birth, but a mother is someone that recognizes and encourages and who is unselfish to her child or children; teaches them love and understanding which strengthen their direction as they develop.

Able to provide transportation to and from school, help with homework, provide love and support.

Object Relations

Although there were no statistically significant differences in object relations between the two groups based on their descriptions of their mothers and children, the mean rankings for both representations of mother and representations of child were higher for mothers whose children returned home compared to those whose children remained in care (Table 6-2). Also, there were subtle differences in the perceptions of significant objects. While most mothers from both groups focused their descriptions of their mother on their direct need gratifications for themselves and internal or external qualities that were unidimensional, more of those whose children had not been returned to their care described strained relationships with their mothers.

Substance Abuse Problem Severity

Mean problem severity ratings were lower for six of the seven problem areas for mothers whose children had been returned to their care compared to mothers whose children had not been returned to their care (see Table 6-3). While there were no statistically significant differences at the .05 level, differences between the two groups approached statistical significance at the .10 level, for drug use and psychopathology.

Similar findings were observed in comparisons of composite scores, which are the ratings based on self-reports by the mothers regarding problems in the seven areas, as well as their own ratings regarding their need for treatment (see Table 6-4). Again, differences between the two groups of mothers approached statistical significance at the .10 level for drug abuse

**Table 6-2. Wilcoxon-Mann-Whitney Rank Sum Test
for Levels of Object Representations of Mother
and Child for Mothers Whose Children Returned Home
and Mothers Whose Children Remain in Kinship Foster Care**

	Child Returned Home	Child Remains in Kinship Care		
	Mean Rank	Mean Rank	U (2-tail)	p
Representation of Mother	11.65	9.35	38.5	.3577
Representation of Child	11.50	9.50	40.0	.4337

**Table 6-3. Comparison of Severity Ratings for Addiction
Severity Index Problem Areas for Mothers
Whose Children Returned Home and Mothers
Whose Children Remain in Kinship Foster Care**

	Child Returned Home		Child Remains in Kinship Care			
	Mean	Standard Deviation	Mean	Standard Deviation	t (2-tail)	p
Physical Health	2.00	3.30	4.30	4.05	1.39	.181
Employment	2.40	3.40	4.70	4.11	1.36	.190
Alcohol Use	3.10	3.34	5.20	4.05	1.26	.222
Drug Use	3.10	3.34	5.80	3.64	1.72	.102
Legal	1.50	3.06	1.30	2.66	.16	.878
Family/Social	2.80	3.42	4.90	3.10	1.44	.168
Psychopathology	3.10	3.57	5.80	3.49	1.77	.105

and psychopathology ratings. Five respondents whose children had been returned to their care reported a history of substance abuse problems as opposed to nine whose children remained in kinship foster care. Mothers whose children remained in kinship care also had a higher rate of recurrent substance abuse than those whose children had been returned to their care.

Table 6-4. Comparison of Composite Scores for Addiction Severity Index Problem Areas for Mothers Whose Children Returned Home and Mothers Whose Children Remain in Kinship Foster Care

	Child Returned Home		Child Remains in Kinship Care			
	Mean	Standard Deviation	Mean	Standard Deviation	*t* (2-tail)	*p*
Physical Health	.22	.37	.38	.44	.88	.391
Employment	2.51	.30	1.90	1.01	1.83	.096
Alcohol Use	.00	.00	.05	.34	.42	.683
Drug Use	.00	.00	.02	.03	1.86	.096
Legal	.00	.00	.00			
Family/Social	1.90	1.45	2.01	.26	1.19	.253
Psychopathology	.14	.17	.35	.26	1.93	.085

There were no reports of mental illness by mothers in the group whose children had been returned to their care. However, four mothers whose children had not been returned to their care had been diagnosed as being mentally ill and had received treatment as inpatients at a mental hospital. Three of these mothers reported that they were currently receiving outpatient mental health treatment, which included individual psychotherapy and psychotropic medication. One mother whose child had not been returned to her care reported five suicide attempts.

The one area in which mothers whose children had returned home displayed greater problems was employment, approaching the .10 level of statistical significance. It appears that employment problems were of greater concern to mothers who had their children returned to their care than it was for mothers whose children remained in kinship foster care.

Extended Family Support

The quality of extended family support reported by mothers whose children had returned to their care was compared to that reported by mothers whose children remained in care. Mothers in both groups were deeply rooted in their extended family networks. All of the mothers whose children had returned home and nine of the ten mothers whose children remained in care reported that they had relatives who played an important part in their lives. The two mothers whose children had been legally adopted by their maternal grandmothers reported continued close relationships with their children as well as with their family members. These mothers assisted in caring for their children on a daily basis and helped with their homework. One mother walked with her child to and from school because the school was in a dangerous area. The mothers whose children had been returned to their care reported a strong degree of encouragement from their extended family members to do whatever the child welfare system required to have their children returned to their care.

The mean number of close relatives identified by mothers whose children had returned was higher (3.8) than the number reported by mothers whose children remained in care (2.7), but the difference was not statistically significant. There was no statistically significant difference between the groups with regard to the mothers' ratings of the degree to which their relatives go out of their way to help. Seven of the mothers in each group indicated that their family members go out of their way "a great deal" or "a very great deal." Mothers in both groups expressed positive feelings about their families helping them in hard times. Slight differences were observed in the amount of help that the family provided since IDCFS became involved in their lives, although the differences were not statistically significant. Four mothers whose children had returned to them reported that their families' help had increased since IDCFS became involved compared to only two mothers whose children remained in care. Two mothers in each group reported that their families' help had decreased since IDCFS involvement. Mothers in both groups expressed positive feelings about the care that their relatives provided for their children while in kinship foster care.

Responses to the Help Received Scale revealed no statistically significant differences between groups. Child care and emotional support were the most frequently received types of support.

Summary and Conclusion

This study compared ten mothers whose children had been returned to their care after kinship foster care placement and ten mothers whose children remained in kinship foster care. The two groups of study participants were similar in terms of age and religious preference, with slight differences in marital status. Their income and employment levels varied. Mothers whose children had been returned to their care had a higher income level than those whose children had not been returned to their care, were more likely to be employed, and were more concerned about employment-related problems. There were no statistically significant differences in object relations between the two groups of study participants based on their descriptions of their mother and child; however, mean rankings suggest that mothers whose children returned to their care were functioning at a somewhat higher level of development and experienced more positive relationships with their own mothers.

Both the severity ratings and composite scores on the ASI suggest that mothers whose children remained in kinship foster care were more likely to display problems in drug abuse and mental illness compared to mothers whose children had returned to them. There were no statistically significant differences in the quality of extended family support between the two groups. Mothers in both groups had close relatives who provided help to them, except one respondent whose child had not been returned to her care. Extended family support was available to and valued by 19 of the 20 study participants, but it was not associated with children returning home in this sample.

Implications for Practice

The findings of this study do suggest that child welfare practitioners should more carefully assess object relations, substance abuse problem severity, and extended family support in their practice with mothers and children placed in kinship care. This study provided an opportunity to improve understanding of object relations and expand research that focused on African American mothers' mental representations of their external objects and the quality of their relationships to their own children. This study suggests that discussing the mother's relationship with her own mother may be a way of understanding and possibly enhancing parenting capacity.

Many of the African American mothers in this study reported multiple problems. This study suggests that child welfare caseworkers should take an in-depth look at drugs, income, and mental illness in their work with African American mothers whose children have been placed in kinship care. It would certainly seem that intensive services to mothers and children are required during periods of separation and after reunification, given the types and severity of problems identified by the mothers in this study.

Although not associated with children returning home or remaining in care in this study, extended family support was valued by mothers in both groups. The high level of participation of a couple of mothers with their children and their extended family suggests that focusing on the mother's relationship with her family is likely to have benefits to children whether they return to the mother's care or remain with kin. The importance of extended family in child rearing in African American families is well documented but not always supported in child welfare practice [McAdoo, 1978; Brown & Gary 1985]. Enhancing the capacity of child welfare practitioners to work with mothers and extended families is one way of addressing the need identified by Cahn and Johnson [1993] for culturally appropriate services provided to children of color in the custody of the child welfare system.

Implications for Research

Although it had substantial limitations, this study lays the groundwork for future studies regarding African American mothers and their children placed in kinship care. In some ways the limitations of this study are as important to attend to as the substantive findings, because they provide suggestions for future research. Probably the most severe limitations of this study are related to the size of the sample and the sample selection procedures. The small sample size severely limited statistical power, which made it impossible to detect subtle differences that may exist between the two groups of mothers in this study. The small sample and the convenience sampling procedures that were used suggest that this group of parents is probably not representative of the population of mothers whose children have been placed in kinship care and reunified or those who remain in kinship care.

Also, since the study was cross-sectional, the women who participated in this study had been involved with the child welfare system for varying amounts of time, and in the case of reunification, children had been returned home also at varying times, some very important questions could not be answered by this study. For example, did the mothers whose children returned home and those whose children remained in kinship care differ on the object relations, substance abuse severity, and extended family support measures at the time the reunification decision was made? Did changes occur in each of these areas over time, once the children returned home? Would the differences between the two group of mothers be greater or would there be greater similarities on these measures if they were compared as the child entered care and at regular intervals thereafter? Does the mother's functioning improve or deteriorate over time, once children are returned to her care, and what factors predict positive or negative changes in functioning?

Clearly, studies that are prospective, longitudinal, and include larger samples are needed. For example, a large sample of mothers could be obtained at the point when their children are placed in kinship care and their object relations, substance abuse problems, and extended family support measured at this time and at repeated intervals that span substantial periods of time. Self-report measures are important because they elicit the perspective of the mother, yet it is best if these measures are supplemented with other sources of data as well as direct observation. Future research should be geared to gaining a greater understanding of the barriers and conditions, both individual and systematic, that interfere with the successful reunification of African American mothers and their children placed in kinship care. Also, studies of effectiveness of interventions with mothers, which focus on object relations, substance abuse, extended family support, and other important areas of functioning, could contribute to the development of effective practice models in kinship care.

References

Barth, R. P. (1997). Family reunification. In R. Barth, J. D. Berrick, & N. Gilbert (Eds.), *Child welfare research review: Volume two* (pp. 219-228). New York: Columbia University Press.

Barth, R. P., Courtney, M. E., Berrick, J. D., & Albert, V. (1994). *From child abuse to permanency planning: Child welfare services, pathways and placements.* New York, Aldine de Gruyter.

Berrick, J. D., & Barth, R. P. (1994). Research on kinship foster care: What do we know? Where do we go from here? *Children and Youth Services Review, 16*(1/2), 1-5.

Berrick, J. D., Needell, B., Barth, R. P., & Jonson-Reid, M. (1998). *The tender years: Toward developmentally sensitive child welfare services for very young children.* New York: Oxford University Press.

Blatt, S. J., Brenneis, C. B., Schimek, J. G., & Glick, M. (1976a). A developmental analysis of the concept of the object on the Rorschach. Unpublished scoring protocol.

Blatt, S. J., Brenneis, C. B., Schimek, J. G., & Glick, M. (1976b). Normal development and psychopathological impairment of the concept on the Rorschach. *Journal of Abnormal Psychology, 85,* 7-28.

Blatt, S. P., Chevron, E. S., Quinlan, D. M., & Wein, S. (1981). *The assessment of qualitative and structural dimensions of object representations.* New Haven, CT: Yale University.

Blatt, S. J., & Lerner, H. (1983). The psychological assessment of object representation. *Journal of Personality Assessment, 47,* 7-28.

Brown, D. R., & Gary, L. E. (1985). Social support network differentials among married and unmarried black females. *Psychology of Women Quarterly, 9,* 229-241.

Cahn, K., & Johnson, P. (1993). Critical issues in permanency planning: An overview. In K. Cahn & P. Johnson (Eds.), *Children can't wait: Reducing delays for children in foster care* (pp. 1-12). Washington, DC: Child Welfare League of America, Inc.

Courtney, M. E., & Needell, B. (1997). Outcomes of kinship care: Lessons from California. In R. Barth, J. D. Berrick, & N. Gilbert (Eds.), *Child welfare research review: Volume two* (pp. 129-159). New York: Columbia University Press.

Courtney, M. E., Piliavin, I., & Entner Wright, B. R. (1997). Transitions from and returns to out-of-home care. *Social Service Review, 71*(4), 652-667.

Fairbairn, W. R. D. (1952). *Psychoanalytic studies of personality*. London: Routledge & Kegan Paul.

Fishler, P. H., Sperling, M. B., & Carr, A. (1990). Assessment of adult relatedness: A review of empirical findings from object relations and attachment theory. *Journal of Personality Assessment, 55*(3 & 4), 499-520.

Gleeson, J. P., O' Donnell, J., Altshuler, S., & Philbin, C. (1994). *Current practice in kinship care: Case workers's perspectives*. Chicago: University of Illinois, Jane Addams College of Social Work & Jane Addams Center for Social Policy and Research.

Gleeson, J. P., O'Donnell, J., & Bonecutter, F. J. (1997). Understanding the complexity of practice in kinship foster care. *Child Welfare, 76*(6), 801-826.

Goerge, R. M. (1990). The reunification process in substitute care. *Social Service Review, 64*, 422-457.

Greenberg, J., & Mitchell, S. (1983). *Object relations in psychoanalytic theory*. Cambridge, MA: Harvard University Press.

Hale, J. (1982). *Black children: Their roots, culture and learning styles*. Provo, UT: Brigham Young University Press.

Hill, R. B. (1972). *The strengths of Black families*. New York: Emerson Hall.

Hill, R. B. (1977). *Informal adoption among Black families*. Washington DC: National Urban League Research Department.

Hill, R. B. (1997). *The strengths of African American families: Twenty-five years later*. Washington, DC: R & B Publishers.

Martin, E., & Martin, J. M. (1978). *The black extended family*. Chicago, IL: University of Chicago Press.

McAdoo, H. P. (1977). *The impact of extended family variables upon the upward mobility of black families*. Final report under contract no 90-C-631 (1). Washington, DC: U. S. Department of Health, Education and Welfare, Office of Child Development.

McAdoo, H. P. (1978). Factors related to stability in upwardly mobile black families. *Journal of Marriage and the Family, 40*, 716-776.

McAdoo, H. P. (1980). Black mothers and the extended family support networks. In L. F. Rodgers-Rose (Ed.), *The black woman* (pp. 125-144). Beverly Hills, CA: Sage Publications.

McLellan, A. T., Luborsky, L., Woody, G. E., & O' Brien, C. P. (1980). An improved evaluation instrument for substance abuse patients: The Addiction Severity Index. *Journal of Nervous and Mental Disease, 168,* 26-33.

McLellan, A. T., Luborsky, L., Woody, G. E., & O' Brien, C. P. (1981). Are the addiction-related problems of substance abusers really related? *Journal of Nervous and Mental Disease, 169,* 232-239.

McLellan, A. T., Luborsky, L., Woody, G. E., & O' Brien, C. P. (1983). Predicting response to alcohol and drug abuse treatment: Role of psychiatric severity. *Archives of General Psychiatry, 40,* 620-625.

Meyer, B. S., & Link, M. K. (1990). *Kinship foster care: The double-edged dilemma.* Rochester, NY: Task Force on Permanency Planning for Foster Children, Inc.

Stack, C. (1974). *All our kin: Strategies for survival in the black community.* New York: Harper and Row.

Wilson, M. N. (1984). Mothers' and grandmothers' perception of parental behavior in three generational black families. *Child Development, 55,* 1333-1339.

Wulczyn, F. H., Harden, A. W., & Goerge, R. M. (1997). *Foster care dynamics 1983- 1994: An update from the multistate foster care data archive.* The Chapin Hall Center for Children at the University of Chicago.

Wulczyn, F. H., & Goerge, R. M. (1992). Foster care in New York and Illinois: The challenge of rapid change. *Social Service Review, 66,* 278-294.

7

Casework Practice with Fathers of Children in Kinship Foster Care

John M. O'Donnell

Marsiglio [1995] notes that fatherhood has become a popular topic for scholarly inquiry, particularly in the disciplines of sociology and psychology. In the past three decades, much of the inquiry has focused on whether and how fathers influence the well-being of their children [Biller 1993; Lamb 1995; Levine 1993; Parke 1996]. Many studies have found positive outcomes associated with paternal involvement with their children, particularly in regard to children's cognitive and psychosocial development, although not all studies have confirmed these findings. An increasing amount of research is now being directed toward identifying the ways in which paternal influence operates and exploring how factors such as the quality of the father-child relationship and the child's gender may affect paternal influence on developmental outcomes. This continuing scholarly interest is consistent with the emergence of fatherhood as an issue of national concern and attention.

Social work literature has been slow in reflecting this interest. Examining the output of five major social work periodicals from 1961 to 1987, Grief and Bailey [1990] found only 21 articles specifically pertaining to fathers. Most of these articles dealt with problems caused by fathers, such as sexual abuse, or problems experienced by single-father families. By comparison, Quam and Austin [1984] reviewed eight social work journals from 1970 to 1981 and found 286 pertaining to women's issues such as motherhood and female-headed households. In a follow-up to their earlier inquiry, Grief and Bailey [1997] found a substantial increase in the number of articles about fathers in the five social work journals they had previously surveyed. In the nine-year period from 1988 to1996, these journals contained 22 articles concerning fathers, approximately one article for every 12 issues of the journals. Many of the recent articles addressed the nurturing capacities of fathers rather than focusing on negative or problematic aspects of fatherhood.

Despite this increased attention, the social work literature pertaining to fathers still has many gaps. One of the major weaknesses is the lack of research on the involvement of fathers in social services, particularly in fields such as child welfare where paternal participation in services may help to secure safe, permanent, and nurturing environments for abused and neglected children. With the exception of services to adolescent fathers, child welfare literature provides few descriptions of whether or how fathers are involved in child welfare interventions. Child welfare texts and journal articles on programs such as permanency planning and family preservation often assume that child welfare work involves two-parent families even though single-parent, mother-headed households constitute a large segment of families served by child welfare agencies. Typically, the literature does not discuss how the roles of fathers and mothers may vary within families, identify how intervention with fathers may differ from work with mothers, or offer guidance on how to engage fathers. Little has been written about the importance of involving nonresident fathers or ways of working with these fathers to determine how they may contribute to their children's material and psychological well-being.

This study was undertaken to increase knowledge about casework practice with biological fathers of children involved with the child welfare system. The study was based on data gathered from caseworkers in two kinship foster care programs. Kinship foster care was considered a particularly opportune child welfare service in which to study practice for two reasons. First, the use of relatives as foster parents for maltreated children has increased significantly in the past decade. In some states, such as

Illinois, kinship foster home placements now outnumber placements in nonrelated homes. Secondly, kinship foster care inherently promotes the involvement of biological family in the care and treatment of placed children.

This study describes casework practice with the biological fathers of a sample of children in kinship foster care and examines relationships between casework practice with these fathers and characteristics of the caseworker. The study includes comparisons of casework practice with fathers when the child is placed with paternal relatives and maternal relatives and comparisons of casework practice with mothers and fathers of children in the sample. Caseworkers' reactions to the lack of paternal involvement are also described.

Methodology

This study involved a secondary analysis of data collected as part of a federally funded research and demonstration project designed to improve permanency outcomes for abused and neglected children who had been placed in kinship foster care.* The first phase of the project involved the collection of data regarding current casework practice with children who had been removed from the custody of their parents by the public child welfare system and placed in foster homes with related caregivers. Two private child welfare agencies in Chicago, Illinois provided services to the children, their parents, and the relative foster parents under a contract with the public child welfare system. The data were collected during 1993 and 1994 in interviews with the caseworkers in the two private agencies who were assigned to the cases.

* Supported in part by Grant No. 90-CO-0595, awarded to Dr. James P. Gleeson, from the Adoption Opportunities Office of the Administration for Children, Youth, and Families, U.S. Department of Health and Human Services, with in-kind contributions from the Jane Addams College of Social Work, Central Baptist Family Services, Lutheran Social Services of Illinois, the Jane Addams Center for Social Policy and Research, the Jane Addams Hull House Museum, Loyola University of Chicago School of Social Work, Life Concerns, and the Assistance of the Illinois Department of Children and Family Services.

To ensure a history of casework services, the sample was limited to families with children who had been in placement at least one year. Ninety-one eligible families were randomly selected from the agency caseloads and one child was randomly chosen from each family. Interviews were completed for 77 (85%) of the 91 cases. Case closings, case transfers, and recent caseworker turnover prevented completion of interviews on the remaining 15%. Analysis of the 77 completed interviews revealed that only 10 (13%) involved children placed with a relative of the father. To obtain more information about casework practice with paternal kinship foster homes, a second sample of 23 families was randomly selected from all of the cases in which a child was placed with a relative of the father. One child was then randomly chosen from each of the 23 families and interviews were completed on all of these cases.

The Instrument

Project staff developed an instrument that probed several major dimensions of casework practice with the children and their families, including case assessment procedures, permanency planning activities, service provision, frequency and content of contacts with the child and family, and case consultations. The instrument elicited primarily factual data that were either known to the caseworker or that could be obtained from the case record, which was brought to the interview. The instrument was developed by project staff, all of whom had extensive experience in child welfare services. A project steering committee, which included child welfare professionals from the public and private child welfare service sectors as well as social work faculty from other areas of practice, provided consultation on the design of the instrument and commented on individual items.

Project staff conducted a field test of the instrument that involved three interviewers and 35 cases. The field test identified several ambiguously worded questions that were subsequently modified to ensure consistency in interpretation and response. The final instrument consisted of 195 questions. One-hundred seventy-three required fixed-alternative responses and 22 were open-ended.

Data Collection

Project staff collected data on the cases through in-person interviews with the 54 caseworkers who were responsible for services to the 100 selected children and their families. The interviews lasted from one to three hours; the mean length was one hour and 50 minutes. Social work faculty, doctoral students, and masters-level students in social work conducted the interviews.

Description of the Sample:
The Children and Their Fathers

The children selected as the focus of the original research and demonstration project consisted primarily of young African American children. The mean age of the children was 7.9 years, the median was 6.8 years. Ninety-five percent of the children were African American. Most (83%) had been placed because of neglect that was usually associated with the mother's drug use. Other reasons for placement included physical and sexual abuse (10%), a combination of abuse and neglect (4%), and dependency (3%). Most of the children (55%) had only been in placement one or two years; 31% had been placed three to five years, and 14% from six to 10 years.

Caseworkers knew the identity of 91 of the 100 fathers. Five of the fathers were deceased. Five had lost parental rights to the child, including one whose identity was unknown. This study was limited to the 82 fathers whose identity was known to the caseworker, who were living and whose parental rights had not been terminated. Table 7-1 summarizes the major descriptive characteristics of these 82 fathers.

Almost all of the fathers were African American. Caseworkers knew the ages of 55 fathers, which ranged from 21 to 44 years. Both the mean and the median ages were 31 years. One of the most striking aspects of Table 7-1 is the high percentage of missing data. Caseworkers did not know the marital status of 41% of the fathers or the housing status of 54%. Of the 48 fathers whose marital status was known, 71% had never married and only 6% were married to the mother of the child in placement. Fifteen fathers were known to be living in their own home or apartment, and 12 were

---

Table 7-1. Characteristics of Fathers (*N*=82 fathers)

	Number	Percent
Race		
African American	74	90
Caucasian	4	5
Latino	1	1
Caseworker did not know	3	4
Age in Years		
21-25	13	16
26-30	13	16
31-40	25	30
41-44	4	5
Caseworker did not know	27	33
Marital Status		
Never married	34	41
Divorced	5	6
Married to mother of placed child	3	4
Married to another woman	6	7
Caseworker did not know	34	41
Education		
Less than high school	13	16
High school graduate	7	9
Some college or vocational training	4	5
Caseworker did not know	58	71
Housing		
Own apartment/house	15	18
Lives with others	12	15
Lives in institution	8	10
Other	3	4
Caseworker did not know	44	54
Sources of Income		
Employment	17	21
Public assistance	6	7
Social Security/SSI	6	7
Other	5	6
Caseworker did not know	48	59

Note: Percentages do not always total to 100 because of rounding error.

---

living with family and friends. Eight fathers lived in institutions, primarily prisons. Caseworkers had no information about the education or income of most of the fathers. Seventeen were known to be employed and 12 were receiving public benefits. Caseworkers did not know the educational attainment of 71% of the fathers; among those whose educational status was known, more than half had not completed high school.

Fathers' Problems and Strengths

For 55 of the 82 fathers (67%), caseworkers were able to identify one or more problems that affected the father's ability to care for the placed child. The most frequently mentioned problem was drug abuse or alcoholism (33% of the 82 fathers), followed by current or recurrent incarceration (16%), lack of cooperation with the caseworker or agency (9%), housing problems (7%), lack of interest in the child (7%), history of abusing children (5%) or abuse to the mother (4%), and lack of parenting skills (5%).

Caseworkers reported less about the fathers' strengths than their problems. In 50% of the cases, caseworkers stated that they did not know whether the fathers had any strengths in regard to caring for their children; in an additional 15%, caseworkers responded that the father had no strengths. Among the 35% for whom one or more strengths were identified, the most commonly cited were love for the child, maintenance of contact with the child, giving the child gifts, and expressing interest in the child's affairs.

Casework Practice with Fathers

Casework practice with fathers was defined and measured by two variables: the frequency of contact between the caseworker and the father during the preceding six months, and the father's involvement in nine activities pertaining to service planning and service delivery. Table 7-2 displays the frequency of in-person and telephone contacts that the caseworker had with fathers during the six months preceding the interview. In-person and telephone contacts are also combined and summarized in Table 7-2.

Caseworkers' accounts of their contacts with fathers were consistent with their general lack of knowledge about this client group. In a majority

Table 7-2. Frequency of Caseworker Contact with Fathers During Six Months Preceeding Interview
(*N*=82 fathers)

	Number	Percent
In Person		
0	59	71.9
1	9	11.0
2-4	9	11.0
5-7	3	3.6
8-14	0	0.0
15-19	2	2.4
Telephone		
0	61	74.4
1	8	9.8
2-4	6	7.3
5-9	4	4.9
10-13	3	3.7
In Person and Telephone Contact Combined		
0	52	63.4
1-3	16	19.5
4-7	7	8.5
8-16	4	4.9
17-20	3	3.7

Note: Percentages do not always total to 100 because of rounding error.

of cases (63.4%), caseworkers reported no contact with the father in the preceding six months. While caseworkers did have at least one telephone communication or in-person meeting with 30 of the 82 fathers, only a small percentage of fathers had contact with caseworkers on a regular basis.

Nine activities were used to measure fathers' participation in case planning and service delivery:

- the caseworker's discussion with the father of the reasons for the child's placement;
- exploration of the father's feelings about the placement;
- discussion of the role of the caseworker;

- the father's participation in an initial family assessment following case opening;
- the father's participation in periodic reassessments;
- the father's participation in the development of the most recent case plan for the child by providing background information;
- the father's participation in the development of the most recent service plan by contributing recommendations for planning objectives, case goals, and services;
- the father's participation in the most recent case review; and
- the father's receipt of services from the agency.

These activities were chosen to measure service participation because they are either required of child welfare caseworkers or are generally acknowledged as good practice. For example, the first three activities are basic steps in engaging parents to work with the caseworker on behalf of the child [Maluccio et al. 1986]. Social work practice literature in general has stressed the need for helpers to involve clients in assessing their problems as well as working with clients to identify and implement solutions to the problems. These principles of client involvement are also embodied in child welfare policy. Federal funding legislation requires the development of written case plans every six months for children in substitute care. The plans must identify a desired permanency outcome for the child and the services that will be provided to the child and parents. The case plans are to be reviewed for appropriateness every six months by a panel that includes someone who is not responsible for services to the child or family. Parents must be allowed to participate in this review [Allen et al. 1983]. Illinois policy requires caseworkers to seek parental input for the semi-annual case plan as well as for the initial and periodic case assessments that include identification of parental strengths and weaknesses in regard to caring for the child.

Table 7-3 lists fathers' participation in the nine planning and services delivery activities. The data indicate that few fathers were engaged in helping efforts on behalf of their child. Small percentages of fathers partici-

---

Table 7-3. Fathers' Involvement in
Service Planning and Service Delivery
(*N*=82 fathers)

	Number of Fathers Involved in Activity	Percent
Exploration of father's feelings about the child's placement	30	37
Exploration of the father's understanding of why the child was placed	27	33
Discussion of the role of the caseworker	21	26
Participation in the initial case assessment	7	9
Participation in updated assessments	14	17
Contributing background information for semi-annual service plan	12	15
Contributing recommendations for case objectives and services	5	6
Participation in services through child welfare agency	5	6
Attendance at administrative case review in past year	2	2

Note: Percentages do not always total to 100 because categories are not mutually exclusive. Each father could participate in multiple activities.

---

pated in decisionmaking activities such as contributing recommendations for the most recent service plan (6%) or participating in the most recent administrative case review (2%). At the time of the interviews with the caseworkers, only five of the eighty-two fathers were receiving services to assist them in assuming greater responsibility for the child.

Caseworkers' Characteristics and Father Involvement

Forty-five of the 54 caseworkers interviewed in this study were female. Twenty-six were African American, 24 were white, three were Latino, and one was a Native American. Forty-four of the caseworkers had only a bachelor's degree, seven had master's degrees in fields other than social work, such as psychology and counseling, and three had master's degrees in social work. The mean length of experience in human services among the caseworkers was 3.2 years, ranging from nine months to four and one-half years. The mean length of experience in kinship foster care was one year, ranging from one month to three and one-half years. These caseworkers served an average caseload of 22 children from eight families. The number of children on a caseload varied from 15 to 29 and the number of families varied from five to 16. The average length of time that a caseworker had served a case was 12 months, with a range of one month to nearly four years.

Analysis of relationships between caseworker characteristics and involvement of the father was limited to cases in which the current caseworker had been assigned the case for six months or longer and therefore had sufficient time to involve fathers. Thirty-seven caseworkers met this criterion. Since the unit of analysis was the caseworker, one case was randomly selected from the interviews completed by each caseworker.

There was no statistically significant difference between the 18 white and 19 African Americans caseworkers in regard to the average number of contacts with fathers (Table 7-4). Similarly there was no significant difference in the average number of service activities among fathers served by white and African American caseworkers. Bivariate correlation analyses using Pearson's *r* revealed no significant associations between the length of caseworkers' professional experience in kinship foster care or all human services and either the number of contacts (Table 7-5) or service participation. Similarly, practice did not vary significantly by the size of the caseworkers' caseload or the length of time the caseworker had served a case. The latter finding was particularly interesting as lower caseloads and greater familiarity with a case would provide more favorable conditions for contact with fathers. The low number of male caseworkers precluded an assessment of whether gender or gender combined with race influenced paternal participation.

Placement with Maternal and Paternal Relatives and Father Involvement

As Table 7-6 shows, fathers whose children were placed with paternal relatives had more contact on average with caseworkers in the six months

Table 7-4. Mean Number of Contacts Caseworkers Had with the Father and Service Involvement of the Father by Race of the Caseworker

	Caucasian Caseworkers	African American Caseworkers	*t*-value	*df*	2-tailed significance
Contact with Father[a]	2.78	2.37	-.23	35	.82
Service Involvement of Father[b]	1.22	1.31	.14	35	.89

a   Includes in-person and telephone contacts with the caseworker in the last six months.
b   Number of service activities, out of nine possible activities, in which the father participated in the last six months.

Table 7-5. Zero-Order Correlations Between Caseworker Experience and Number of Contacts with Father, Service Involvement of Father, in the Last Six Months

	Contact with the Father[a]	Service Involvement of Father[b]
Experience in Kinship Foster Care (in years)	-.11	-.04
Experience in All Human Services (in years)	.18	.02
Caseload Size	.11	.05
Length of Time Serving Case	-.15	.04

Note: None of the observed correlations were statistically significant at the .05 level.
a   Includes in-person and telephone contacts with the caseworker in the last six months.
b   Number of service activities, out of nine possible activities, in which the father participated in the last six months.

**Table 7-6. Mean Number of Contacts Caseworkers
Had with the Father and Service Involvement
of the Father by Placement of the Child
with Maternal or Paternal Relatives**

	Maternal Relatives	Paternal Relatives	*t*-value	*df*	2-tailed significance
Contact with Father[a]	1.22	3.45	-2.36	80	.02
Service Involvement of Father[b]	.90	2.45	-3.57	80	.00

a   Includes in-person and telephone contacts with the caseworker in the last six months.
b   Number of service activities, out of nine possible activities, in which the father participated in the last six months.

preceding the project interview than those whose children were placed with maternal relatives. The mean number of contacts with fathers of children placed with paternal relatives was 3.45 for six months as contrasted with 1.22 contacts for fathers whose children were placed with maternal relatives. They also had more involvement in planning and service delivery. The fathers with children in paternal family homes were engaged in a mean number of 2.45 activities compared to a mean of .90 for those with children in maternal relatives. *T*-tests indicated that both of these differences were significant at the .05 level. The most plausible explanation for this finding is that placement with paternal relatives usually afforded caseworkers greater access to the father.

Comparison of Casework Practice with Mothers and Fathers

Comparisons were made between caseworker practice with mothers and with fathers to determine whether the findings regarding fathers were unique. The comparisons involved matched pairs of mothers and fathers from the 80 cases in which the identity of the father was known, both parents were living, and parental rights had not been terminated. Table 7-

7 indicates that, on average, caseworkers had significantly more contact with mothers than fathers during the six months preceding the project interviews, and that mothers, on average, participated in significantly more services activities than fathers.

Caseworkers' Responses to the Lack of Involvement by Fathers

The study also explored the extent to which caseworkers developed strategies for working successfully with fathers, pursued opportunities to connect with noninvolved fathers or even identified lack of paternal involvement as a concern. Caseworkers' responses suggested that they seldom gave attention to the fathers of the children in their caseloads. For example:

- Sixty-seven (82%) of the fathers had not contributed to the most recent case assessment. When asked what additional information they would have liked to have had for this assessment, caseworkers mentioned information from or about the father in only three (4%) of these 67 cases.

- Seventy-four (90%) of the fathers had not participated in drafting the most recent service plan for the child and family; in 12 (16%) of these cases caseworkers cited fathers' lack of participation as an impediment to case planning.

- Caseworkers had at least monthly conferences with their supervisors and were asked to identify all of the topics discussed in these conferences during the six months preceding the project interview. In 69 (84%) of the 82 cases, caseworkers reported no discussions about the father with the supervisor.

- Similarly, in 68 (83%) of the cases, caseworkers did not note any discussions about the father in their contacts with external agencies such as the juvenile court, the public child welfare agency, and community service providers.

- Caseworkers typically made monthly visits to the homes of 31 foster parents who were related to the father. In 19 (61%) of these 31 cases, caseworkers' descriptions of their discussions with the relatives dur-

**Table 7-7. Comparison of Casework Practice
with Mothers and Fathers**
(*N*=80 mothers and fathers)

	Father	Mother	*t*-value	*df*	2-tailed significance
Mean number of caseworker contacts in last six months[a]	2.10	8.28	-6.00	79	.00
Mean number of service activities in which parent participated[b]	1.50	4.00	-6.69	79	.00

a Includes in-person and telephone contacts with the caseworker in the last six months.
b Number of service activities, out of nine possible activities, in which the father participated in the last six months.

ing the previous six months did not include a single reference to the father, even though the caseworker had reported not knowing the father's whereabouts in many of these 19 cases.

• In 28 cases, caseworkers also noted that they had at least one contact with noncustodial paternal relatives in the six months preceding the interview. According to caseworkers' accounts, no mention of the father was made in 24 (86%) of theses 28 cases.

Discussion

Data from caseworkers in the two agencies involved in the study revealed that fathers seldom participated in interventions on behalf of their children and that caseworkers rarely engaged fathers in discussions that might lead to involvement. Several factors beyond the control of the caseworkers probably contributed to these findings. In cases where the mother was the most immediate source of knowledge about the father, obtaining reliable information may have been difficult. Most of the mothers suffered from drug addiction and many were not consistently available to provide information to the caseworker. They may also have been reticent to provide information about the father's whereabouts and circumstances either from reluctance to involve the father or because of anger toward the child welfare system for placing their children.

Many of the fathers also had difficult problems. Thirty-two percent were known to use drugs or alcohol and the actual prevalence may have been higher. Sixteen percent of the fathers were either in jail or had a history of incarceration. The fathers often proved elusive to caseworkers. In several cases, the caseworkers noted the difficulty in maintaining contact because the father did not have stable housing. Caseworkers also complained in several cases about fathers who failed appointments.

Client characteristics and behavior, however, do not fully explain why so many of the fathers in this study were not involved in helping efforts on behalf of their children. Caseworkers' perceptions of, and attitudes toward, fathers also played a role, as did agency expectations regarding casework with fathers. Given the low levels of paternal involvement, it is remarkable, for example, that caseworkers' problems in working with fathers appeared rarely either in accounts of supervisory conferences or in reported contacts with other agencies, such as the public child welfare system that monitored service provision. Even more extraordinary is the reported silence about the father in most of the caseworkers' contacts with members of the father's own family.

The silence about fathers in professional and family contacts was consistent with caseworkers' apparent disinterest about who the fathers were or how they felt about their children. As indicated above, lack of information about the father was rarely identified as an obstacle to assessing the problems that caused or perpetuated the child's placement; lack of input from the father was seldom perceived by the caseworker as an impediment to planning for the child's current and future needs, even in cases where the father was apparently available to provide input. In the small percentage of cases where caseworkers did make face-to-face contact with fathers, meetings usually took place in formal settings, such as courts and offices, rather than in informal settings such as the father's home, where the caseworker would have been better able to gain an understanding of the father.

Much more information would be needed to explain the casework practice revealed in this study. For example, understanding the caseworkers' perceptions of fathers and fathers' views of the child welfare system would probably help to clarify why so few fathers participated in service planning. A greater knowledge about the service needs of those fathers who had the willingness and capacity to contribute to their children's well-being would also help to determine whether the agencies' resources would have been sufficient to meet those needs.

While the study's limitations prevent a conclusive interpretation of the findings, several factors that may have influenced the findings can be identified from the social policy and social services literatures. For example, one explanation for the finding of low paternal participation in child welfare services involves conventional cultural perceptions of fathers and the paternal role in American society. Traditionally, fathers have been depicted as uninvolved in child rearing. The paternal role involved breadwinning and providing a visible but somewhat distant role model to children while child care responsibilities were delegated to the mother [Parke 1996]. Until recently, social policy and the legal system in the United States reflected this cultural view of fathers. Policy emphasized the economic responsibility of fathers toward their children but generally ignored other dimensions of fathering, such as caregiving and nurturing, that also might benefit children [Elllwood 1993; Kamerman 1983].

In the same vein, courts generally favored mothers as custodians on the assumption that, by nature, they were better parents than were fathers [Erickson & Babcock 1995]. Social work has traditionally exhibited a similar bias toward mothers and the maternal role in relation to services for children and families. As noted earlier, social work literature until quite recently contained few positive references to fathers and largely ignored fathers' capacities to nurture their children. In regard to practice, Jaffe [1983] observes that social services have not exhibited an understanding of the importance of the father's role and, historically, were not structured to accommodate fathers. He attributes these shortcomings to several factors, including the predominance of women in the social work profession, the focus in early social work practice on the problems of mothers and children, and the greater availability of women than men to social service workers during regular working hours. Thus, the low level of paternal involvement observed in this study, and caseworkers' apparent lack of concern about the fathers, may largely reflect an indifference to fathers in professional work that has traditionally been viewed as mother-focused.

A second factor that probably influenced the findings was the racial composition of the sample. The small number of white and Latino fathers in the sample did not allow an adequate exploration of the extent to which paternal participation varied by race. However, the low paternal participation in planning and services may stem in part from the preponderance of African American fathers in the study. Although there is little research on use of social services by African American fathers, studies suggest that utilization rates are quite low [Hendricks et al. 1981; Hendricks 1980]. The reasons for this low utilization are often attributed to established attitudes and practices of social service professionals toward African American men. Traditionally, social service agencies have held a deficit view of African Americans that focused on weaknesses and failures and did not acknowledge strengths or achievements [Chestang 1970; Leigh & Green 1982]. African American men, particularly inner-city residents, have often been treated as marginal or unproductive by middle class social service professionals who often lack the knowledge needed to work effectively with them [Bryan & Ajo 1992; Hopkins 1973]. The experiences of many African American fathers have led them to avoid social service agencies, including child welfare agencies, because they are seen as coercive organizations that expect financial responsibility of fathers but provide little help or support to meet these expectations [Leashore 1981, 1997]. If this perception of the child welfare system is widespread among African American fathers, it is not surprising that most of the African American fathers in this study did not seek out caseworkers or cooperate with them.

If many child welfare caseworkers and their agencies do hold deficit views of the fathers of children involved with the child welfare system, this may explain their apparent reluctance to pursue engagement of the fathers. For these caseworkers, most of these fathers probably constituted an extremely difficult clientele, one whose behaviors appeared hostile, indifferent, or perplexing, and one whose needs far exceeded whatever help that caseworkers could offer. In these circumstances, even experienced and dedicated caseworkers might well have declined any rigorous efforts to involve these fathers.

Policy and Practice Implications

The findings of this study have several implications for child welfare practice and policy. Briefly, these include the following:

- The low level of paternal involvement in planning and services, coupled with the caseworkers' apparent disinterest in paternal involvement, raises serious concerns about their willingness and ability to work with fathers. One of the first steps in addressing this issue would be to develop child welfare caseworkers' knowledge about fathers, fatherhood, and the findings from current research on the paternal role in families.

- Particular attention needs to be paid to caseworkers' perception of minority fathers. In conducting training for experienced child welfare staff in Detroit, Gray & Nybell [1990] found that caseworkers admitted to having preconceived, negative views of inner-city African American fathers but were eager to learn how to work more effectively with them. The findings of this study point to the need for similar training among professionals at all levels in child welfare agencies.

- One of the major limitations of this study was the lack of information about whether or how the fathers in the sample could have contributed to the well-being of their children. Although current research indicates that fathers can play several roles in their children's lives beside that of breadwinner, the findings of this research suggest that child welfare staff do not know how to assess the full range of paternal capacities or to match these capacities to the needs of individual children. In addition to training, the development of paternal assessment instruments would also help to ensure that staff consider a broad range of roles and responsibilities in determining fathers' parenting potential.

- The needs of many of the fathers in this study span several service areas such as job training, drug treatment, and parental skill development. The current fragmentation of these services thwarts the development and implementation of comprehensive service packages. Until policy redresses this fragmentation, even the most skilled caseworkers will be challenged to help these parents meet the needs of their children on a timely basis.

Conclusion

This study is one of a small number that has looked at casework practice with fathers in child welfare. Much more research is needed to understand the scope of, and variations within, this practice. Any research agenda should include at a minimum:

- more descriptive studies of the characteristics and circumstances of the fathers of children involved in the child welfare system;
- comparative studies of casework practice involving fathers of different race and socioeconomic status to identify whether and how such practice varies by ethnicity and culture;
- exploration of the extent of paternal involvement across a spectrum of services that target children and families, such as mental heath and early child development;
- descriptions of service interventions and outcomes involving fathers, including the effects of paternal involvement on the child's well-being;
- identification of factors associated with successful inclusion of fathers; and
- identification of barriers that inhibit fathers from entering into partnership with social service providers.

Finally, the inclusion of service recipients in research on the effectiveness of social service programs is always a good practice that satisfies ethical concerns and promotes desirable program outcomes. The findings of this study are especially persuasive of the need to involve fathers in the development of programs to identify and strengthen their parenting capacities.

References

Allen, M. L., Golubock, C., & Olson, L. (1983). A guide to the adoption assistance and child welfare act of 1980. In M. Hardin (Ed.), *Foster children in the courts* (pp. 575-611). Boston: Butterworth Legal Publishers

Biller, H. B. (1993). *Fathers and families: Paternal factors in child development*. Westport CT: Auburn House

Bryan, D. L., & Ajo, A. A. (1992). The role perception of African American fathers. *Social Work Research & Abstracts, 28*(3), 17-21.

Chestang, L. W. (1970). The issue of race in casework practice. In *Social work practice 1970*. Selected papers. 97th Annual Forum, National Conference on Social Welfare, Chicago, Illinois, May 31-June 5, 1970. New York: Columbia University Press.

Ellwood, D. T. (1993). The changing structure of American families: the bigger family planning issue. *Journal of Economic Perspectives, 4*(4), 65-84.

Erickson, R. J., & Babcock, G. M. (1995). Man and family law: From patriarchy to partnership. *Families and Law, 21*(3/4), 31-54.

Gray, S. S., & Nybell, L. M. (1990). Issues in African-American family preservation. *Child Welfare, 69*(6), 513-523.

Grief, G. L., & Bailey, C. (1990). Where are the fathers in social work literature? *Families in Society, 71*(2), 88-92.

Grief, G. L., & Bailey, C. (1997). Where are the fathers in social work literature? Revisiting the question. *Families in Society, 78*(4), 433-435.

Hendricks, L. E. (1980). Unwed adolescent fathers: Problems they face and their sources of social support. *Adolescence, 15*(60), 861-869.

Hendricks, L. E., Howard, C. S., & Ceasar, P. P. (1981). Help-seeking behavior among select populations of Black unmarried adolescent fathers: Implications for human service agencies. *American Journal of Public Health, 71*, 733-735.

Hopkins, T. J. (1973). The role of the agency in supporting Black manhood. *Social Work, 18*(1), 53-58.

Jaffe, E. D. (1983). Fathers and child welfare services: The forgotten clients? In M. Lamb & A. Sagi (Eds.), *Fatherhood and family policy* (pp. 129-137). Hillsdale, NJ: Lawrence Erlbaum Associates.

Kamerman, S. B. (1983). Fatherhood and social policy: Some insights from a comparative perspective. In M. Lamb & A. Sagi (Eds.), *Fatherhood and family policy* (pp. 129-137). Hillsdale, NJ: Lawrence Erlbaum Associates.

Lamb, M. (1995). Paternal influences on child development. In M. van Dongen, G. Frinking, & M. Jacobs (Eds.), *Changing fatherhood: A multidisciplinary perspective* (pp. 145-157). Amsterdam: Thesis Publications.

Leashore, B. R. (1981). Social services and Black men. In L. E. Gary (Ed.), *Black men* (pp. 257-267). Beverly Hills: Sage.

Leashore, B. R. (1997). African American men, child welfare, and permanency planning. *Journal of Multicultural Social Work, 5*(1/2), 39-48.

Leigh, J. W., & Green, J. W. (1982). The structure of the Black community: The knowledge base for social services. In J. W. Green (Ed.), *Cultural awareness in the human services* (pp. 94-121). Englewood Cliffs, NJ: Prentice-Hall.

Levine, J. A. (1993). Involving fathers in Head Start: A framework for public policy and program development. *Families in Society, 74*(1), 4-21.

Maluccio, A. N., Fein, E., & Olmstead, K. A. (1986). *Permanency planning for children: concepts and methods.* New York: Tavistock Publications.

Marsiglio, W. (1995). Fatherhood scholarship: An overview and agenda. In W. Marsiglio (Ed.), *Fatherhood: Contemporary theory, research, and social policy* (pp. 1-20). Thousand Oaks: Sage.

Parke, R. D. (1996). *Fatherhood.* Cambridge: Harvard University Press.

Quam, J. K., & Austin, C. D. (1984). Coverage of women's issues in eight social work journals, 1970-81. *Social Work, 29,* 360-365.

8

Kinship Care When Parents Are Incarcerated

Creasie Finney Hairston

The support and care of children whose parents are in prison is becoming a major social concern and an issue of significance for child welfare agencies and organizations. As the U.S. correctional population (which exceeded more than 5.5 million adults in 1998 [Beck 1998]) continues to escalate at unprecedented levels, so do the numbers of children whose parents are unable to provide for their daily care and protection.

Historically, prisoners' parenting roles have been of little concern to the social services community and there have been few advocacy and family-oriented support services for prisoners and their children and families. The relatively small number of women who were incarcerated was likely to be summarily dismissed, by the public and service providers alike, as being unfit parents. If fathers were considered at all, they were viewed primarily in terms of being absent parents or in terms of the negative influences their criminal behavior was believed to have on children. Children whose parents were in prison were cared for by relatives during their parent's absence. Since they were not usually under state custody, their families were not eligible for, or perceived to be in need of, child welfare prevention or intervention services.

The dramatic increase of the female correctional population throughout the 1990s [Gilliard & Beck 1998], along with the emergence of strong advocacy organizations for women, has directed the recent public attention toward prison parenting issues and the importance of maintaining parent-child bonds when incarceration separates parents and children. Similarly, responsible fatherhood initiatives, though focusing primarily on fathers' financial support of children, have increased recognition and awareness of the fact that incarceration does not negate fathers' parental responsibilities, roles, or commitments. (See, for example, Brenner & Orr [1996].) Factors that are pushing parental incarceration to the forefront as a public child welfare issue include shortened permanency planning time frames, new laws governing permanency options and the termination of parental rights, and welfare reform laws offering only temporary financial assistance to poor families.

The formalization of kinship care as a major child welfare strategy for providing care and protection for poor African American children in large urban areas has also been significant in this regard. As the relationship among parental incarceration, children's well-being, and the achievement of child welfare and other public policy goals becomes more apparent, social welfare policymakers and social services providers are seeking the knowledge and understanding to guide effective interventions. Similar to other emerging interest areas, however, the scientific knowledge base to support the effective care and well-being of children when parents are incarcerated has not been well defined or articulated. Research in this area has been limited and the findings of research in related areas are often overlooked.

Determining Research Priorities

This chapter discusses the research knowledge base on kinship care when parents are incarcerated. It expands current understandings about parental incarceration and child welfare practice and recognizes families' historical use of care by relatives as a primary means of meeting children's needs during parental incarceration. The chapter defines what we currently know and can use and what we need to know to provide more effective, relevant, and compassionate child welfare services.

The research findings and research priorities presented here are based on a review of the literature on prisoners and families, three empirical studies of parents in prison conducted by the author, and forums on families and the correctional system convened by the Jane Addams Center for Social Policy and Research at the Jane Addams College of Social Work, University of Illinois at Chicago. The three studies included interviews of women incarcerated at a midwestern jail [Hairston 1991] and two surveys of men confined in southeastern prisons [Hairston 1989, 1995b].

The forums included a national meeting of individuals who had been pioneers in the development of family-oriented programs in correctional settings; a midwest conference on children, families, and the correctional system [Hairston et al. 1997]; a dialogue on children of incarcerated parents in the Illinois child welfare system [Wall 1997]; and a dialogue on the implications of attachment and bonding research for child welfare policy and practice. The forum participants were individuals with knowledge and understanding of issues faced by families whose lives are affected by criminal justice and child welfare system involvement. They included corrections and child welfare administrators, social services staff, family members of incarcerated individuals, attorneys and other court representatives, former prisoners, researchers from different academic disciplines, and children and family advocates. To facilitate discussion, research studies and literature on parental incarceration and child welfare issues were distributed to the participants prior to each meeting. Each participant also received a list of general discussion issues and questions.

Determining the Numbers

On the one hand we know a lot, and on the other we know very little, about care arrangements and outcomes for children when their parents go to prison or jail. We do know that the problem of parents in prison is one of enormous proportions and one that disproportionately affects poor families of color. Surveys of incarcerated populations consistently show that the majority of male and female prisoners are parents of dependent children. A national survey of state prisoners conducted in 1991 indicated that 56% of male prisoners and 67% of women prisoners had a child or children under the age of 18 [U.S. Department of Justice 1993]. Given the average of about two children per parent and a prison population of more than 1.2 million people [Gilliard & Beck 1998], we know that on any given day the parents of more than 1 million children are in state and federal institutions alone. The number of children affected by parental involvement in the criminal justice system increases considerably when we include children whose parents are awaiting trial or sentenced to local jails and those whose parents are under community correctional supervision. It increases even further when we include the millions of children whose parents have been in prison during some period of their growing-up years.

Children from families who are poor or are African American are affected more adversely than others. The majority of persons in prison and jails are poor [McGuire & Pastore 1996]. African Americans constitute about 50% of the state and federal prison population [Gilliard & Beck 1998] and in some states such as Illinois make up as much as two-thirds of the prison population [Illinois Criminal Justice Authority 1997]. The problem becomes even more pronounced when one considers that in 1995 one in three (up from one in four only five years earlier) African American males between the ages of 20 and 29 was under some form of correctional supervision [Mauer & Huling 1995].

We also know that neither the child welfare system nor the criminal justice system maintains a database that provides current information on incarcerated parents and their children. Although the criminal justice system maintains and updates annually an extensive database on prisoners and jail inmates, the last national survey and report of statistics on prisoners' family status and structure was done in 1991 [U. S. Department of Justice 1993]. There is similarly no national child welfare system report that provides information on parents' incarceration status. Only a few states are even willing or able to give rough estimates of these numbers. In 1997, the Child Welfare League of America asked state child welfare agencies if they could identify the number of children in their caseloads with a parent in prison. Of the 37 agencies who responded, only five were able to give any data at all [Seymour 1998].

Determining the Arrangements for Children's Care

Surveys of parents in prison indicate that parents rely primarily on their relatives for child care and other forms of social and financial support during incarceration. Most male prisoners report that their children's mothers are the primary care providers during the fathers' absence [Hairston 1995b; Lanier 1987, 1993; Sharp & Marcus-Mendoza 1998]. Grandparents and maternal aunts are the primary caregivers of children of female prisoners, though a small but significant number of women report that the children's fathers are children's providers during the mothers' absence [Bloom & Steinhart 1993; Hairston 1991; Sharp & Marcus-Mendoza 1998].

Prisoners rarely indicate that their children are in foster homes or in other child welfare system care arrangements. The percentage of parents who say they have a child in foster care is usually lower than 10%. (See, for example, studies by Bloom & Steinhart [1993], Hairston [1991], Sharp & Marcus-Mendoza [1998], and U.S. Department of Justice [1993].) It is highly likely, however, that the number of children involved in the child welfare system is much larger, and the percentages much higher, than parents report. The family characteristics and living conditions (i.e., poor, drug involvement, young, etc.) that parents involved in child welfare processing share with families involved in the criminal justice system suggest that this is the case.

Prisoners' limited involvement in day-to-day decisionmaking about their children may limit their knowledge of children's child welfare status. Some fathers may not know if their children are under state custody, since fathers are seldom included in child welfare decisionmaking even when paternal relatives are children's relative foster parents [Hairston 1998; O'Donnell 1995, Chapter 7]. Most fathers have limited contact with their children during incarceration [Hairston 1989, 1995b; Lanier 1993]; some acknowledge that they do not know where their children are [Sharp & Marcus-Mendoza 1998]. Fathers may, therefore, base their statements about children's caregivers or residences on their knowledge of children's whereabouts prior to their incarceration, rather than on more recent developments or family changes. The most recent information they have about their children's whereabouts could be several months or even years old. Mothers, on the other hand, may be aware that children are under state custody, but since the children are living with relatives they do not regard this as being in foster care.

The research methodology used in studies of parents in prison also contributes to confusion regarding families' involvement in the child welfare system, particularly their involvement in relative foster care. Research questions with preset response categories do not usually allow for the fact that a child may be living with a relative and still in foster care. Without additional probing, even open-ended questions such as "Who does your child live with?" may not elicit responses that would allow an accurate assessment of whether or not a child is a ward of the state.

There are similar problems in obtaining information about children's parents from child welfare agency records or reports. Child welfare records do not typically state whether or not a parent is incarcerated; data of this nature are not usually compiled in any systematic way and information on parental incarceration is seldom, if at all, presented in any formal agency reports. The exception for individual case records might be when neglect due to maternal incarceration is the reason for placement. Parental incarceration is not the reason for placement, however, in many situations involving mothers as a significant number of children are placed or lived with relatives prior to a parent's imprisonment [Hairston 1991; Bloom & Steinhart 1993; U.S. Department of Justice 1993]. Studies that rely on case records or agency reporting forms noting reason for placement could, therefore, easily understate the extent of maternal incarceration. Since data on fathers are seldom maintained in any systematic way, and often never even obtained, the agency documents approach would certainly underestimate significantly the number of children whose fathers are in prison [Hairston 1998].

The establishment of a child welfare data collection and reporting system that accurately identifies the number of children in state care whose parents are incarcerated should be a core component of a child welfare research program. It is, furthermore, a prerequisite for effective policy development and program planning. In the absence of this basic information, it is difficult to determine how many children are affected, to trace trends and patterns, and to assess the financial and service implications of specific or general policies whether they cover kinship care, parental incarceration, or more general child welfare issues.

Child Welfare System Processing and Outcomes

Just as we know little about the numbers of children in formal kinship care arrangements whose parents are, or have been, incarcerated, we know little about their system experiences. We do know that caseworkers occupy a central role in the child welfare delivery system, influence the processing of cases, and shape children and families' experiences as child welfare service recipients. We also know that though caseworkers provide needed services and sometimes serve as children's advocates, they are often viewed as being less than helpful. Comments made in the attachment and bonding dialogue session crystallize one image of child welfare staff. One participant proclaimed to the group that the research they were discussing wouldn't make any difference in decisions for poor, African American families. He reasoned that the public defenders assigned to the families didn't care and their social workers didn't like their jobs. Others expressed concerns that children's caseworkers failed to present themselves in court as being knowledgeable about families and children's real situations or about the principles, theory, or research underlying their recommendations. The notion that caseworkers felt victimized themselves permeated "sidebar" conversations.

The general perception of caseworker inadequacy expressed in the dialogue is prevalent in studies of incarcerated parents and their children's relative caregivers. Surveys of parents and relative caregivers indicate that many do not find child welfare caseworkers to be helpful [Beckerman 1994; Hairston 1991; Hungerford 1996; Johnston 1995b; Poe 1992]. Parents and relative foster parents report that caseworkers have limited, if any, contact with parents themselves and do little to help relative caregivers maintain contact between parents and children. One study of incarcerated women with children in foster care found that almost half of the women had no correspondence from their children's caseworkers and almost two-thirds had not received a copy of their reunification plan [Beckerman 1994]. Another found high numbers of women who had not received appropriate reunification services including communication from caseworkers, notification of custody hearings, and opportunities to participate in case planning [Johnston 1995b]. Black grandmothers serving as parents for their grandchildren describe myriad encounters with social service agencies that resulted in major frustrations, but few benefits to assist them in their roles as parents [Poe 1992].

Focused discussions on this issue among caseworkers, corrections staff, and family advocates revealed that child welfare practice with correctional populations and with relative caregivers is extremely challenging and involves a number of complex individual and systemic factors. Child welfare workers' attitudes about parents involved in the criminal justice system, fear of and/or distaste for prison visits, limited understanding of parent-child attachment and extended family networks in African American communities, and the demands of other less burdensome cases are all factors believed to affect caseworkers' practices [Hairston et al. 1998]. No less important, however, in cases of parental incarceration and kinship care is the absence of agency expectations and guidance regarding caseworkers' roles and responsibilities and the absence of organizational and interorganizational resources and agreements and working protocols to support more than cursory service to preserve or strengthen family ties [Hairston 1998; Seymour 1998].

The critical role that caseworkers have in altering children's futures mandates a better understanding of their work with parents, caregivers, and children; the factors that influence their service approaches and strategies; and the outcomes of their services for children and families. Cross-sectional studies of workers' attitudes, knowledge, and service practices in cases involving parental incarceration and kinship care; process and out-come evaluations of special programs and projects; and case studies of practice in child welfare agencies that devote resources for casework ser-vices with incarcerated parents and relative caregivers are all approaches to use in obtaining this understanding. The results and benefits of these research investigations should be broadened understanding of the factors that influence practice as well as the delineation of principles, program models, and training to guide more responsive, relevant, and effective practice.

Paralleling the need for system identification of children whose parents are imprisoned and assessments of casework practice involving them is the need for basic information on system processing and general outcomes. An important research activity will be tracing the system pathways or "ca-reers" of children who enter state custody because of parental incarcera-tion or who may enter for a different reason but their ability to return home or maintain relationships with their parents is exacerbated or influ-enced by parental incarceration. We need to understand how these chil-dren move through the system and how their movement is similar to or different from other groups of children. Assessments using common sys-tem indicators such as length of stay, number of placements, reunification rates, returns to care following reunification, and permanency outcomes should be undertaken. Both the individual and dual impact of kinship care and parental incarceration need to be assessed. Accordingly, compari-sons on the above indicators between children in relative and nonrelative foster care, informal and formal kinship care, and incarcerated and nonincarcerated parents are all appropriate means of defining and assess-ing differential system impact.

Public Policies and Administrative Regulations

We know that most mothers and fathers in prison want to maintain rela-tionships with their children and plan to reunify with them upon their release from prison [Baunach 1985; Bloom & Steinhart 1993; Hairston 1991, 1995b]. We also know that regular, ongoing communication be-tween parents and children is essential for maintaining parent-child attachments and important in reunifying households following separation. Children who have limited contact with their parents may begin to view their parents as strangers or even forget who they are. Moreover, parents who have little contact with their children and the individuals responsible for their children's daily care have few opportunities to carry out parental roles, responsibilities, and commitments and are not significant individuals in their children's upbringing. They may forsake their role as parents long before any legal action is undertaken to do so.

There is evidence that imprisonment can lead to the permanent, legal severance of parent-child relationships. The author's review of confidential papers provided by families residing in different states indicates that parental incarceration and criminal lifestyles can and are used as reasons for the termination of parental rights. In addition, a parent's failure to demonstrate ongoing communication with children under state custody during imprisonment is a justification for the termination of parental rights under the provisions of the Adoption and Safe Families Act of 1997 [Beckerman 1998; Raimon & Kopperman 1998]. Termination can occur even when children live with relatives during a parent's absence and when the children were not under the custody of the state when the parents first entered prison.

Despite the importance of ongoing communication in maintaining family ties, most parents in prison and jails seldom see their children [Baunach 1985; Hairston 1989, 1991, 1995b; Hungerford 1996], and face-to-face parent-child contact depends on children making prison visits. Some imprisoned parents give personal or familial preferences as the reasons they do not see their children. Parents serving short sentences in city and county jails reason, for example, that they will be away from home only a few weeks or months and that children are better off not seeing them under conditions of confinement [Hairston 1991].

Other parents do not see their children because they or their children's care providers do not tell children that the parents are incarcerated [Hairston 1991, 1995b]. Children are told that parents are away attending college, in the military, or in the hospital. Still other parents do not see their children because of care providers' preferences [Hairston et al. 1997]. Some parents indicate that the kids are better off not having parental contact when there is serious conflict between parents and caregivers; others in these circumstances may still want to see their children but know that the relatives who are taking care of their children will not permit children to visit.

Notwithstanding the importance of individual and family preferences, the primary impediment to communication between parents and children revolves around public policies, administrative regulations, and staff practices. Public policies are key in this regard. Policies demonstrate the value that states place on parent-child relationships and the protection and well-being of children when parents are incarcerated. They also guide the allocation of resources for parent-child visiting and parental and caregiver involvement in child welfare decisionmaking, and shape caseworkers' practice with incarcerated parents and their children and families.

Corrections Policies

Corrections policies present major barriers to the maintenance of family relationships as they affect and control the behavior not only of the individuals who are incarcerated but also the behavior and options of their children and their children's caregivers. Several studies provide evidence of the problems correctional communication policies present for relative care providers when they try to help children maintain contact with their parents.

Hairston and Hess' [1989] report of their comprehensive study of visitation policies governing state prisoners provides extensive documentation of the many problems noted by several researchers prior to and after their study. They reported that visiting policies varied considerably from one state to another and within states from one institution to another. Children's ability to spend time with their parents was restricted by the days and hours for visits, the length and conditions of visits, and inflexibility around the adult who could approve visits or would be required to escort children on visits. Often these requirements and accompanying staff practices bore little relevance to the extended family networks and com-

plex legal and social relationships found in poor, African American families or to their resources, work schedules, or other family obligations. Follow-up reviews of states' visiting policies and administrative practices, in a
few states, suggests that in many jurisdictions visiting regulations have
become even more stringent during the 1990s get-tough-on-crime era
[Hairston et al. 1997].

Parent-child communication by phone, while not as physically arduous
and emotionally exhaustive as prison visits, is also difficult [Hairston 1998].
The costs for calls from parents to their children are borne by relative
caregivers. Most phone calls must be made collect and at expensive rates
that generate lucrative profits which are shared by corrections departments
and the telephone companies with which they contract. Consequently, many
relatives limit or block collect phone calls. Families' use of phone cards for
long distance service and the absence of residential phones also prohibit
parents' ability to have contact with their children via the phone and
caregivers' ability to confer with parents on important child rearing mat-
ters.

Contact by mail, while not a significant financial cost to families or prisoners, carries a tremendous social burden. Letters from correctional institutions typically carry a large stamped declaimer noting that the letter is
from an inmate at a correctional institution and has not been reviewed by
prison authorities. This stamp and the resulting stigma discourages families who are trying to maintain privacy or secrecy from communicating by
mail. In addition, in this era of instantaneous contact via fax, e-mail, and
telephone, letter writing requiring several days for delivery and then a
delayed response is not a part of the routine experience of the general
public or prisoners' families.

Maintenance of family relationships and relatives' protection and care
of children are exacerbated when children are under the custody of child
welfare departments and their parents are incarcerated [Hairston 1995a].
In these situations, parents and relative caregivers alike must comply with
the demands and requirements of two systems of social control. They must
adhere not only to prison rules but also to child welfare agency regulations

and stipulations. They often do not receive the organizational support they need to meet various mandates and sometimes live in fear of divulging information or making mistakes that would put children's permanent relationships with parents or caregivers in jeopardy [Hungerford 1996; Poe 1992].

Parents who are prisoners have no choice but to give first priority to adherence to corrections policies, procedures, and the nuances of correctional staff practices. This adherence, more often than not, affects their ability to comply with child welfare department regulations and children's care providers' expectations. No matter how much they may want to spend time with their children, attend an administrative hearing, or participate in a self-help program as required by a child welfare case plan, their ultimate ability to do so depends not on their desires, but on prison rules and what staff allow them to do.

Child Welfare Policies

Unlike correctional policies, empirical studies examining the nature and impact of child welfare policies on families involved in the criminal justice system have been limited. Much of what we know is based on different scholars' informed analyses of child welfare policies. These analyses show controlling features for prisoners and their children's relative caregivers that are similar to and as harmful as those found in institutional settings. Beckerman [1994, 1998] and Hairston [1995a] caution, for example, that while maintaining parent-child relationships during imprisonment is desirable, it is difficult for parents whose children are under the state's' custody. Child welfare policies and resource allocations do not support the kind of communication between parents and children that is needed to prevent the termination of parental rights. Child welfare laws are explicit about the need for imprisoned parents to have regular contact with their children and plan for their children's futures. Yet, states do not generally allocate monies for parent-child visits or mothers' presence at hearings involving their children. There are also seldom established protocols, practice guidelines, or agency administrative units to provide mothers information about custody issues or to facilitate their involvement in case planning.

Phillips and Bloom [1998] discuss how families are undermined when relatives providing informal care have to allege parental abuse or neglect to obtain the services and financial assistance that formal kinship foster care provides; even then they are not assured that children will be allowed to remain in their care. While Phillips and Bloom view subsidized guardianship plans as appropriate means for providing relatives the legal and financial assistance they need to keep children during a parent's prison term, they note that these plans kick in only after a child has been in foster care for a designated period.

Other scholars voice particular concerns about the impact of the provisions of the Adoption and the Safe Families Act of 1997 on families involved in the criminal justice system. Genty's [1998] review of the provisions of the Adoption and Safe Families Act of 1997 also describes potentially negative implications for incarcerated mothers and their children. He notes the adoption orientation of the law, the vulnerability of parent-child relationships, and the kinship caregiving arrangements that most incarcerated mothers use for their children. Despite the presence of a provision that allows states to use placement with a relative to avoid the strict adoption orientation, the absence of agency focus on families separated by incarceration places these children at risk of permanent separation from their parents and extended family members.

Many family advocates question policies that pressure relative caregivers to adopt children in their care or risk having the children removed from their homes and placed with strangers. Aside from questioning this pressure as an ethical issue they note that adoption of one's relatives is considered foreign and culturally insensitive by many families [Hairston et al. 1997]. They also express concerns regarding agency policies and practices that are used to remove or threaten the removal of children from relatives' homes if the relatives allow children to visit or maintain contact with imprisoned parents.

We do not know the predominant or prevailing approaches that states use to carry out responsibilities to children and their relative caregivers when children's parents are in prison, as no systematic investigations have been conducted and reported. The author's requests for and examination of policies from select states suggests, however, that child welfare policy-makers, planners, and system administrators devote little attention to parental incarceration. Policy statements either did not exist, were unknown to workers, and, in one case, to top administrators, or were seriously out-dated [Hairston 1998]. The Illinois policy, for example, was several years old, pertained only to mothers, and covered only one institution though women are incarcerated in different Illinois state prisons and several local jails.

Along the same line, there are no published reports and comparative analyses of different states' plans for implementing the relative placement provisions in the new child welfare law or of the implications of these plans for safety, stability, or family connections of prisoners' children. Neither the policies affecting family ties during or after imprisonment, nor the service programs and casework practices emanating from these policies have been the subject of child welfare research. These topics have also not been included in the research programs of related areas such as family preservation, kinship care, permanency planning, and family reunification.

National level studies of state policies and plans should constitute a fundamental component of the research program on kinship care when parents are incarcerated. Assessment of current state policies will identify how parental incarceration is viewed in current child welfare practice and define general system expectations about the nature of practice, including how family and kinship networks are to be involved in decisionmaking and caregiving. Systematic reviews and comparisons of different states' policies similar to Gleeson and Craig's [1994] national study of how the states view kinship care can help delineate the different philosophical ideas that underlie policy directives and clarify the approaches that dominate different philosophical orientations. They may also be used to define the desired role of kinship care under conditions of parental incarceration in decisions related to permanency goals, termination of parental rights, and family reunification. These types of examinations can provide the background and knowledge essential for establishing national child welfare standards and policy guidelines as well as practice principles for adaptation and use by different states and child welfare agencies.

More detailed studies of different policy directives should focus on purpose and goals, the specific activities that are to be undertaken to achieve these goals, the organizational supports to be provided, and the individuals responsible for goal achievement. These studies should also describe and analyze the monitoring procedures to be used to assure compliance with policy directives, the plans for evaluation of system results and client outcomes, and the means by which polices are to be reviewed and changed. Policy implementation and impact studies covering similar areas must also be conducted if we are to understand the differences between intent and results and the influential factors affecting the ultimate ends for children.

Among the substantive topics to explore are the purpose of involving or not involving children's birth parents, including fathers, in care and decisionmaking; the role that incarcerated parents are to have in children's lives; supports that are to be provided to parents, children, and children's caregivers to maintain parent-child relationships; supports that are to be provided to parents in meeting case plans for children; and formal arrangements with departments of corrections to facilitate caseworker-parent communication. Also important are the conditions under which parental rights are to be terminated and the procedures to facilitate permanency planning when parents' rights must be terminated or long-term relative foster care is an appropriate case goal.

Determining Families' Day-to-Day Experiences

We know that parental imprisonment presents family disruptions and creates major changes for children. Many children are subjected to enduring and ongoing trauma resulting from their parents' criminal life styles, arrest, incarceration, and recidivism [Kampfner 1995; Johnston 1995a]. Not unlike other children who are separated from parents with whom they are bonded, they often experience social and emotional difficulties. Some display problem behaviors including withdrawal, acting out, rebellion, excessive crying, etc. [Gabel 1992; Poe 1992; Johnston 1995a; Sack & Seidler 1976]. Most writings on children's experiences when their parents are sent to prison have focused on these negative impacts or on children's increased risks for other problematic life experiences including delinquency, teenage pregnancy, and intergenerational incarceration [Johnston 1995a].

Despite what appears to be a tangled web of pathology and negativism, however, many children whose parents are involved in the criminal justice system function quite well. Although they endure difficult experiences, they manage to survive childhood trauma and become successful, caring, and law-abiding adults. Studies of the factors that influence children's well-being when they are separated from their parents provide some clues as to why and how this is the case. These studies consistently point to the quality of care children receive following separation and their ongoing relationship with their parents as instrumental forces in shaping outcomes for children. Sack [1977], for example, found that children's problem behaviors following their fathers' incarceration improved considerably once they were able to see and spend time with their fathers. Widom's [1994] research on foster care and delinquency showed that delinquency outcomes for children depended on several quality of care factors including such variables as the number of placement disruptions.

Altshuler's [1996, Chapter 5] qualitative assessment of children's experiences in relative foster care also points to quality of care as a major consideration in children's views of what constitutes and makes for their well-being. Among the factors she identified as important to children are the attention and care that relative foster parents provide, the acts of kindness they demonstrate to children, and the high level of future expectations and hopes they help children feel and see. These studies, along with the literature on resiliency and the strengths perspective in social work practice, indicate that we need to look beyond pathology and examine the factors that sustain and support children and families during periods of adversity.

There have been few published studies of kinship care and parental incarceration and, therefore, we know little about the quality of families' lives as reflected in their day-to-day experiences. We do know from research, however, that many caregivers and families of prisoners are poor and lack the resources—nice houses, money, access to health care, etc.—

that are often equated with quality of care [Bloom & Steinhart 1993; Gaudin & Sutphen 1993]. We also know that many relative caregivers love the children under their care and want to, and do, care for them, despite the major adjustments they must make and the absence of basic resources [Bloom & Steinhart 1993; Phillips & Bloom 1998].

We know further that parental incarceration and related lifestyles often create family tensions that affect child rearing and caregivers' responses to their relatives in prison. The social stigma of having an adult child who is a prisoner or drug addict, the behavior and disrespect that prisoner parents may have shown toward the caregiver, and the callous disregard that some have shown for children's well-being before going to prison have caused deep hostilities among the members in some families [Hungerford 1996; Poe 1992]. As protective measures for children and themselves, some grandparents don't have contact with children's parents or do what they can to make sure that children won't be returned to their parents. Poe [1992] and Bloom and Steinhart [1993] also found, in contrast, many grandparents and other relative caregivers who actively promoted children's contact with their incarcerated parents. The caregivers took children to visit their parents, accepted collect phone calls from parents, and planned for the time when children would be able to return to their parents' homes. They had high hopes that parents would be able to get their lives together and resume caring for their children in responsible ways.

Social service providers' ability to make decisions that really are in the best interest of the children in relative care situations when parents are incarcerated requires a deeper understanding than is currently reflected in the child welfare literature. A major question that must be answered is how relatives, particularly grandparents and elderly individuals, manage the caregiving experience including ties and contact with parents in prison, when children are under the custody of the state and their parents are under correctional supervision. Related questions abound. What differences do maternal and paternal family networks make in the care of children and in subsequent outcomes for children? How and to what extent is caregiving shared among the extended family network and how are decisions made about who will do what? Do children who have successful outcomes as measured by academic achievements, avoidance of the juvenile justice system, job success, etc., have different relationships with their caregivers and parents than those who are not successful? How do family relationships change over time, and in relationship to the stage of criminal justice processing, and what impact do they have on child care arrangements? How do children feel about and relate to their parents, relative caregivers, and living situations? What makes the difference and what difference does it make?

A serious program of research must examine such questions about children and families' lived experiences from their perspectives. Answers to questions such as these will broaden our understanding of the impact of parental incarceration on children and of the effectiveness of different formalized care arrangements in mediating that impact and promoting positive child development. This type of research program will also help us better understand how to promote and support care arrangements that are sensitive to different family preferences, cultures, and living environments.

Conclusion

Although there has, historically, been little public recognition of the placement and care of children of incarcerated parents, there is a tremendous need to address this issue now. The rising prison population, along with changing child and public welfare policy, have pushed this issue to the forefront of attention of child welfare policymakers and social services providers.

The movement from recognition, awareness, and concern to effective and compassionate public policies and programs requires a comprehensive knowledge base that is shaped by empirical study and theoretical understanding. As shown here, studies of incarcerated parents, kinship care, and child welfare system processing, as well as informed analyses of policy statements provide a useful reference point. By and large, this body of literature does not address the circumstances unique to families' simultaneous involvement in two different systems of social control. It is also limited by its focus on narrow topics or special projects and on intent or likely impact, as opposed to actual results.

A broad, more comprehensive research program regarding the use of kinship care as a formal child welfare approach when parents are incarcerated is needed to enhance understanding and shape future program and policy directions. This chapter presents what we already know and can use from related work and previous research. It also identifies major substantive areas for exploration, methodological issues and concerns, and reality-based philosophical and practical challenges that must be faced in forging ahead to new discoveries and understandings.

References

Altshuler, S. J. (1996). *The well-being of children in kinship foster care.* Unpublished doctoral dissertation, University of Illinois at Chicago.

Baunach, P. J. (1985). *Mothers in prison.* New Brunswick: Transaction Books.

Beck, A. J. (1998). *Understanding the growth in U.S. incarceration rates.* Paper presented at the Annual Conference on Criminal Justice Research and Evaluation, Washington, D.C.

Beckerman, A. (1998). Charting a course: Meeting the challenge of permanency planning for children with incarcerated mothers. *Child Welfare, 77*(5), 513-529.

Beckerman, A. (1994). Mothers in prison: Meeting the prerequisite conditions for permanency planning. *Social Work, 39*(1), 9-14.

Bloom, B., & Steinhart, D. (1993). *Why punish the children? A reappraisal.* San Francisco: National Council on Crime and Delinquency.

Brenner, E., & Orr, D. (1996). *What the states are doing to promote responsible fatherhood: A national survey.* Washington, DC: Council of Governors Policy Advisors.

Gabel, S. (1992). Behavioral problems in sons of incarcerated or otherwise absent fathers: The issue of separation. *Family Process, 31*, 303-314.

Gaudin, J., & Sutphen, R. (1993). Foster care vs. extended family care for children of incarcerated mothers. *Journal of Offender Rehabilitation, 19*(3/4), 129-147.

Genty, P. H. (1998). Permanency planning in the context of parental incarceration: Legal issues and recommendations. *Child Welfare, 77*(5), 543-560.

Gilliard, D., & Beck, A. (1998). *Prisoners in 1997.* Washington, DC: U.S. Department of Justice, Bureau of Justice Statistics.

Gleeson, J. P., & Craig, L. C. (1994). Kinship care in child welfare: An analysis of states' policies. *Children and Youth Services Review, 16,* 7-31.

Hairston, C. (1989). Men in prison: Family characteristics and parenting views. *Journal of Offender Counseling, Services & Rehabilitation, 14,* 23-30.

Hairston, C., & Hess, P. (1989). Family ties: Maintaining child-parent bonds is important. *Corrections Today, 51,* 102-106.

Hairston, C. (1991). Mothers in jail: Parent-child separation and jail visitation. *Affilia, 6* (2), 9-27.

Hairston, C. (1995a). Family views in correctional programs. In R. Edwards & J. Hopps (Eds.), *Encyclopedia of social work* (19th ed.) (pp. 991-996). Washington, DC: NASW Press.

Hairston, C. (1995b). Fathers in prison. In D. Johnson & K. Gables (Eds.), *Children of incarcerated parents* (pp. 31-40). Lexington, MA: Lexington Books.

Hairston, C., Wills, S, & Wall, N. (1997). *Children, families, and correctional supervision: Current policies and new directions.* Chicago: University of Illinois at Chicago, Jane Addams College of Social Work.

Hairston, C. (1998). The forgotten parent: Understanding the forces that influence incarcerated fathers' relationships with their children. *Child Welfare, 77,* 617-838.

Hungerford, G. P. (1996). Caregivers of children whose mothers are incarcerated: A study of the kinship placement system. *Children Today, 2,* 23-27.

Illinois Criminal Justice Authority. (1997). *Trends and issues 1997.* Chicago: Author.

Johnston, D. (1995a). The care and placement of prisoners' children. In D. Johnston & K. Gables (Eds.), *Children of incarcerated parents* (pp. 103-123). Lexington, MA: Lexington Books.

Johnston, D. (1995b). Child custody issues of incarcerated mothers. *The Prison Journal, 75*(2), 222-238.

Kampfner, C. (1995). Post traumatic stress reactions in children of imprisoned mothers. In D. Johnston & K. Gabel (Eds.), *Children of incarcerated parents* (pp. 89- 99). Lexington, MA: Lexington Books.

Lanier, Jr., C. S. (1987). *Fathers in prison: A psychosocial exploration.* Unpublished master's thesis, New Paltz College of the State University of New York.

Lanier, C. S. (1993). Affective states of fathers in prison. *Justice Quarterly, 10*, 49-65.

Mauer, M., & Huling, T. (1995). *Young Black Americans and the criminal justice system: Five years later.* Washington, DC: The Sentencing Project.

McGuire, K., & Pastore, A. L. (1996). *Bureau of Justice Statistics sourcebook of criminal justice statistics.* Albany, NY: The Hindelang Criminal Justice Research Center, University of Albany.

O'Donnell, J. M. (1995). *Casework practice with fathers in kinship foster care.* Unpublished doctoral dissertation, University of Illinois at Chicago.

Phillips, S., & Bloom, B. (1998). In whose best interest? The impact of changing public policy on relatives caring for children with incarcerated parents. *Child Welfare, 77*(5), 531-532.

Poe, L. (1992). *Black grandparents as parents.* Berkeley, CA: Author.

Raimon, M., & Kopperman, W. (March 1998). Federal foster care law imposes new hardships on incarcerated mothers and their children. *Policy Updates.* New York: Women's Prison Association.

Sack, W. (1977). Children of imprisoned fathers. *Psychiatry, 40*, 163-174.

Sack, W., & Seidler, J. (1976). Children of imprisoned parents: A psychosocial exploration. *American Journal of Orthopsychiatry, 46*(4), 618-628.

Seymour, C. (1998). Children with parents in prison: Child welfare policy, program and practice issues. *Child Welfare, 77*(5), 469-493.

Sharp, S., & Marcus-Mendoza, S. (1998). *Gender differences in the impact of incarceration on children and spouses of drug offenders.* Paper presented at the 35th Annual Conferenceof the Academy of Criminal Justice Sciences, Albuquerque, New Mexico.

U.S. Department of Justice. (1993). *Survey of state prison inmates, 1991.* Washington, DC: Bureau of Justice Statistics.

Wall, N. (1997). Policies affecting children whose parents are incarcerated. *Dialogues on Child Welfare Issues Report.* Chicago: Jane Addams Center for Social Policy and Research.

Widom, C. S. (1994). The role of placement experiences in mediating the criminal consequences of early childhood victimization. In R. P. Barth, J. D. Berrick, & N. Gilbert (Eds.), *Child welfare research review. Volume 1* (pp. 298-322). New York: Columbia University Press.

Part IV
Kinship Caregivers

9

Child-Rearing Perspectives of Grandparent Caregivers

Olga Osby

This chapter relates the experiences of ten grandparent caregivers as they shared their stories of how they, their children, and grandchildren became involved with the Illinois child welfare system. The intent of this chapter is not to generalize these experiences to all grandparent caregivers, but to provide some insight into the lives and world views of a small group of grandparents who suddenly found themselves with the responsibility of becoming parents for a second, and for some a third, time. The narratives presented here provide insight into the lives of these grandparent caregivers in their own voice.

World Views Perspective

The grandparents interviewed in this study are representative of a phenomenon faced by an increasing number of persons across this country who are rearing their grandchildren [Burton 1992; Minkler et al. 1994; Woodworth 1996]. While the overwhelming majority of grandparents who are primary caregivers for their grandchildren provide this care through informal kinship care arrangements, the grandparents interviewed for this study shared responsibility for their grandchildren with the child welfare system. Although these grandparents see themselves as family members, the child welfare system views them as "kinship caregivers" or "relative foster parents," and therefore part of the formal child welfare system. Like the majority of relatives caring for children in the custody of the child welfare system, the grandparent caregivers interviewed for this study were persons of color.

A theoretical construct that can be used to place the life experiences of this group of grandparent caregivers into context with their experiences in the child welfare system is the world view perspective [English 1983, 1991]. Social scientists define world views as perceptions of one's relationship to other people, institutions, objects, and nature. World views are the lenses through which experiences are viewed and given meaning [Jackson & Sears 1992]. World views are shaped in large part by one's culture.

The world views of African Americans and other persons of color are likely to differ significantly from the world views of European Americans and the child welfare system [English 1991]. That world views differ by culture is not only expected, it is healthy. In their review of the research literature, Jackson and Sears [1992] summarize results of studies that support the importance of Africentric world views as mediators of stress for African American women. Africentric world views were described as a high value placed on spirituality, a collective orientation that emphasizes cooperation and interdependence, oneness and harmony with nature, an emphasis on self-knowledge, and a past and present orientation rather than a future orientation. These same values have been described as world views held by Latino [Montalvo 1997] and Native Amercan [Cross 1995] families. While similar world views are held by many persons within a cultural group, there is considerable diversity among persons in any group. English [1991] points out that world views held by members of a cultural group vary across at least two dimensions: (1) the level of participation in and commitment to one's own culture, and (2) the level of participation in and commitment to mainstream and other culture. To effectively share the responsibility for child rearing, it is imperative that child welfare caseworkers and the child welfare system understand the world views of relative caregivers.

Understanding a person's world view also helps one interpret how individuals react to certain life and environmental stressors, since perceptions of these stressors influence major decisions [English 1991]. Interviews with grandparent caregivers in this study provided a glimpse into the world views of a generation of individuals who never imagined that they would be involved with the child welfare system or the court system. For many of them, the fact that they were caring for their grandchildren was not as surprising as the reasons that they were required to do so. The caregivers assumed their child-rearing responsibilities with various degrees of willingness and acceptance. The degree of their acceptance of their new role in the lives of their grandchildren was seemingly dependent upon their view of their role in relationship to their family, community, and society at large. In many African American families, grandparents play a significant, and often central role, in the extended family and especially in the rearing of their grandchildren [George & Dickerson 1995]. This traditional role for African American grandparents has continued to have a major and significant impact on African American families [Burton 1996; Jendrek 1994].

The world view construct is also useful in giving an understanding of the life perspective of this group of grandparents. As English has noted, "World views are shaped by such factors as age, place of birth, education, occupation, socio-economic status, and where a person lives and work" [1983, p.21]. Views about caregiving and child rearing, relationships with children and grandchildren, as well as positive and negative experiences with the court and child welfare system are all rooted in life experiences, and continue to shape the decisions and choices made each day.

In many cultures, grandparents have assumed a role in the child rearing and caregiving of their grandchildren due to parental illness, unemployment, or single parenthood. The grandparents interviewed in this study, however, found themselves dealing with their adult children's substance abuse, criminal behavior, and child abuse and neglect; all of which, in their view, mandated that they assume the caregiving of their grandchildren. The world views perspective is especially apt in examining the experiences of this group of caregivers and how they have guided themselves and their grandchildren through the foreign territory of the child welfare system.

Methodology

Grandparent caregivers of children who were in the custody of the child welfare system were interviewed as part of a curriculum development and training project for child welfare caseworkers.* The interviews were intended to elucidate the perceptions and experiences of these caregivers. The results of these interviews were helpful to curriculum developers as they attempted to develop materials that were relevant to the families and children served in kinship foster care.

Caregivers were recruited for this study by the staff of a social service agency who were in the process of developing support groups for relatives caring for children in the custody of the child welfare system. The agency was responsible for supervising the care of these children, through a purchase of service contract with the Illinois Department of Children and Family Services. More than 30 relative caregivers were invited to participate in these interviews. Caregivers were offered a $20 grocery certificate as an incentive and partial compensation for sharing their experiences and perceptions with the researcher. Ten caregivers agreed to be interviewed.

At the time the study was conducted, all of the caregivers were residents of the south side of Chicago and the interviews were conducted in their homes. The interviews lasted from approximately one hour to an hour and a half, depending on the caregivers and how much they wanted to share about the circumstances that brought them into contact with the child welfare system and their experiences within the system. The interviewer also spent time getting to know the grandparents before beginning the interviews and visiting with them after the interviews, spending a total of two hours in most of the caregivers' homes. Eight of the caregivers who agreed to be interviewed for this study were grandmothers and two were grandfathers. Nine of the grandparents were African American. One grandmother was Latina.

---

* Innovative Training for Exemplary Practice in Kinship Foster Care, supported by Grant Number HHS05CT5037 from the U.S. Children's Bureau and a contract with the Illinois Department of Children and Family Services.

The interviews were ethnographic in nature. English [1991] indicates that an ethnographic approach is an effective way of facilitating understanding of a person's world view. Through a set of open-ended questions the caregivers were allowed to freely answer the questions posed to them. The intent of ethnography, a qualitative research method used heavily in anthropology, is to comprehend the ideology, rituals, behaviors, and social structures foreign to the investigator, without the influence of preconceived judgements or prejudicial attitudes [Goodson-Lawes 1994]. Ethnography also seeks to understand the meaning of actions, events, and physical objects for the people who are teaching the investigator, rather than what they mean to the investigator directly. One of the treasures of ethnographic research is the opportunity to listen to people talk about their lives and experiences, and to have these experiences presented in a forum and format from which others can hear and learn. The grandparent caregivers interviewed for this study not only answered the questions posed to them, but also provided invaluable insight into their background, life experiences, child-rearing beliefs, and values related to family and home. Most interviews ended with these caregivers engaged in a seemingly traditional grandparent ritual of proudly showing off family pictures, family mementos, school awards, or even the children themselves.

The data collected from the interviews were analyzed using a grounded theory approach through which major themes were identified and grouped together [Gilgun 1994]. This method allows the researcher to identify ideas and concepts in each interview, establish if a relationships exist between the ideas and concepts discussed by each study participant, and highlight the patterns found across the spectrum of interviews. This process has also been termed constant comparison, which denotes the continuing search for comparisons in themes and issues both within and across the interviews [Gilgun 1994]. For example, themes continually emerged in the interviews that centered around such issues as substance abuse and child neglect when grandparents talked about what brought them into contact with the child welfare system. These issues or themes were present even for caregivers who could not bring themselves to directly admit to their children's drug addiction or neglect of their children, using such phases as, "She left the children alone for hours or days," or "She would run off and stay all night without someone to watch the children."

The survey instrument was divided into two parts. The first section of the instrument consisted of a series of open-ended questions. The questions pertained to the issues that were present when the children were first taken into the custody of the child welfare system, what support systems existed for the caregivers, perceptions of the legal and child welfare system, as well as their advice on changing the system. The second part of the instrument was demographic in nature, and asked for detailed information about age, income sources, marital status, etc. The findings of the study and the responses of the caregivers were organized by both the major themes that cropped up during the interviews and the questions that caregivers were asked in the survey instrument.

All interviews were conducted by the author. Conducting the interviews in the caregivers' homes allowed the investigator to observe the caregivers in their home and communities and their interactions with the children. These observations and experiences while in the homes of the grandparents also informed the author's understanding of the world view of these grandparents.

Description of the Grandparent Caregivers

The caregivers ranged in age from 49 to 72 years. The mean age of the caregivers was 58 years of age. Five of the caregivers were currently married. Two of the caregivers reported being widowed and two reported that they were separated from their husbands. Only one of the caregivers identified herself as single, never married. While these caregivers had experiences of working outside of the home, only one was currently employed. Three caregivers were supported primarily by a pension, five received social security, and only one reported receiving TANF. The caregivers also received monthly financial subsidies from the child welfare system for the care of their grandchildren, except for two who were waiting for these payments to begin. While several of the caregivers retired as they had always planned, some reported that they decided to end their employment to provide full-time care to their grandchildren.

The caregivers were evenly split between those who owned their own homes, and those who were currently renting. Those who were homeowners were a stable group, reporting that they lived in that same neighborhood for 20 to 40 years and raised their children in their current home.

Perspectives of the Grandparents

The survey instrument for this study allowed the grandparent caregivers to talk freely and openly about the issues that brought them, their children, and grandchildren into the Illinois child welfare system. While most of these issues were sensitive for the caregivers to discuss, they appeared to appreciate the opportunity to share some painful experiences with someone outside of the court and child welfare system. How the grandparents formed decisions based on their world view of issues affecting their lives, family, and grandchildren can be seen and heard in the statements they made during the interviews.

At the time of the interviews, these grandparents shared responsibility for the care of their grandchildren with the child welfare system. Some of the grandparents had begun the process of assuming permanent legal responsibility for their grandchildren through adoption. As their perceptions and life histories unfolded during the interviews, it became evident that many of the grandparents remained hopeful that their children would one day become emotionally and physically able to resume their child-caring responsibilities and provide the type of family they would like their grandchildren to have.

Why are the children in the care of the grandparents?

Most of the grandparents were caring for their grandchildren because their children's substance abuse problems contributed to neglect or abuse that had been discovered by the child welfare system. For many of the grandparents, this was difficult to admit. Some talked around this issue before finally stating that their children had problems with alcohol or drug abuse that placed their grandchildren in harmful situations. For many of the caregivers, the full-time care of these children turned out to be an unexpected responsibility at this phase of their lives. Almost all of the caregivers reported that at the time that the child welfare system became involved, many of the children had a history of living with or being taken care of by the grandparent who already assumed a sense of responsibility for full-time care of the child. This finding is typical in that most African American grandparents, especially in low-income families, tend to be actively involved in the rearing and support of their grandchildren from birth [George & Dickerson 1995].

The grandparents in this study reflected the traditional roles of caregivers as resources for their families. In fact, for some caregivers, this was not the first time that they had assumed child care responsibilities for someone else's children, and several stated that they saw this as their role in life. For others, taking on the full-time responsibility of caregiving and essentially becoming parents again was unexpected and forced upon them.

This 49-year-old caregiver's response was typical of explanations that grandparents gave of the way the children ended up in their care:

> I guess the mother was neglecting her. She used to go out and leave 'em in the apartment by themselves. But ever since this [child] was born, I loved this child, and I'd bring her home with me, and watch her. But since she wasn't in the system yet, her mother had a right to come and get her anytime. She was the first born. But when (her daughter) had other children it became too much and she was neglecting them. I suppose somebody must have called on her, that she had left the kids alone. So I was always with the little ones, but the oldest was [child], so I just brought her to my home, and all the other children were taken away to different foster homes where they've been very well taken care of.

Other identified reasons for the children in their care were homelessness and mental illness. One caregiver dealing with the mental illness of her daughter had this to say:

> This is how I came to get [child]. It was due to ignorance of illness. I did not know about the illness of my daughter.

> I thought that what she was going through at that time was drug related, but turned out it was illness related. The police was called in, and after the police were called in, child protection was called in. They all came in to investigate, and one stage lead to the other stage. I made the commitment that I was not, I was not, going to let anybody take my grandchild unless through force or death. And so far, that is the way it ended up, and that is how I came to have him.

Generational factors are apparent in the narratives of the caregivers. For the most part, this group of grandparent caregivers is composed of senior citizens who are retired with adult children. The decisions and choices that they made about caregiving are rooted in their view of family, their work ethic, and how they view their relationship to grandchildren and their own children.

Who else was available to care for the children?

When asked who else was available to care for the children other than this particular caregiver, only four grandparents could provide the name of someone else in the family who would or could take the children and prevent them from entering the foster care system. One of these caregivers admitted that the three siblings in her care would probably have been split up among various family members if she had not been able to care for the children.

What systems of support were available to caregivers?

The caregivers who were the most satisfied with their role reported that there was someone else in the family who could take care of the children in the event of their illness or death. They reported that they had a good deal of family support, from either their other children, who pitched in to help, or from other family members, such as the caregiver's sister or brother.

The 72-year-old caregiver, taking care of her 13-year-old great-grandson reported that family members were in and out most of the day, and that other family members called daily to check to see if she needed anything. She also received a great deal of support from a grandson she helped to rear, who moved back in with her to help with the great-grandson. Several other caregivers reported some assistance from family members, but indicated that they could not depend on them for full-time care of the children. Some were resentful about the lack of support they received.

This 54-year-old grandparent mirrored many of the other responses when talking about that lack of support.

> They visit, my kids and stuff, but they're of no help. I mean what I call help is like if they come over and say, "Well I'll take the kids for the weekend," or they might say, "Well mom, is there anything you need us to do concerning these kids? Did you need us to take 'em to the doctor for you? Or did you need us to do this?" I would say no, cuz they don't. So basically it's just me.

The most unsettling responses came from caregivers who perceived a lack of support from friends and other network systems. These caregivers reported that they did not have friends or ties with people from church or other associations to whom they could turn for help, assistance, or support. These caregivers seemed extremely isolated as they cared for the children.

The most touching response came from a 56-year-old grandmother who decided to take her six grandchildren to live with her full time. When asked about friends who could help her, her voice started to shake. She said,

> Right now, I don't even have a love life. I can't have a friend. I had a friend but...

Then she started to cry. The investigator turned the tape off for a few minutes while she composed herself. When she continued, she said,

> I had to let him go because he wanted to get involved. You can't have a life with somebody else when you raising somebody else's kids. I don't even have no other friends.

Then she started to cry again. This caregiver really struggled over balancing her love for her grandchildren and her desire to care for them and not allow them to enter the foster care system with the personal sacrifices she made to care for them.

What advice did caregivers have for the child welfare system?

This question to caregivers received a mixture of responses. Many of them reported that they have had a good experience with the child welfare system, including agency caseworkers, lawyers, and judges. This 49-year-old grandmother is typical of the grandparents frustrated, not with the child welfare system, but the parents of the children in care.

> You know, there are so many like my daughter, that it's hard to say what advice. I'm really lost on that part. Some people change, and others never change... as hard as the social workers, and judges and other attorneys work on people like my daughter, you know, it doesn't sink into their head that they should change and take care of their kids, they just continue on doing what they wanna do. It's like they have a mind on their own. Oh, they go in front of the judge and say "Yes, your honor I did group, I went to school, I got a certificate, I'm a better parent." Then they walk out of there and they forget everything they just talked about, you know. And the poor social workers are there racking their brains trying to get the families together and I've seen 'em there, they're just like, it's a big joke. I really don't have no advice. I think they've probably tried everything they can think of.

Others reported that the most difficult aspect of dealing with the child welfare system was the court process. This process was frightening for both the caregivers, many of whom had never had to go to court before for anything, and for the children, who harbored the fear that they would be "snatched away" from their grandparent(s).

There was also a sense from the statements of the caregivers that, despite the fact that they were providing care for the grandchildren, power and control was still in the hands of their adult children who abandoned their responsibilities. As caregivers, they felt that they had been left holding the bag, given all the rules and regulations to follow, while the parents of the children were given all the freedom. Several of the caregivers expressed frustration with the courts for allowing visitation rights to the parents. According to these caregivers, these visits caused adjustment problems for the children and temporarily altered the children's attitudes toward the caregivers.

What are caregivers' attitudes about child rearing and discipline?

The world view perspective of the caregivers on the issue of child rearing differed greatly from that of the social service agency and the child welfare system. The gap in the parenting styles and approaches to discipline held by the grandparents and the child welfare system is seen in the statement of this 72-year-old caregiver. Like other caregivers, she felt some resentment about being told how to rear children. She stated,

> I already knew everything they was telling us, you know, because I had been through it with my kids, raising them. Of course these modern things, you know that you're not s'pose to spank 'em all like that, but see when I was coming up they'd get their little behinds popped, not all the time, but I'm telling you, you'd go through that, they'd do something, and do it two or three times, they'd get on punishment. If they did it again, they'd get a spanking on their hands. If they did it again, they'd get a spanking on their behinds. And, I never had no trouble with none of 'em. I have never had to go to jail to get none of them out, and I had four boys and two girls. So I think I did a good job.

This caregiver also stated firmly, "You do not let a child rule you, you rule the child." With many of the caregivers, they felt that the system allowed children to rule. The requirements placed on the caregivers, which are much more strict than when they reared their own children, also caused resentment. This 58-year-old grandfather talked about the expectations and demands placed on him to provide for the children. He said,

I would tell the judge to not push me to do this and do that. They require that each child has their own room. We are not rich people. Each child has their own bed. That is the important thing. I told the judge, I have done the best I can since they were two weeks old. They eat better than me. I eat at Burger King, they don't. I make sure they have good food and sleep good. They are my grandchildren, and I make sure they taken care better than any other children. I know kids. I raised seven of them. My wife had ten children, but only seven are now living. I talk to the caseworker when I have problems, but I know children.

Perspectives of Male Caregivers in Study

There were two grandfathers who agreed to be interviewed for this study. In addition, three grandfathers were observed as they interacted with the grandchildren in their care while their spouses were interviewed. The interviews with grandfathers were longer than any of the interviews with the female caregivers. These grandfathers had much to say about their experiences with the system, were more critical of the child welfare system, but were much more willing to acknowledge the child neglect and abuse of their adult children. They had quite a bit to say about how intrusive the system had become in the lives of their families. The grandfathers who were interviewed, and others who were observed, were active in the lives of their grandchildren. They were present and interacting with the children. Their wives reported that these grandfathers were sources of support to them in caring for the children. The two grandfathers who participated in interviews were quite forthcoming, sharing a wealth of information about their perspective of how the system impacts families and about their roles as caregivers.

The Investigator's Observations and Reactions

These families made a lasting impression on the investigator. One of the most impressive characteristics of the caregivers was their dedication to family—both their grandchildren and children. Conversations with caregivers and observations of their interactions with their grandchildren provided evidence of the traditional strengths of African American families:

> strong kinship ties and obligations, care of the elderly and absorption of children into households by other relatives and fictive kin, strong religious consciousness, strong community ties, socialization of the young with emphasis on group welfare over individual welfare, strong helping and mutual-aid tradition, and strong achievement orientation. These patterns are rooted in the African American experience. [English 1991, p. 23]

English [1991] notes that not all African American families share all of these values and that variations in families are due to such factors as social mobility, urban experiences, exposure to racism and discrimination, and childhood socialization. The same can be said of the families interviewed in this study, but when examining the list of strengths and values outlined by English, a majority of these values could be viewed in the families in this study.

Another impression gained from interviews and observations was the amount of anger that clearly lay just under the surface of most of the caregiver statements during the interviews. This anger was expressed by some of the caregivers. Anger was focused at their adult children for not taking care of their responsibilities, but it was clear that they did not want their children to be judged unfairly. They were able to recognize where mistakes and neglect occurred, but none of the grandparents talked about turning their children away if they appeared at the door. They still hoped that their children would someday turn their lives around and take care of their own children.

It was clear from the interviews and postinterview discussions that if they had to do this all again, take in their grandchildren and make the same sacrifices, they would do so without hesitation. Many of the caregivers acknowledged that since their grandchildren were born they had a certain bond that transcended the grandparent-grandchild relationship. There was some sadness that these grandparents missed out on having that special grandparent-grandchild type relationship with these children, and instead had been forced to become full-time parents and caregivers. But when asked where they thought the children would be living three years in the future, caregivers often responded with, "I hope right here."

Another lasting impression that the investigator will always have of this group of caregivers is how open they were in discussing their families and sharing their experiences. In almost every case, the interview process would have to pause as caregivers would suddenly leap from their seats to proudly show family pictures, school certificates, and awards or to show off the children themselves. This aspect of the interview process pointed clearly to the richness of the ethnographic method and the benefit of the world view perspective in gaining an insight into why the caregivers made the decision to provide full-time care for their grandchildren, despite personal and financial sacrifices. Interviewing these caregivers was like becoming part of their families for two hours. They shared their personal backgrounds, family stories and events, hopes and dreams in a way that one would not expect with any other research method. Often, caregivers insisted that the investigator not leave without having at least a cup of coffee. On several occasions the investigator was invited to come back and just sit and talk. One caregiver invited the investigator to Sunday dinner. For these grandparents, to share their stories was also to share their lives and to make the interviewer part of their families. The investigator was accepted by them and made to feel a part of their life experience.

Implications of the World Views Perspective for Child Welfare Workers

English first raised the issue of practitioners failing to recognize the world views of clients with the mental health profession. He stated,

> To ignore or fail to understand and consciously recognize the world views of minorities is to engage unwittingly or otherwise in a form of cultural oppression. When mental health practitioners fail to take into account world views

of minorities or, in the absence of doing so, substitute their own views (especially when they differ from their clients), they are likely to impute negative traits to their clients and to contribute to the high drop-out rates of minority clients in mental health services. [1983, p 23]

The same concerns expressed about mental health practitioners have been applied to caseworkers in the child welfare system as well. The social, economic, and political realities that bring families of color into contact with the child welfare system are often unique and complex. With the grandparent caregivers represented in this study, it was clear that there were generational, cultural, community, and gender issues that made each family's experience unique, but there were also common themes among these families that child welfare workers could utilize to bridge the gap between caregivers' perspectives and their own.

Listed below are some of the common themes heard from the caregivers:

- a sense that their many years of experience in child rearing has not been acknowledge or valued;

- a lack of acknowledgment that for many of these families, this was their first exposure to the legal and child welfare system and a failure by child welfare caseworkers to help them maneuver through the maze;

- a failure to recognize that, despite their anger, and even embarrassment, with their adult children, there was still love and concern for these children; and

- a sense of isolation for many of the caregivers from friends, family, and associates, especially after the caregiver made personal and professional sacrifices to assume responsibilities that he or she considered to be a duty within the family.

The assessment of a client's realities, stressors, and world views perspective is an invaluable source of information that should be used by child welfare practitioners to design best practice approaches and to enhance service delivery. According to English [1991], the world views perspective, as a practice tool, can assist the child welfare field in several ways:

- by assessing the client's cultural background and understanding his or her overall orientation toward life,
- by gaining a better understanding of the client's presenting problems and developing a relevant and effective service plan,
- by empowering racial and ethnic minority families, and
- by creating innovative programs and interventions.

Conclusion

The caregivers interviewed for this study were a remarkable group of men and women. Sitting with them, surrounded by their grandchildren, it was evident in their words, actions, and deeds that there was tremendous strength, pride, love and joy within their families. It is important as researchers, social service providers, and child welfare practitioners to know that due to substance abuse, crime, incarceration, and mental illness there has been a dramatic increase in the numbers of children dependent on kinship care provided most often by grandparents. The tool of ethnography and the construct of world views aid in understanding the realities which these families face that brought them into the legal and child welfare system, the stressors which these families endure, and ways that these stressors are sometimes compounded by the very systems that should ease some of their burdens. Ethnography can also help one develop a better perspective of the resilience of these caregivers and identify the gaps in services and support systems that could aid these caregivers.

References

Burton, L. M. (1996). Age norms, the timing of family role transitions, and intergenerational caregiving among aging African American women. *The Gerontologist, 36,* 199-208.

Burton, L. A. (1992). Black grandparents rearing children of drug-addicted parents: Stressors, outcomes, and social service needs. *The Gerontologist, 32,* 744-751.

Cross, T. (1995). Resiliency in families: Racial and ethnic minority families in America. In H. I. McCubbin, E. A. Thompson, A. I. Thompson, & J.

E. Fromer (Eds.), *Ethnic minority families: Native and immigrant American families* (Vol. 1) (pp. 143-158). Boston: Sage.

English, R. A. (1991). Diversity of world views among African American families. In J. E. Everett, S. Chipungu, & B. Leashore (Eds.), *Child Welfare: An Africentric Perspective* (pp. 19-35). Rutgers University Press: New Jersey.

English, R. A. (1983). *The challenge for mental health: Minorities and their world views.* Austin, TX: Hogg Foundation for Mental Health, University of Texas.

George, S. M., & Dickerson, B. J. (1995). The role of the grandmother in poor single-mother families and households. In B.J. Dickerson (Ed.), *African American single mothers.* Thousand Oaks, CA: Sage Publications.

Gilgun, J. F. (1994). Hand into glove: The grounded theory approach and social work practice research. In E. Sherman & W. Reid (Eds). *Qualitative research in social work.* Columbia University Press: New York.

Goodson-Lawes, J. (1994). Ethnicity and poverty as research variables: Family studies with Mexican and Vietnamese newcomers. In E. Sherman & W. Reid (Eds.), *Qualitative research in social work* (pp. 21-31). New York: Columbia University Press.

Jackson, A. P., & Sears, S. J. (1992). Implications of an Africentric worldview in reducing stress for African American women. *Journal of Counseling & Development, 71*, 184-190.

Jendrek, M. P. (1994). Grandparents who parent their grandchildren: Circumstances and decisions. *The Gerontologist, 34*, 206-216.

Minkler, M., Roe, K. M., & Robertson-Beckley, R. J. (1994). Raising grandchildren from crack-cocaine households: Effects on family and friendship ties of African-American women. *American Journal of Orthopsychiatry, 64*, 20-29.

Montalvo, E. (1997). Programs with a cultural fit: Working with Latino families. *Children's Voice, 6*(4), 4-5 & 15.

Woodworth, R. S. (1996) You're not alone... You're one in a million. *Child Welfare, 5*, 619-635.

10

The Effect of Caregiver Preparation and Sense of Control on Adaptation of Kinship Caregivers

Donna D. Petras

The welfare of tens of thousands of children in state custody rests with relatives who have been delegated responsibility for their day-to-day care by the child welfare systems within the United States [Kusserow 1992]. This is an especially vulnerable and often fragile population of children due to prior experiences of child abuse, neglect, and subsequent separation from parents [Child Welfare League of America 1994; Dubowitz et al. 1994]. Meeting the needs of these children and promoting their healthy development requires that kinship caregivers have the willingness, ability, and resources to accomplish this. Yet, little is known about the unique needs of kin as caregivers of children involved in the child welfare system. The lack of empirical data that can inform the development of policy and programs to support kinship caregivers is due in part to the relatively recent emergence of kinship care as a predominant form of care for children in state custody.

Although the care of children within extended families is not a new phenomenon, it has traditionally taken place through private, informal arrangements between family members outside the legal responsibility of the child welfare system [Child Welfare League of America 1994]. The involvement of the state in placing children in state custody with kin represents a significant departure from traditional practices that primarily involved placing children with unrelated families and creates new program and policy challenges. Despite their great and increasing dependence on kinship care, few states have clearly articulated the purposes, goals, or distinct program models for this service [Gleeson & Craig 1994]. Rather, states most often tend to view kinship care as a component of foster care services.

Once viewed as a way to divert children from the formal child welfare system, kinship care placements are increasingly viewed as preferred alternatives for permanent homes for children. Caregivers are encouraged to adopt or assume legal guardianship when children placed with them cannot be safely reunited with their parents. Efforts to enlist relatives as permanent families for children are often made without adequate consideration of the impact on the caregiver and without provision of supports and services to assure the success of the placement for the children [Magruder 1994].

This chapter describes a study that examined the impact of providing care on kinship caregivers. The influence of kinship caregivers' preparation for caregiving and sense of control on their adaptation to caregiving provides the focus of study. The chapter begins with a review of relevant literature on forces that influence family caregivers' adaptation to their caregiving roles, followed by a description of the study methodology, and a summary of the results. The chapter ends with a discussion of the implications of these results for child welfare policy, practice, and future research.

Several forces point to the need to critically examine kinship care providers' adaptation to their caregiving role and to clarify the forces that are influential in that regard. Among these are the fact that kinship caregivers are less likely to receive services for children and support for their caregiving role than unrelated foster parents [Berrick et al. 1994; Kusserow 1992]. This occurs despite the fact that they take on the caregiving role in the midst of severe family breakdown, often without prior planning or preparation. The assumption of the caregiving role is often under difficult and painful circumstances, precipitates an abrupt transition, and requires many changes in the way caregivers live their lives [Minkler & Roe 1993].

Caregivers must respond to the day-to-day care demands of young children who have experienced the trauma resulting from child abuse or neglect and separation from their parents and who have a high incidence of physical and behavioral problems [Berrick et al. 1994; Dubowitz et al. 1994; Iglehart 1994]. They must, at the same time, respond to the demands, and often intrusions, of a governmental bureaucracy that has authority to make major decisions regarding the care and future of the child. Adjusting to the changes in relationships within the extended family and managing the changes within one's own daily life required to accommodate the caregiving situation can leave kinship caregivers with a sense that they have little control over important events in their lives [Crumbley & Little 1997].

Family Caregiving Research

Although research on the adaptation of child welfare kinship caregivers to their caregiving role has been sparse, a considerable body of literature documents factors related to adaptation to the caregiving role for other family caregivers [Miller 1991]. The literature on caregiving for elderly, disabled relatives is informative as there are some similarities in caregiving for children. The physical demands of daily caregiving, the emotional strain of responding to behavioral difficulties and developmental delays, and the management of children's medical problems are quite similar to some elderly caregiving arrangements and are likely to create similar stresses [Minkler & Roe 1993]. These similarities provide the basis for the assumption that research addressing other populations of familial caregivers are sufficiently relevant to kinship caregivers to inform the present study.

Whereas caregiver adaptation can be assessed in terms of both positive and negative outcomes, adaptation has basically been studied in terms of negative outcomes for the caregiver. Caregiver depression is one of the most commonly identified symptoms of caregiver distress noted in the literature on familial caregiving of the frail elderly [Chenoweth & Spencer 1986; George & Gwenther 1986; Rabins et al. 1982]. Studies of grandparent caregivers of children also focus on those negative factors and suggest that rates of depressive symptomatology in this population are also higher than in the general population [Burton 1992; Minkler & Roe 1993]. Many scholars note, however, that both positive and negative consequences of caregiving are intrinsic to most caregiving situations [Lawton et al. 1989]. In fact, caregivers who provide more care have been found to simultaneously experience more satisfaction and more psychological distress [Lawton et al. 1992].

Adaptation to the stresses of caregiving is influenced not only by the demands of caregiving itself but also by a variety of personal and interpersonal factors attendant upon the caregiving situation [Pearlin et al. 1990]. Higher levels of perceived caregiver preparation are associated with lower levels of caregiver role strain among caregivers of older individuals [Archbold et al. 1990]. The relationship of sense of control to psychological well-being has been studied extensively and an internal sense of control has been consistently found to be associated with decreased depression [Mirowsky & Ross 1990]. However, the applicability of traditional conceptualizations of sense of control in studies of African American adults has been questioned [Barbarin 1983; Miller et al. 1994].

This study examines whether caregiver preparation and sense of control demonstrate similar relationships to measures of adaptation for kinship caregivers involved with the child welfare system as has been demonstrated in the general literature on family caregiving. As the child welfare system becomes increasingly dependent upon kin to provide care to children in state custody, the importance of understanding adaptation to this caregiving role and the issues that influence adaptation also increases.

Description of the Study

Using a cross-sectional approach, the study examined relationships between kinship caregivers' perceptions of their preparation for caregiving, their sense of control, and adaptation to the caregiving role. Extensive data were collected to describe the study sample, including demographic data as well as information regarding their experiences of caregiving.

A convenience sample of 80 caregivers of related children in state custody was recruited in Cook County, Illinois. While random selection of the study sample would have produced data with greater generalizability to the population of kinship caregivers, sample selection was constrained by the difficulty of recruiting a sufficiently large sample to complete the study. Approximately 2,000 caregivers were contacted either by mail or through distribution of invitations at foster parent conferences or support group meetings to recruit the study sample of 80 caregivers [Petras 1998].

One-time structured interviews were conducted primarily in caregivers' homes between May and September, 1997. The interview guide included questions on demographics, experiences in caring for children, relationships with caseworkers, health of members of the household, as well as existing measures for caregiver preparation, sense of control, caregiver depression, caregiver satisfaction, and child behavior problems. The instruments selected to measure the independent and dependent variables have been used in studies of adaptation to various types of familial caregiving situations, particularly familial caregiving to the frail elderly.

Two multiple regression analyses were conducted to test the hypotheses that kinship caregivers' perceptions of their preparation for caregiving and their sense of control would be negatively associated with depression and positively associated with caregiver satisfaction. Two additional variables were entered into each regression equation to control for the difficulty of caregiving: the number of children living in the home and a rating of the behavioral problems displayed by the most difficult to manage child in the home.

Description of the Sample

Caregivers in this study were primarily middle-aged, Protestant, African American women living singly and providing care for their maternal grandchildren (Table 10-1). They had a mean of 12.65 years of schooling with 48.9% of caregivers reporting some education beyond high school.

Twenty-one percent of the caregivers had spouses or partners who lived in the home with them. Most caregivers in the study sample were employed outside the home with 41% employed full time. Those who worked outside the home were engaged in a wide variety of occupations but were

Table 10-1. Characteristics of Kinship Caregivers

Characteristics	Number	Percent
Age	N=80	
23-42 years	17	21.3
43-52 years	23	28.7
53-59 years	23	28.7
60-71 years	17	21.3
Sex		
Female	78	97.5
Male	2	2.5
Race		
African American	77	96.1
Latino	1	1.3
Native American	1	1.3
Caucasian	1	1.3
Religion		
Protestant-Baptist	41	51.2
Protestant-Other	24	30.0
Catholic	6	7.5
Other	8	10.0
None	1	1.3
Education		
Grade school only	7	8.8
Some high school	18	22.6
High school graduate	16	20.0
Some college	26	32.6
College graduate	6	7.5
Graduate level	7	8.8
Marital Status		
Single, never married	19	23.8
Divorced	20	25.0
Widowed	13	16.3
Separated	11	13.8
Married, living together	14	17.5
Live-in partner, not married	3	3.8

most likely to be employed as laborers, secretaries, or health care workers. The median income from all sources for all members of the household for the year prior to data collection was $20,000–$24,999 with most receiving income from multiple sources. All caregivers received some foster care board payments for the children in state custody, either the full foster care board rate for licensed foster parents or the reduced amount provided unlicensed caregivers.

Exploration of previous experiences caring for children revealed that the caregivers in this sample were highly experienced. Ninety-three percent had at least one child of their own and 70% had at least three children. The average caregiver in this sample cared for two or three related children who were in the custody of the child welfare system. Also, 60% of caregivers in the study sample had held at least one job in which they cared for children and 80% had cared for another friend's or family member's child prior to caring for the children currently in their homes. In addition to being highly experienced, 71% of caregivers rated their performance as caregivers as "very good." This finding is consistent with the finding of Gleeson, O'Donnell, Altshuler, and Philbin [1994] who found that caseworkers rated more than 79% of the kinship caregivers as providing "good care without help" or "needs a little help on occasion."

The majority of caregivers included in the study sample were managing significant health issues for themselves, other adults in the household, and/ or children in the household. Most caregivers suffered from at least one chronic illness and/or disability, with many caregivers reporting multiple chronic illnesses and/or disabilities. Several caregivers were caring for other adults with significant health problems, including four caregivers who were caring for frail, elderly parents. The most frequently reported chronic illnesses affecting caregivers and other adults in the household were high blood pressure, asthma, diabetes, heart disease, and arthritis. Also, more than one-third of caregivers reported that one or more children living in their home suffered from at least one disability and almost one-third of caregivers reported that at least one other child in their home suffered from at least one chronic illness. Many children in these households suffered from multiple disabilities and chronic illnesses.

Caregivers included in this study were similar to those in other studies on most demographic measures: age, race, gender, religion, marital status, education, income, relationship to the children for whom they are providing care, number of children for whom they were providing care, frequency of working outside the home, and level of satisfaction with the caseworker for their related children [Berrick et al. 1994; Dubowitz et al. 1993; Gleeson et al. 1994; Testa 1993; Thornton 1991]. However, caregivers who participated in this study were more likely to suffer from a chronic illness or disability and to be caring for at least one child with a disability or chronic idleness than caregivers in other studies [Berrick et al. 1994; Gleeson et al. 1994; Dubowitz et al. 1993].

Measurement of Variables

Measurement of each of the variables included in the regression equations is described in this section. Caregiver adaptation was defined as the positive and negative ways kinship caregivers accommodate to the demands of caring for related children involved in the child welfare system and was measured by assessing caregiver depression and caregiver satisfaction. Depression was measured using the Epidemiologic Studies Depression (CES-D) Scale. Caregiver satisfaction was measured using the Caregiver Satisfaction Index. The two independent variables were caregiver preparation, measured by the Preparedness for Caregiving Scale, and sense of control, measured by the Denying Responsibility for Success subscale of the Control Index. The two control variables were number of children receiving care and behavior problems of the most difficult to manage child living in the home. The number of children receiving care was measured by asking caregivers to identify all persons residing in their home on the date of the in-person interview and the age of each person residing in the home as of their last birthday. The number of children 18 years of age and younger was computed for each caregiver. The level of child behavior problems was measured by the Child Behavior Checklist (CBCL). Each of the standardized measures is described below.

The CES-D Scale

The CES-D Scale is a 20-item self-report that has been widely used in studies of depression with nonpsychiatric populations, especially in studies of adaptation of familial caregivers in a variety of caregiving situations [Radloff 1977]. The scale has been used in studies of African American and white English-speaking American populations of both sexes and with a wide range of age and socioeconomic status [Radloff 1977; Pruchno & Resch 1989; Miller et al. 1992]. Scores range from 0 to 60. The higher the score, the higher one's level of depression. The CES-D scale demonstrated high internal consistency reliability with a Cronbach's *alpha* of .87 for the current study.

The Caregiver Satisfaction Index

The Caregiver Satisfaction Index is a five-item Likert-like scale that asks caregivers to respond to items that address the positive aspects of caregiving [Lawton et al. 1989]. Empirical tests found that the index, which is positively correlated with affect, caregiver ratings of the quality of their relationship with the care receiver, and the help given by caregivers, has modest internal consistency reliability. For this study the Caregiver Satisfaction Index demonstrated modest internal consistency reliability with a Cronbach's *alpha* of .69.

The Preparedness for Caregiving Scale

The Preparedness for Caregiving Scale developed by Archbold, Stewart, Greenlick, and Harvath [1986], is a six-item Likert-like scale that asks respondents to indicate their perception of how well-prepared they are to manage several caregiver tasks. In eliciting responses to items in the Preparedness for Caregiving Scale, participants were first asked, "At the present time, how well-prepared do you think you are?" They were then asked, "When you began providing care for your grandchild, niece, etc., how well-prepared do you think you were?" In this way, two preparation for caregiving scales were created. One scale, labeled "Preparation for Caregiving Now," represents caregivers' perceptions of their preparation at the time of data collection and the other, labeled "Preparation for Caregiving When Began," represents caregivers' perception of their preparation at the time they began caring for the children currently in their homes. In prior research, the scale demonstrated modest internal consistency reliability. For this study, the Preparation for Caregiving Now scale had a Cronbach's *alpha* of .78 and the Preparation for Caregiving When Began scale had an *alpha* of .84.

Denying Responsibility for Success Subscale of the Control Index

Sense of control was measured using the Denying Responsibility for Success subscale of the Control Index [Mirowsky & Ross 1990; 1991]. This was the only Control Index subscale that demonstrated minimally acceptable internal consistency reliability with this sample; therefore, it was the only subscale used to measure the sense of control that caregivers had over outcomes in their own lives. The Denying Responsibility for Success subscale had a Cronbach's *alpha* of .69. High scores on this subscale indicated that the caregivers did not believe that they were responsible for positive outcomes in their own lives.

Child Behavior Checklist (CBCL)

The 120-item behavioral problem scale of the CBCL [Achenbach 1991] was used to measure children's behavioral problems. It records in a standardized format the behavioral problems and competencies of children ages 4 through 18 years. In the present study, kinship caregivers were asked to complete the checklist for only one child, regardless of the number of children residing in their home. Caregivers were asked to provide information requested on the CBCL for the child for whom they were providing care who had reached his or her fourth birthday, resided in the caregiver's home for at least six months, was a ward of the state, and for whom it was most difficult to provide care. The children so identified by caregivers had a mean age of 9.9 years and a median age of 9.4 years, were predominately male, African American, and in a regular fourth grade classroom.

The CBCL is highly correlated with other measures of difficulty of child behavior problems and highly effective in differentiating clinically referred children from children in the general population. The scale has high reliability with a reported intraclass correlation coefficient (ICC) from one-way analysis of variance of .959 and a Cronbach's *alpha* of .96 [Achenbach

1991]. Reliability scores for the present study were consistent with the published findings cited above.

Results

Bivariate relationships among all the variables included in the analysis were examined by computing the Pearson's *r* correlation coefficients (Table 10-2). As expected, a significant positive relationship was found between the dependent variable caregiver depression and the control variable child behavior problems ($r = .263$, $p < .05$). Contrary to the prediction of the study hypothesis, a significant positive relationship was found between the dependent variable caregiver satisfaction and the Denying Responsibility for Success subscale ($r = .313$, $p < .01$). A significant positive relationship was also found between the independent variables preparation for caregiving now and preparation for caregiving when began ($r = .581$, $p < .01$). While the correlation coefficient for these two independent variables indicated a strong association, it was substantially below the Pearson's *r* value of .9, which suggests multicollinearity [Tabachnick & Fidell 1989]. A significant negative relationship was found between the independent variable preparation for caregiving when began and the control variable child behavior problems ($r = .248$, $p < 05$).

Two hierarchical multiple regression procedures were computed to test the study hypotheses controlling for child behavior problems and number of children receiving care. The first was performed to test the hypothesis that a significant inverse relationship would be found between caregiver preparation, caregiver sense of control, and caregiver depression. In this procedure, caregiver depression was entered as the dependent variable. Child behavior problems and number of children receiving care were entered into the regression equation first as a block to act as control variables. Next, preparation for caregiving now, preparation for caregiving when began, and sense of control as measured by the Denying Responsibility for Success subscale were entered as a block using the SPSS enter method. The results of this procedure are presented in Table 10-3 and summarized in this section.

Table 10-2. Zero-Order Correlations Between Variables Included in the Analysis

Variables	1	2	3	4	5	6	7
1 Caregiver depression	1.000						
2 Caregiver satisfaction	-.134	1.000					
3 Preparation for caregiving now	-.179	.216	1.000				
4 Preparation for caregiving when began	-.128	.116	.581**	1.000			
5 Sense of control[a]	.072	.313**	.055	.032	1.000		
6 Child behavior problems	.263*	-.149	-.111	-.248*	.032	1.000	
7 Number of children receiving	-.095	.067	.192	.111	.152	.062	1.000

* $p \le .05$ (two-tailed)
** $p \le .01$ (two-tailed)
a   Denying Responsibility for Success Subscale

In Step 1 of the hierarchical regression, approximately 8% of the variation in caregiver depression was accounted for by child behavior problems and number of children receiving care. The contribution of the variable, number of children receiving care, was found to be nonsignificant. However, level of child behavior problems was found to have a significant positive relationship with caregiver depression.

In Step 2 of the regression procedure, the independent variables were added to the equation to determine whether they increased the amount of variance in caregiver depression explained by the model. The multiple R^2 of .107 obtained at this stage was not found to be significantly different from zero. Addition of the three independent variables (preparation for caregiving now, preparation for caregiving when began, and sense of control) added only 3% to the amount of variance in caregiver depression explained by the model. Evaluation of the *Beta* scores revealed that level of child behavior problems was the only variable included in the model that

Table 10-3. Hierarchical Multiple Regression
Predicting Caregiver Depression

Variable	B	SE B	β
Step 1			
Child behavior problems	.208*	.086	.265
Number of children receiving care	-.597	.613	-.107
$R^2 = .082$ $F = 3.425^*$			
Step 2			
Child behavior problems	.201*	.089	.258
Number of children receiving care	-.546	.632	-.098
Preparation for caregiving now	-.706	.617	-.157
Preparation for caregiving when began	.083	.330	.035
Sense of control[a]	.393	.507	.086
$R^2 = .107$ $R^2 = .697$			

* $p \leq .05$
a   Variable measured by Denying Responsibility for Success Subscale of the Control Index

made a significant contribution to the explanation of the variance in caregiver depression.

A second hierarchical multiple regression procedure was performed to test the study hypothesis that a significant positive relationship would be found between caregiver preparation, caregiver sense of control, and caregiver satisfaction. In this procedure, caregiver satisfaction was entered as the dependent variable (Table 10-4). The control variables, child behavior problems, and number of children receiving care were entered into the equation in Step 1 of the regression procedure. The model at Step 1 explained only 3% of the variance in caregiver satisfaction and was not statistically significant. Neither of the control variables, child behavior problems, or number of children receiving care were significantly associated with caregiver satisfaction.

In Step 2 of the regression procedure, the independent variables preparation for caregiving now, preparation for caregiving when began, and sense

---

Table 10-4. Hierarchical Multiple Regression Predicting Caregiver Satisfaction

Variable	B	SE B	ß
Step 1			
Child behavior problems	-.035	.026	-.153
Number of children receiving care	.124	.184	.076
$R^2 = .028$ $F = 1.105$			
Step 2			
Child behavior problems	-.034	.025	-.148
Number of children receiving care	-.010	.180	-.006
Preparation for caregiving now	.285	.175	.216
Preparation for caregiving when began	-.039	.094	-.055
Sense of control[a]	.413**	.144	.309
$R^2 = .159$ $R^2 = .131*$			

* $p \leq .05$
** $p \leq .01$
a Variable measured by Denying Responsibility for Success Subscale of the Control Index

---

of control as measured by the Denying Responsibility for Success subscale of the Control Index were added to the equation. Sixteen percent of the variance in caregiver satisfaction was explained by the model, which was statistically significant at the .05 level. Only sense of control contributed significantly to the prediction of caregiver satisfaction. The results of the regression analysis indicate that as denial of responsibility for success increases, caregiver satisfaction also increases. The results of the multivariate analysis not only confirm the bivariate finding of a significant relationship between the two variables but also show that denying responsibility for success continues to explain a statistically significant proportion of the variance in caregiver satisfaction even with child behavior problems and number of children receiving care controlled.

Discussion

While the literature on caregiving and sense of control reports that an external sense of control is one of the most consistent predictors of caregiver depression in female caregivers of the frail elderly [Parks & Pilisuk 1991], the results of this study do not support this conclusion. Perhaps the most surprising finding of the study was an inverse relationship between sense of control and caregiver satisfaction. The study finding indicates that as caregiver denial of responsibility for success increases, so does caregiver satisfaction. This contradicts the literature regarding familial caregivers of the elderly, which suggests that as the caregivers' internal sense of control increased so does their satisfaction with the caregiving role. There are several possible explanations for this finding. First, the literature on sense of control and African American adults has questioned the applicability of traditional conceptualizations of sense of control to African American populations. Some researchers have suggested that experiences with discriminating practices may predispose African Americans to view negative events as being out of their control while maintaining high levels of personal efficacy [Barbarin 1983]. If this interpretation is correct, it would explain why African Americans could simultaneously maintain high levels of denial of responsibility for successful outcomes and high levels of caregiver satisfaction.

Another possible explanation of the finding of a positive relationship between denying responsibility for success and caregiver satisfaction relates to the severity of problems that lead to family breakdown and placement of children by the child welfare system. For most of the families included in the study sample, the major precipitating factor to child placement was alcohol and/or drug abuse by one or more of the children's parents. Resolution of these problems depends upon the decisions and behavior of the parents of the children in care who are most often the children of the kinship caregivers. The degree to which kinship caregivers are able to absolve themselves of personal responsibility for successfully resolving these problems could directly affect their satisfaction as caregivers.

A third possible explanation for the finding of a positive relationship between denying responsibility for success and caregiver satisfaction derives from caregivers' comments as they responded to items included in the sense of control measure. Numerous caregivers made comments when responding to these items such as, "I don't believe in luck, I believe in God's grace." These comments reflect the central importance of faith and spirituality in the lives of the caregivers included in this sample. Caregivers repeatedly stated that their deep religious faith provided the basis for their emotional strength and ability to cope with the multiple problems that characterize their daily lives.

Caregivers' perceptions of their preparation for caregiving were not found to be significantly related to either of the dependent variables, caregiver depression or caregiver satisfaction. This finding also differs from reported findings from studies of caregivers of the frail elderly in which caregiver preparation was found to be a significant predictor of caregiver role strain [Archbold et al. 1990]. The finding of no significant relationship between caregiver preparation and either caregiver depression or caregiver satisfaction may be attributable to a variety of explanations. Two measures of caregivers' perceptions of their preparation for caregiving were included in the present study, preparation for caregiving now and preparation for caregiving when began. The univariate analysis of the data revealed that the caregivers in the present sample rated their preparation for caregiving on both measures substantially higher than samples of caregivers to the frail elderly who comprised the samples for other studies in which the measure had been used.

Caregivers' scores on preparation for caregiving may be related to the amount of prior experience as caregivers reported by the study sample. More than 90% of the caregivers in this sample had reared at least one child of their own and more than 70% had reared three or more of their own children. In addition, 60% of the study sample had held at least one job caring for children and 80% had cared for another family member or friend's child prior to caring for the children currently in their home. The high scores on the preparation for caregiving scales may well reflect the sense of competence in caring for children derived from considerable previous experience.

A second explanation for caregivers' high sense of preparedness may derive from their assessments of their performance as caregivers. More than 70% of caregivers in the study sample rated their performance "very good." When asked to explain their rating, a large number of caregivers talked about the improvement in the condition of the children since they began providing care. Frequently cited accomplishments were improved child health, better school grades, improved behavior, and greater emotional security. The genuine accomplishments resulting from caregiver performance serves to bolster a sense of competence and preparedness as caregivers. As a consequence, caregivers' perceptions of their preparation for caregiving may have too little variance to show a relationship with the dependent variables.

This study did demonstrate a significant positive relationship between child behavior problems and caregiver depression. This finding is consistent with studies of caregivers of the frail elderly, which have consistently shown that as the level of functional or mental impairment of the care receiver increases so does the degree of stress experienced by the caregiver [Cicirelli 1981, 1983; Horowitz 1982; Robinson 1983; Wilder et al. 1983]. The CBCL scores for children in this study indicate that not only did these children have substantially more behavior problems than children in the general population, they also were far more likely to externalize their problems and act out with behaviors that are difficult to manage than to internalize those problems.

The literature on familial caregivers to the frail elderly has repeatedly found that symptoms of caregiver distress, such as depression and caregiver satisfaction, are not mutually exclusive [Lawton et al. 1989]. The results of the present study support these findings. Caregivers in the present study were found to have a moderate degree of depressive symptomatology, as measured by the CES-D Scale, suggestive of exogenously induced, low grade, chronic depression. They simultaneously reported a high level of caregiver satisfaction.

Many observations made in the process of data collection were outside the confines of statistical findings yet provide a contextual understanding of the experience of caregiving in kinship care. As kinship caregivers expanded on their responses to questions contained in the study questionnaire, they described their lives in vivid detail. These descriptions provide a broader framework within which to understand the experience of caring for related children in state custody.

Almost all the caregivers included in the study sample were providing care amid the heartbreak and tragic loss that families experience when one or more of their members become embroiled in the alcohol and drug epidemic rampant in American society. Many of the caregivers had experienced first hand the impact of violence within their communities. They and their families were struggling to cope with ever present danger as well as the aftermath of victimization. A large number of the caregivers interviewed for this study were facing these challenges with virtually no support from the agencies responsible for the children in their care. Although the majority of caregivers indicated they were receiving at least minimally adequate support from the child welfare system, the one-third of caregivers who indicated they were not receiving such support were often at a complete loss regarding how and where essential services could be obtained. Finally, the strengths of the caregiving families, their commitment to the children in their care, and the quality of care they provide regardless of external circumstances inspire profound respect.

Implications

The findings of the present study provide data that can assist child welfare caseworkers in developing appropriate models for role definition, assessment, and support of persons caring for related children served by the child welfare system. The child welfare literature has long acknowledged the importance of kinship care as a placement of choice for many children who require out-of-home care. Kinship care placements last longer and result in fewer placement disruptions than any other type of placement utilized by the child welfare system [Testa 1993]. Further, children in kinship care have been found to fare better than children in other types of placements on various indicators of child well-being [Fein et al. 1983].

The findings of this study provide some initial indications of factors that may contribute to these positive outcomes for children. Kinship caregivers in the study sample were found to bring many strengths to the caregiving situation. These strengths include a strong sense of competence as caregivers based upon a high level of prior experience in caregiving; a solid record of accomplishment as caregivers, which is reflected in improvement in the physical, emotional, and behavioral conditions of the children in their care; and a high level of satisfaction with their role as caregivers. These findings contribute to an understanding of specific strengths of kinship caregivers that can serve as a foundation for the development of strengths-based models for child welfare practice with kinship caregivers.

The inverse relationship observed between sense of control and caregiver satisfaction, combined with statements that caregivers made about their reliance upon God, faith, and spirituality, suggest that child welfare practitioners need to be open to exploring spirituality as a source of support for caregivers. While the central role of the church as an organizing mechanism for African American society has long been recognized, the importance of religious faith as the basic premise upon which many individuals within the African American culture ascribe meaning and find personal fulfillment has not been appropriately incorporated into child welfare practice. Child welfare practitioners need to be cognizant that, at least for some kinship caregivers, their faith in God allows them to transcend the woes of daily life and to persevere in the face of adversity. An important implication of the present study is the need to incorporate these findings into the development of more culturally responsive service models and intervention strategies for kinship caregivers and into education and training curricula for child welfare caseworkers.

The high number of children in kinship care placements who scored in the clinical range on the Child Behavior Checklist has important implications for child welfare practice. Children with this level of functional impairment are in need of services to assist caregivers in addressing both the disruptive behaviors and the underlying emotional trauma the children have experienced. Yet fully one-third of caregivers reported that they received less than adequate support from the child welfare agencies responsible for the children in their homes. The lack of responsiveness by child welfare practitioners to the real needs of the caregivers and the children in their care is a monstrous disservice to the children and families in need. The gap in services identified here calls for the development of service delivery structures that support staff in the provision of needed services and guard against the neglect of major segments of the service population.

The findings of the present study also suggest that kinship caregivers, themselves, have their own problems and needs that must be addressed if they are to provide adequate care for children. The age of caregivers, the severity of health problems from which they and other members of their households suffer, the level of difficulty of behavior problems the children in care bring, and elevated levels of depressive symptomatology experienced by kinship caregivers are only a few of the findings of the present study that suggest kinship caregivers require strong support from the child welfare system. On the other hand, findings such as the high level of experience as caregivers, successful performance as caregivers evidenced by improvement in the condition of children in care, high levels of commitment to the children, and satisfaction as caregivers are indicative of the many strengths kinship caregivers bring to the caregiving situation. These findings provide a deeper insight into the dynamics of kinship care and can inform the development of policies and programs that build on identified strengths while addressing identified needs of kinship caregivers.

References

Achenbach, T. M. (1991). *Manual for the Child Behavior Checklist/4-18 and 1991 Profile.* Burlington, VT: University of Vermont Department of Psychiatry.

Archbold, P. G., Stewart, B. J., Greenlick, M. R., & Harvath, T. (1990). Mutuality and preparedness as predictors of caregiver role strain. *Research in Nursing and Health, 13,* 375-384.

Barbarin, O. A. (1983). Coping with ecological transitions: A psychosocial model. *Journal of Community Psychology, 11,* 308-322.

Berrick, J. D., Barth, R. P., & Needell, B. (1994). A comparison of kinship foster homes and foster family homes: Implications for kinship foster care as family preservation. *Children and Youth Services Review, 16,* 35-63.

Burton, L. M. (1992). Black grandparents rearing children of drug-addicted parents: Stressors, outcomes, and social service needs. *The Gerontologist, 32*(6), 744-751.

Chenoweth, B., & Spencer, B. (1986). Dementia: The experience of family caregivers. *Journal of Gerontology, 26*(3), 267.

Child Welfare League of America. (1994). *Kinship care: A natural bridge.* Washington, DC: Author.

Cicirelli, V. G. (1981). *Helping elderly parents: The role of adult children.* Boston: Auburn House.

Cicirelli, V. G. (1983). A comparison of helping behavior to elderly parents of adult children with intact and disrupted marriages. *The Gerontologist, 23,* 619-625.

Crumbley, J., & Little, R. L. (1997). *Relatives raising children: An overview of kinship care.* Washington, DC: Child Welfare League of America.

Dubowitz, H., Feigelman, S., Harrington, D., Starr, R., Zuravin, S., & Sawyer, R., (1994). Children in kinship care: How do they fare? *Children and Youth Services Review, 16,* 85-106.

Dubowitz, H., Feigelman, S., & Zuravin, S. (1993). A profile of kinship care. *Child Welfare, 72*(2), 153-169.

Fein, E., Maluccio, A. N., Hamilton, V. J., & Ward, D. E. (1983). After foster care: Outcomes of permanency planning for children. *Child Welfare, 62*(6), 485-558.

George, L., & Gwenther, L. (1986). Caregiver well-being: A multidimensional examination of family caregivers of demented adults. *The Gerontologist, 26*(6), 253-259.

Gleeson, J. P., & Craig, L. C. (1994). Kinship care in child welfare: An analysis of states' policies. *Children and Youth Services Review, 16,* 7-31.

Gleeson, J. P., O'Donnell, J., Altshuler, S., & Philbin, C. (1994). *Current practice in kinship care: Caseworker's perspectives.* University of Illinois at Chicago, Jane Addams College of Social Work and Jane Addams Center for Social Policy and Research.

Horowitz, A. (1982). *The impact of caregiving on children of the frail elderly.* Paper presented at the Annual Meeting of the American Orthopsychiatric Association, San Francisco.

Iglehart, A. (1994). Kinship foster care: Placement, service and outcome issues. *Children and Youth Services Review, 16,* 107-127.

Kusserow, R. P. (1992). *Using relatives for foster care* (DHHS Publication No. OEI-06- 90-02390). Washington, DC: U.S. Department of Health and Human Services, Office of Inspector General.

Lawton, M. P., Kleban, M., Moss, M., Rovine, M., & Glicksman, A. (1989). Measuring caregiver appraisal. *Journal of Gerontology: Psychological Sciences, 44*(3), 61-71.

Lawton, M. P., Rajagopal, D., Brody, E., & Kleban, M. H. (1992). The dynamics of caregiving for a demented elder among black and white families. *Journal of Gerontology: Social Sciences, 47*(4), S156-S164.

Magruder, J., (1994). Research Note: Characteristics of relative and non-relative adoptions by California public adoption agencies. *Children and Youth Services Review, 16,* 123-132.

Miller, B. (1991). Elderly married couples, gender, and caregiver strain. *Advances in Medical Sociology, 2,* 245-266.

Miller, B., Davis, L., Farran, C., & Campbell, R. T. (1992). Project CASA: *Caregiver adaptation to spouses with Alzheimer's.* Chicago: University of Illinois at Chicago.

Miller, B., Campbell, R. T., Farran, C. J., Kaufman, J. E., & Davis, L. (1994). *Race, control, mastery and caregiver distress.* Chicago: University of Illinois at Chicago.

Minkler, M., & Roe, K. M. (1993). *Grandmothers as caregivers: Raising children of the crack cocaine epidemic.* Newbury Park, CA: Sage.

Mirowsky, J., & Ross, C. E. (1990). Control or defense? Depression and the sense of control over good and bad outcomes. *Journal of Health and Social Behavior, 31,* 71-86.

Mirowsky, J., & Ross, C. E. (1991). Eliminating defense and agreement bias from measures of sense of control: A 2 x 2 index. *Social Psychology Quarterly, 54,* 955-969.

Parks, S. H., & Pilisuk, M. (1991). Caregiver burden: Gender and the psychological costs of caregiving. *American Journal of Orthopsychiatry, 61*(4), 501-509.

Pearlin, L. I., Mullan, J. T., Semple, S. J., & Skaff, M. M. (1990). Caregiving and the stress process: An overview of concepts and their measures. *The Gerontologist, 30*(5), 583-594.

Petras, D. D. (1998). *The effect of caregiver preparation and sense of control on adaptation of kinship caregivers.* Unpublished doctoral dissertation, University of Illinois at Chicago.

Pruchno, R., & Resch, N. (1989). Husbands and wives as caregivers: Antecedents of depression and burden, *Gerontology, 29*(2), 159-165.

Rabins, P. R., Mace, N., & Lucas, M. (1982). The impact of dementia on the family. *Journal of the American Medical Association, 248*, 333-335.

Radloff, L. S. (1977). The CED-D scale: A self-report depression scale for research in the general population. *Applied Psychological Measurement, 1*(3), 385-401.

Robinson, B. (1983). Validation of a caregiver strain index. *Journal of Gerontology, 38*, 344-348.

Tabachnick, B. G., & Fidell, L. S. (1989). *Using multivariate statistics* (2nd ed.). New York: Harper Collins.

Testa, M. F. (1993). *Home of relative (HMR) program in Illinois: Interim report* (rev. ed.). Chicago: University of Chicago, School of Social Service Administration.

Thornton, J. L. (1991). Permanency planning for children in kinship foster homes. *Child Welfare, 70*, 593-601.

Wilder, D. E., Teresi, J. A., & Bennett, R. G. (1983). Family burden and dementia. In R. Mayeux & W.G. Rosen (Eds.), *The dementias.* New York: Raven Press.

11

Caregiver Burden in Kinship Foster Care

Rocco A. Cimmarusti

According to Scannapieco and Jackson [1996], kinship foster care has great potential for linking child welfare services with the child's family system, culture, and community. They conclude that placing the child with extended family is preferable to placements with strangers, because it preserves the child's history. Further, relatives may more easily serve as role models for the child's birth parents. Additionally, kinship foster care is seen as sensitive to the long tradition of kinship care in the African American community [Billingsley 1992; Boyd-Franklin 1989; Scannapieco & Jackson 1996; Yusane 1990].

The critics of kinship care [Dubowitz et al. 1993], on the other hand, contend that placing children with the same relatives who reared an abusive or neglectful parent is not a defensible decision. They also contend that the child welfare field provides inadequate case planning and services for abused and neglected children placed with relatives.

Little can be said of a definitive nature about the effects of such care arrangements [Berrick & Barth 1994]. There is growing evidence, however, that some of the intended benefits of kinship foster care, as it is currently practiced, have not been achieved. Data gathered to this point indicate, for example, that children in kinship foster care have a lower rate of adoption or return home than the rate for children in other foster care arrangements, although their placements are less likely to disrupt [Berrick et al. 1994; Gleeson & Craig 1994; Iglehart 1994; Thornton 1991; Wulczyn & Goerge 1992]. Kinship foster parents have reported less contact with agency caseworkers than other foster parents and the children in relative placements have reportedly been less likely to see their caseworker than other foster children [Gebel 1996; Iglehart 1994]. Berrick et al. [1994] found that fewer social services were received by children in kinship foster care compared to those in traditional foster care, but visitation between children and their parents was more likely to occur in kinship foster care arrangements than in traditional placements.

Kinship foster care placements are primarily found in urban inner-city settings [Gleeson 1995]. The children are by and large children of color, poor, and being cared for by their grandmothers [Dubowitz et al. 1993; Meyer & Link 1990] whose average age is about 50 years old [Hegar & Scannapieco 1995]. Kinship caregivers are typically older than traditional foster parents, report more health problems, and fewer financial resources than traditional foster parents [Berrick & Barth 1994; Berrick et al. 1993; Gebel 1996]. Further, recent social and economic decline experienced by many African Americans living in poor inner-city neighborhoods may have reduced the capacity of kin networks to provide support to each other [Burton 1992].

The needs of these relative caregivers have not been addressed [Le Prohn 1994]. While there are indications that kinship caregivers suffer more health and emotional problems than other foster parents [Berrick et al. 1994], little is known about the degree of caregiver burden, increased stress, and resulting emotional distress that is experienced by kinship caregivers [Minkler et al. 1992]. Research on other forms of caregiving, however, provides ample evidence that caregiver burden results in increased symptoms of emotional distress [Anthony-Bergstone et al. 1988; Barnes et al. 1992; Bulger et al. 1993; Eisdorfer 1991] and that social support can buffer these deleterious effects [Furstenberg 1980; Greene & Monahan 1989; Halevy 1993; Koeske & Koeske 1990; Lindblad-Goldberg & Dukes 1985; Tausig 1992].

Studies of extended family caregiving in African American families suggest that caregiver burden is an important area for further study. Burton's

[1992] qualitative study of African American maternal grandmothers providing care to the children of their drug-addicted offspring identified three sources of stress that were named by the participating grandmothers: contextual, familial, and individual. Contextual stressors involved dangers associated with the community: drug trade, burglaries, violence, and the like. Familial stressors included the drain of caregiving on family income, caregiving of other children and adults in the household, and the many tasks associated with caregiving. Individual stressors included loss of employment and loss of time for oneself. This sample of grandmothers reported a sense of personal reward for caregiving, despite the various stressors. They also reported needing more formal assistance for providing care, including financial help, legal counseling, parenting classes, job counseling, and assistance in dealing with their drug-addicted offspring.

Unfortunately, contrary to the beliefs about African American extended family's supportiveness, little support by other family members for caregiving was reported by grandparents in Burton's [1992] study. Though the empirical evidence is strong that the extended family [Taylor 1985, 1986, 1990; Wilson 1986] and the church [Taylor & Chatters 1986a;, 1986b; Walls & Zarit 1991] are generally beneficial social supports for African Americans, they may not be of uniform benefit. There is, for example, empirical evidence that indicates older African Americans may be providing more support than they receive [Taylor 1986]. African American males may also receive disproportionately more social support from extended family than their female counterparts [Dressler 1985; Taylor 1986].

The research on family caregiving and grandparent caregiving in the African American community suggests that there is a need to closely examine caregiver burden, social support, and emotional distress, which may be a consequence of caring for a related child who is in the custody of the child welfare system. The relationship between these variables has not been examined in kinship foster care. The child welfare system's increasing reliance on related caregivers makes it imperative that research focus on this area so that kinship foster care arrangements are utilized in a fashion that does not further tax the well-being of caregivers, which ultimately and directly benefits the well-being of the children in substitute care.

Purpose of the Study*

This research focused on the variables of caregiver burden, social support, and emotional distress as related to kinship foster care. Specifically, this study identified the degree of perceived caregiver burden experienced by a sample of kinship caregivers, identified the degree of perceived social supports experienced by these kinship caregivers, and examined the relationship between perceived caregiver burden, perceived social support, and the emotional distress experienced by these kinship caregivers. In addition, caregivers were asked to describe the child's arrival to their home, sources of caregiver burden, sources of social support, and recommendations for improving the child welfare system.

Caregiver burden was conceptualized in this study as the perceived impact on time-dependence, social, physical, emotional, and developmental aspects of the caregiver's life. Emotional distress was conceptualized as the degree of depression, anxiety, hostility, somatization, interpersonal sensitivity, obsessive-compulsiveness, paranoid ideation, phobic anxiety, and psychoticism experienced by the caregiver as a result of the degree of perceived caregiver burden. Social support was conceptualized within an interactional perspective as the caregiver's perception of being cared for, loved, and accepted.

Methodology

A purposive sample of caregivers who had children in their home for at least 90 days was recruited from March to December 1998. Invitations to participate in the interview were sent to more than 1,500 caregivers in Cook County, Illinois. A $20 grocery certificate was offered to each caregiver

*   This project was supported by the Children and Family Research Center, School of Social Work, University of Illinois at Urbana-Champaign which is funded in part by the Illinois Department of Children and Family Services; grant #2010919027, subcontract #97272.

willing to participate in an interview. In all, 80 appointments were scheduled and 65 interviews were completed. Of the 65 participants who were interviewed for the study, 63 were female. Two of these women identified themselves as traditional foster parents after the interview was initiated. Their responses were not included in this study. Responses of the two male caregivers were included. Consequently, the final size of the sample was 63 kinship caregivers. The majority of these caregivers lived in Chicago, with a smaller number residing in the southern suburbs. At the time they were interviewed, all of these caregivers were rearing at least one child who was in the custody of the child welfare system because of abuse or neglect by the biological parents.

A cross-sectional research design was employed using face-to-face interviews with kinship caregivers in their own homes. The interview questionnaire included existing measures for caregiver burden, perceived social support, and emotional distress, as well as a series of open-ended questions designed to elicit supplemental feedback from the participating caregivers [Cimmarusti 1998]. Each participant was asked to describe specific concerns facing kinship caregivers and to make suggestions for possible improvements in services that child welfare professionals provide to kinship caregivers and their families. Written responses to the various open-ended question were recorded by the researcher during the interview. Every attempt was made to record the caregivers' responses verbatim. When this was not possible, the respondent's main ideas were recorded.

Instrumentation

The independent variables in this study were caregiver burden and perceived social support. Caregiver burden was measured by the Caregiver Burden Inventory [Novak & Guest 1989]. Perceived social support was measured by the Social Support Appraisals Scale [Vaux et al. 1986]. Emotional distress was the dependent variable and was measured by the Symptom Checklist-90-Revised [Derogatis 1994; Derogatis et al. 1976]. Each of the measures are briefly described in this section.

The Caregiver Burden Inventory (CBI) was developed by Novak and Guest [1989] for use with caregivers of persons with Alzheimer's disease. Psychometric studies have been conducted on the five subscales of the CBI and report high levels of internal reliability [Vitaliano et al. 1991]. Internal consistency reliability coefficients were computed with data collected for this study for each of the five subscales and for the full-scale CBI. The reliability coefficients were .79 for the time-dependence burden subscale, .82 for the developmental burden subscale, .78 for the physical burden subscale, .65 for the social burden subscale, and .85 for the emotional burden subscale. The reliability coefficient for the full scale CBI was .91.

The Social Support Appraisal Scale (SSAS) was employed to assess the social support dimension. The SSAS is a 23-item instrument developed by Vaux et al. [1986] based upon Sidney Cobb's definition of social support [Cobb 1974, 1976]. The completed instrument provides a total score, a score for the appraisal of support from family, and a score for the appraisal of support from friends. Reported reliability coefficients from a previous study were .90 for the total SSAS scale, .81 for the family subscale, and .84 for the friend subscale [Vaux et al. 1986]. Good convergent validity was also identified. The internal consistency coefficients were computed with data collected for this research resulting in a full-scale (SSASFS) reliability coefficient of .94. The family subscale reliability coefficient was .89, and the reliability for the friend subscale was .90.

The Symptom Checklist-90-Revised (SCL-90-R) consists of nine subscales, including somatization, obsessive-compulsive, interpersonal sensitivity, depression, anxiety, hostility, phobic anxiety, paranoid ideation, and psychoticism [Derogatis 1994]. The SCL-90-R provides three methods for examining the level of emotional distress: the Global Severity Index, the Positive Symptom Total, and the Positive Symptom Distress Index. The Global Severity Index gives an overall estimation of the level of emotional distress, which is considered the best single indicator of the current level of emotional distress [Derogatis 1994; Fiore et al. 1986], and was used for this study. The Positive Symptom Total provides a simple count of the number of symptoms acknowledged and serves as a measure of symptom breadth [Derogatis 1994]. The Positive Symptom Distress Index functions as a measure of response style and reflects the average level of distress reported [Derogatis 1994].

The SCL-90-R is a well-researched instrument. Its reliability, validity, and utility have been tested in more than 940 research studies, with samples similar to the sample in this study [Derogatis 1994]. Reported internal reliability coefficients for the various subscales have ranged from .77 to .90 [Derogatis 1994]. The Cronbach's *alpha* scores computed for this study ranged from .86 to .92 for all except the psychoticism subscale, which had an *alpha* coefficient of .55. The internal reliability coefficient for the full scale SCL-90-R was .97.

Results of the Quantitative Analysis

The characteristics of the caregivers are presented in Table 11-1. The sample compares favorably with other samples of kinship caregivers [Berrick et al. 1994; Dubowitz et al. 1993; Gebel 1996; Heger & Scannapieco 1995]. The typical caregiver in this study was a single-parent female, 50 years old. She lived with three children 9 to 10 years old; at least two of whom have been placed in her home by the child welfare system. The children placed by the child welfare system were typically her grandchildren, male, and had been with her about four years. On average, 2.5 children, placed by the child welfare system, resided with the caregiver. Yet on a daily basis, caregivers provided child care to a median of three children.

Univariate analyses were conducted for the reported caregiver burden, level of emotional distress, and degree of perceived social support (Table 11-2). The mean score for the full scale Caregiver Burden Inventory was 37 and the median was 34, suggesting a moderate degree of overall caregiver burden. The mean score on the social support measure was 37 (median = 39) and suggests that the sample of caregivers perceived themselves to have a moderate degree of social support. The mean value for the Global Severity Index of the Symptom Checklist 90-Revised was .39, placing this sample of caregivers at the 70th percentile on norms for nonpatient adult females. A fair degree of emotional distress is suggested by this value and caregivers reported a wide range of distress, from no distress (minimum = .0) to great distress (maximum = 3.5). The distribution was skewed, however. The median score for the emotional distress measure was .20, a value

---

Table 11-1. Caregiver Characteristics

Characteristics	Number	Percent
Age	N=63	
25-34 years	7	11
35-44 years	14	22
45-54 years	16	25
55-64 years	19	30
65-74 years	6	10
75+ years	1	2
Race		
African American	62	98
Caucasian	1	2
Gender		
Female	61	97
Male	2	3
Marital Status		
Single, never married	11	18
Divorced	15	24
Separated, not divorced	7	11
Widowed	14	22
Married	16	25
Employment Status		
Employed full-time	16	25
Employed part-time	11	18
Unemployed	36	57
Religion		
Baptist	38	60
Jehovah Witness	5	8
Pentecostal	3	5
Catholic	4	6
Other	13	21

---

that placed this population just below the 50th percentile on the norms for nonpatient adult females. While this score also suggests emotional distress, it clearly does not indicate a level of distress comparable to the mean value.

Pearson's correlations were computed for descriptive variables, the Caregiver Burden Inventory, the Social Support Appraisal Scale, and the

Table 11-2. Mean, Median, Range, and Standard Deviation for Caregiver Burden, Social Support, and Emotional Distress Measures

Measure	Mean	Median	Range		S.D.
			Minimum	Maximum	
Caregiver Burden Inventory (Full Scale)	37	34	11	89	16
Social Support Appraisal (Full Scale)	37	39	23	66	10
SCL-90-R Global Security Index	.39	.20	.0	3.5	.58

Symptom Checklist-90-R (see Table 11-3). Results of this analysis indicate that more children were cared for on a daily basis by younger caregivers than by older caregivers. These younger caregivers also experienced greater emotional distress than their older counterparts, as was demonstrated by the inverse slight and significant relationship between caregiver age and the emotional distress scale ($r = -.26$, $p < .05$).

The relationship between the caregiver burden and emotional distress variables demonstrated a strong and significant relationship ($r = .69$, $p < .001$), but no relationship was observed between caregiver burden and social support ($r = .15$, *ns*). Nor was a relationship found between the social support and emotional distress variables ($r = .18$, *ns*). At least with this sample, using these measures, social support did not appear to have an effect on caregiver burden or on emotional distress experienced by kinship caregivers.

Qualitative Results

Responses to the open-ended questions were content analyzed, first aggregating them and organizing them by four general areas: the child's arrival, sources of caregiver burden, sources of social support, and recommendations for improving the child welfare system. The major themes that were repeated by several caregivers are reported in this section.

Table 11-3. Zero-Order Correlations Between Descriptive, Independent, and Dependent Variables

Variables	1	2	3	4	5	6	7	8	9
1 Caregiver's age	1.00								
2 Caregiver's marital status (0=no, 1=yes)	.17	1.00							
3 Caregiver employed (0=no, 1=yes)	.17	.10	1.00						
4 Number of persons in household	-.23	.43**	.01	1.00					
5 Number of relative foster children	-.01	.20	-.10	.80***	1.00				
6 Number of children cared for daily	-.27*	.09	-.11	.70***	.72***	1.00			
7 Caregiver Burden Inventory (Full Scale)	-.06	-.09	.01	.03	.04	.16	1.00		
8 Social Support Appraisal (Full Scale)	.15	.21	-.08	-.07	-.14	-.20	.15	1.00	
9 SCL-90-R Global Severity Index	-.26*	-.10	-.11	.18	.12	.17	.69***	.18	1.00

* $p \leq .05$ (two-tailed)
** $p \leq .01$ (two-tailed)
*** $p \leq .001$ (two-tailed)

The Arrival of the Children

Caregivers reported that placement of the children occurred either as the result of a call from the police or the child welfare system, or the children had lived with them for a long time and the child welfare system intervention with the birth parents only formalized the existing living arrangement. Many of the children in placement with this group of caregivers had lived intermittently with the caregiver for years before coming to the attention of the child welfare system. Often in these situations, it was the caregivers, themselves, who eventually called the birth parents to the attention of the child welfare system, because the caregiver was aware of the child's need for help. For caregivers who made the referral to the child welfare system, taking the children into their home seemed the only way to rescue the children from their parents. Several caregivers reported making repeated calls to ascertain the whereabouts of their related child or to request the child's placement with them.

When caregivers received the children from police or directly from the shelter, they reported that these children often arrived with few articles of clothing and little else in the way of possessions. In these situations, clothes for the children had to be purchased immediately by the caregiver and contributed to making the transition into their home a stressful one. Caregivers reported that once the children arrived they were often uncontrollable or inconsolable at first and that they stole food, broke furniture, or did not even know how to use a knife and fork. Some children were so traumatized by the events of abuse or neglect they had experienced prior to their arrival in the caregiver's residence that they tried to harm themselves or other children living in the home.

Concern for the Children

Caregivers reported a variety of concerns for the children. Most, however, were concerned for the children's general well-being. Caregivers also expressed concerns that the children not become involved with gangs or drugs. In some instances this was stated as concern that the children not act like their parents.

A number of caregivers worried that the children might return home before their parents were ready to care adequately for them. Others were concerned that the parents would never "get themselves together" to warrant return of the children. Still others were concerned that the child welfare system was taking too long to determine a permanent placement for the children.

A group of caregivers expressed grave concern over the children's behavior. Others worried that the children receive needed therapeutic resources and services or that services might be lost if they agreed to adopt or assume legal guardianship of the child. Caregivers also expressed concern over their ability to parent the children. Statements like, "I need to learn discipline styles that work," or "All their rules for disciplining the child make it hamper me," were expressed. Other caregivers were concerned over what might happen to the children if the caregiver could not provide care due to illness or death.

Other Sources of Caregiver Burden

In terms of stress resulting from family conflict, a number of caregivers reported angry feelings toward the parents of the children. Anger was expressed over the parents' irresponsibility with the children, as well as over the child welfare system's continuing work with these parents. Some proposed that the child welfare system should not spend so much time attempting to rehabilitate uncooperative parents.

A number of caregivers reported strained relationships between family members. In some instances, this was regarded by the caregivers as the result of requirements to restrict contact between the children and their parents. In other instances, family conflict seemed to predate the involvement of the child welfare system.

A number of caregivers reported considerable difficulties with child welfare professionals or the services provided by the child welfare system. There were reports of repeatedly lost foster parent license applications or the application process taking up to two years. One caregiver reported being sent to three different locations before being able to obtain her fingerprints to complete the required background check. Others reported not seeing their caseworker for months at a time. In one instance, the caregiver reported not seeing a caseworker for more than one year. Still others reported that it took weeks to receive a return phone call from their caseworker.

Caregivers also reported experiencing considerable turnover among child welfare agency caseworkers. One reported having eight to ten caseworkers in five years. Sometimes caregivers felt that caseworkers lacked respectfulness or a professional demeanor. Some caregivers reported being made to feel suspect by the curtness of the caseworker. Others reported that their caseworkers complained so often about their heavy caseloads that the caregivers regarded this as a message that they should not make more requests of their caseworkers' time. One reported that the caseworker never visited the home but phoned to ask the caregiver to indicate that visits were occurring if asked. Many reported that it often took weeks or months for some action to occur that was promised by the caseworker. Some reported feeling lied to, giving examples of caseworkers promising to reimburse them for something but failing to follow through.

Caregivers reported serious problems with the length of time it took to begin receiving financial support to help them care for the children. A number reported waiting three or four months, which the caregivers regarded as an extremely long time—especially in those instances when the child arrived with inadequate clothing or supplies. Caregivers also complained about the amount of time they waited before receiving a voucher for services (from camp fees to graduation fees). Caregivers reported often paying out-of-pocket for items or services for the children in their care, because the caseworker took too long to process the paperwork, did not respond to the caregiver's request, or the caregiver was not informed by the caseworker that the item could be paid for by the child welfare system.

Many caregivers reported feeling that the child welfare system took advantage of their relationship to the child by using delaying tactics that caused caregivers to pay out-of-pocket for services. These caregivers reported discrepancies between the services available to nonrelated foster parents compared to those available to kinship foster homes, particularly respite for the caregiver. Caregivers reported receiving as little as $10 reimbursement for school supplies. A few others reported that their board payment check was returned for insufficient funds, causing their finances to experience a major upheaval. In a few instances, caregivers of children with handicapping conditions reported that they were unable to receive the same special services and fees to help them meet the children's needs that nonrelated foster parents receive to care for children with identical conditions. One caregiver stated, "I think they hold back on benefits, because they know we're going to do it anyway because we're family." Another stated, "If they weren't my blood, I'd return them."

Sources of Social Support

Caregivers reported that most of the daily and essential social support came from family, church, and friends, respectively. The support of nuclear and extended family and even the children in placement, themselves, were reported as sources of strength for these caregivers. This support primarily came in the form of love received and given and unconditional acceptance, but also through advice, money, food, and other goods. For some caregivers, the very presence of the children, themselves, served to provide meaning and personal reward for the caregiver.

The most often cited source of support, the support that provided the strength to caregivers for providing care on a day-to-day basis, was a deep faith in God. Caregivers related that they relied heavily upon God to provide for them and see them through any challenges or tribulations. They reported that they prayed often and that prayer helped them remain calm and persevere. Various activities at the respective churches were also reported as being helpful in educating and providing activities for the children in their care.

Recommendations for the Child Welfare System

Generally speaking, caregivers recommended more support from the child welfare system. Delays in payments and returned phone calls, lost licensing documents or excessive bureaucratic red tape, disrespectful caseworker behavior or inaccurate information from caseworkers, all added to the burden felt by kinship caregivers. An often-recommended improvement was that kinship foster parents and nonrelated foster parents be treated similarly, that is, receive the same benefits and services. Caregivers seemed to find it difficult to accept this discrepancy since, in their words, "They expect us to do the same job."

Another recommendation included a more thorough monitoring of agencies and caseworkers to ensure that caseworkers behave professionally, respectfully, and are more accurate in the information they dispense. Caregivers felt that caseworkers did not always follow through on their promises to provide services. It was also recommended that the child welfare system process payments for services, referrals for services, or reimbursement vouchers much more quickly. The long delays experienced by caregivers added stress to their role as kinship foster parents.

Conclusions

Results of the quantitative component of this study reveal that the average caregiver in this sample experienced a moderate degree of burden and received scores at the 70th percentile on a standardized measure of emotional distress. There was considerable variance in this sample, with some caregivers displaying very high levels of burden and emotional distress and some caregivers displaying very low levels. Caregivers' scores on the particular measure of social support used in this study were not associated with caregiver burden or emotional distress. This social support measure was based upon a conceptualization of perceived social support as being cared for, loved, and accepted by persons in their social network. It is likely that this is not the type of social support that kinship caregivers need most. It is likely that the type of social support that may help buffer the effects of caregiver burden and reduce emotional distress is much more concrete or much more spiritual.

Caregivers' responses to open-ended questions and the qualitative analysis of these responses suggest that they defined social support not only as unconditional love and acceptance, but also as advice, money, food, and other goods. Also, the majority of caregivers in this study reported that their relationship with God was their primary source of support. Future research efforts that rely on measures of support that incorporate these concrete and spiritual sources of support may better explain the relationship between these sources of support and the effects of caregiving.

Although generalizability of the findings of this study is limited by a sample that cannot make claims of representativeness, the caregivers who were interviewed provided information that can be helpful in understanding the myriad of challenges and obstacles that confront many relatives who care for children involved with the child welfare system. They contend with difficult-to-manage children, perhaps their own personal health issues or family conflicts, and the large bureaucracy of the child welfare system whose rules and policies are unknown to them. For the most part, they are committed to caring for the children no matter how great the challenge posed by the children's difficulties. At the level of meaning, the children's presence adds personal value to the caregiver.

Kinship caregivers often contend with high caseworker turnover and inadequate or improper information from caseworkers. Sometimes they must deal with caseworkers who are too stressed to listen or who have limited training in the use of engagement skills. They also put up with time delays that seem enormous to them and insinuate a disregard for the well-being of their family. As a consequence, they feel as if those who placed the children with them do not listen and do not care. Nonetheless, the caregivers manage to awaken each morning and resume the task of providing kinship care anew. They face each day with tremendous faith in God's ability to provide for them and the children and make everything work out for the best. This deep faith and the love and assistance of family members and friends sustains these caregivers.

The participants in this study reported several sources of stress, and among them were the difficulties caregivers faced due to the trauma experienced by the children in their care. Another source of stress was conflict between family members that either existed prior to the child welfare system's involvement, became exacerbated by this involvement, or resulted from the involvement of the child welfare system. Stress resulting from negative interactions with child welfare professionals or resulting from the intricacies of the child welfare bureaucracy also added to the burden experienced by this sample of caregivers. The meanings attributed by caregivers to the verbal and nonverbal behaviors of family members and child welfare professional alike seemed a significant factor in their experience of caregiver burden.

Practice Implications

The implications for child welfare practice that flow from the caregivers responses to the open-ended questions are straightforward and clear. Caring for related children is difficult. It is important that the child welfare system not make it more difficult. Caseworkers are thus encouraged to shape their practice in the following manner:

- Caseworkers should do what they say they are going to do. It builds the caregiver's trust.

- Caseworkers should dispense accurate information about the child welfare system to caregivers. Inaccurate information is useless, or worse, damaging.

- Caseworkers should help caregivers negotiate the child welfare system by removing barriers, assisting them to access services, and by sharing information about the system's processes.

- Caseworkers should at all times be respectful of caregivers and show some deference for their previous experience with raising children.

The qualitative data also suggest that caseworker practice with kinship foster care families should attend to the caregiver's attribution of meaning to various aspects of caregiving. What meanings are ascribed and the behaviors to which they lead, may all be significant sources of additional burden for the caregiver. The meaning attached to being involved with the child welfare system will also guide the caregiver's behavior with child welfare caseworkers, as well as guide their understanding of the behavior of child welfare professionals. Thus, caseworkers should attend to this aspect of meaning especially to identify those attributions that work against developing a respectful and collaborative casework process.

Implications for Policy

The current policy debate concerning kinship foster care centers on the nature of the government's involvement with these families. On the one side of the debate, there are the proponents of a least intrusion argument. They regard the current level of service provision to kinship foster care families as too intrusive and disruptive to the families. Such proponents argue that it would be better for these families if government was less involved, the child welfare system provided less monitoring, and there was less involvement with juvenile court.

On the other side of the debate, there are proponents of improved services to kinship foster families. They regard the current level of service provision as inadequate to meet the needs of these families. Instead they focus on methods for improving service delivery and some suggest increasing the board rate for kinship foster care families.

This study suggests that some families need little governmental assistance, while others need considerable assistance. To develop a policy that offers a spectrum of responses targeted to the specific family, child welfare policymakers must abandon their traditional categorical approach to families. The categorical approach may have contributed to current problems facing the child welfare system, by financially supporting families who would have otherwise managed, by providing watered-down services to those needing a more intensive approach, and by providing identical services to parents irrespective of their need for the service (e.g., parenting class, drug assessment, psychological testing).

Improved and thorough collaborative and strengths-based assessment make it more possible to target the degree of government involvement necessary in order to achieve permanency with a particular family. Recognizing that family needs change over time, government should respond flexibly with varying degrees of support. What is needed is policy that allows for idiosyncratic responses to the idiosyncratic needs of the families served by the child welfare system.

References

Anthony-Bergstone, C., Zarit, S., & Gatz, M. (1988). Symptoms of psychological distress among caregivers of dementia patients. *Psychology and Aging, 3,* 245-248.

Barnes, C. L., Given, B. A., & Given, C. W. (1992). Caregivers of elderly relatives: Spouses and adult children. *Health and Social Work, 17*(4), 282-289.

Berrick, J. D., & Barth, R. P. (1994). Research on kinship foster care: What do we know? Where do we go from here? *Children and Youth Services Review, 61*(1/2), 1-5.

Berrick, J. D., Barth, R. P., & Needell B. (1994). A comparison of kinship foster homes and foster family homes: Implications for kinship foster care as family preservation. *Children and Youth Services Review, 16*(1/2), 33-63.

Berrick, J. D., Barth, R. P., Needell, B., & Courtney, M. E. (1993). Relative foster care and the preservation of families: What's the difference? In National Association for Family Based Services (Ed.), *Empowering families: Papers from the sixth annual conference on family based services* (pp. 101-115). Cedar Rapids, IA: Author.

Billingsley, A. (1992). *Climbing Jacob's ladder.* New York: Simon and Schuster.

Boyd-Franklin, N. (1989). *Black families in therapy.* New York, Guilford Press.

Bulger, M. W., Wandersman, A., & Goldman, C. A. (1993). Burdens and gratifications of caregiving: Appraisal of parental care of adults with schizophrenia. *American Journal of Orthopsychiatry, 63*(2), 255-265.

Burton, L. M. (1992). Black grandparents rearing children of drug-addicted parents: Stressors, outcomes, and social service needs. *The Gerontologist, 32*(6), 744-751.

Cimmarusti, R. A. (1998). *Caregiver burden in kinship foster care: Impact of social support on caregiver emotional distress.* Unpublished dissertation, Chicago: Jane Addams College of Social Work, University of Illinois at Chicago.

Cobb, S. (1974). Physiological changes in men whose jobs were abolished. *Journal of Psychosomatic Research, 18,* 245-258.

Cobb, S. (1976). Social support as a moderator of life stress. *Psychosomatic Medicine, 38*(5), 300-314.

Derogatis, L. R. (1994). *SCL-90-R: Administration, scoring, and procedures manual* (3rd ed.). Minneapolis, MN: National Computer Systems.

Derogatis, L. R., Rickels, K., & Rock, A. (1976). The SCL-90 and the MMPI: A step in the validation of a new self-report scale. *British Journal of Psychiatry, 128*, 280-289.

Dressler, W. W. (1985). Extended family relationships, social support, and mental health in a southern Black community. *Journal of Health and Social Behavior, 26*, 39- 48.

Dubowitz, H., Feigelman, S., & Zuravin, S. (1993). A profile of kinship care. *Child Welfare, 72*(2), 153-169.

Dubowitz, H., Zuravin, S., Starr, R. H., Feigelman, S., & Harrington, D. (1993). Behavior problems of children in kinship care. *Journal of Developmental and Behavioral Pediatrics, 14*(6), 386-393.

Eisdorfer, C. (1991). Caregiving: An emerging risk factor for emotional and physical pathology. *Bulletin of the Menninger Clinic, 238-247.*

Fiore, J., Coppel, D. B., Becker, J., & Cox, G. B. (1986). Social support as a multifaceted concept: Examination of Important dimensions for adjustment. *American Journal of Community Psychology, 14*(1), 93-111.

Furstenberg, F. (1980). Burdens and benefits: The impact of early childbearing on the family. *Journal of Social Issues, 36*, 64-87.

Gebel, T. J. (1996). Kinship care and non-relative family foster care: A comparison of caregiver attributes and attitudes. *Child Welfare, 75*(1), 5-18.

Gleeson, J. P. (1995). Kinship care and public child welfare: Challenges and opportunities for social work education. *Journal of Social Work Education, 31*(2), 182-193.

Gleeson, J. P., & Craig, L. C. (1994). Kinship care in child welfare:An analysis of states's policies. *Children and Youth Services Review, 16*(1/2), 7-31.

Greene, V. L., & Monahan, D. J. (1989). The effect of a support and education program on stress and burden among family caregivers to frail elderly persons. *The Gerontologist, 29*(4), 472-477.

Halevy, J. (1993). Bigger can be better: Social network intervention with families in acute distress. In National Association for Family-Based Services (Ed.), *Empowering families: Papers from the sixth annual conference on family based services*, (pp. 37-50). Cedar Rapids, IA: Author.

Hegar, R., & Scannapieco, M. (1995). From family duty to family policy: The evolution of kinship care. *Child Welfare, 74*(1), 200-216.

Iglehart, A. P. (1994). Kinship foster care: Placement, service, and outcome issues. *Children and Youth Services Review, 16*(1/2), 107-122.

Koeske, G. F., & Koeske, R. D.(1990). The buffering effect of social support on parental stress. *American Journal of Orthopsychiatry, 60*(3), 440-450.

Le Prohn, N. S. (1994). The role of the kinship foster parent: A comparison of the role conceptions of relative and non-relative foster parents. *Children and Youth Services Review, 16*(1/2), 65-84.

Lindblad-Goldberg, M., & Dukes, J. L. (1985). Social support in Black, low income, single-parent families: Normative and dysfunctional patterns. *American Journal of Orthopsychiatry, 55*(1), 42-58.

Meyer, B. S., & Link, M. K. (1990). *Kinship foster care: The double edged dilemma.* New York: Task Force on Permanency Planning for Foster Children, Inc.

Minkler, M., Roe, K.M., & Price, M. (1992). The physical and emotional health of grandmothers raising grandchildren in the crack cocaine epidemic. *The Gerontologist, 32*(6), 752-761.

Novak, M., & Guest, C. (1989). Application of a multidimensional caregiver burden inventory. *The Gerontologist, 29*(6), 798-803.

Scannapieco, M., & Jackson, S. (1996). Kinship care: The African American response to family preservation. *Social Work, 41*(2), 190-196.

Tausig, M. (1992). Caregiver network structure, support and caregiver distress. *American Journal of Community Psychology, 20*(1), 81-96.

Taylor, R. J. (1985). The extended family as a source of support to elderly Blacks. The *Gerontologist, 25*(5), 488-495.

Taylor, R. J. (1986). Receipt of support from family among Black Americans: Demographic and familial differences. *Journal of Marriage and the Family, 48,* 67-77.

Taylor, R.J. (1990). Need for support and family involvement among Black Americans. *Journal of Marriage and the Family, 52,* 584-590.

Taylor, R. J., & Chatters, L. M. (1986a). Church-based informal support among elderly Blacks. *The Gerontologist, 26*(6), 637-642.

Taylor, R. J. & Chatters, L. M. (1986b). Patterns of informal support to elderly Black adults: Family, friends, and church members. *Social Work, 31,* 432-438.

Thornton, J. L. (1991). Permanency planning for children in kinship foster homes. *Child Welfare, 70,* 593-601.

Vaux, A., Phillips, J., Holly, L., Thomson, B., Williams, D., & Stewart, D. (1986). The Social Support Appraisals (SS-A) Scale: Studies of reliability and validity. *American Journal of Community Psychology, 14*(2), 195-219.

Vitaliano, P. P., Young, H. M., & Russo, J. (1991). Burden: A review of measures used among caregivers of individuals with dementia. *The Gerontologist, 31*(1), 67-75.

Walls, C. T., & Zarit, S. H. (1991). Informal support from Black churches and the well-being of elderly Blacks. *The Gerontologist, 31*(4), 490-495.

Wilson, M. N. (1986). The Black extended family: An analytical consideration. *Development Psychology, 22*(2), 246-258.

Wulczyn, F. H., & Goerge, R. M. (1992). Foster care in New York and Illinois: The challenge of rapid change. *Social Service Review, 66*(2), 278-294.

Yusane, A. Y. (1990). Cultural, political, and economic universals in West Africa in synthesis. In M.K. Asante & K.W. Asante (Eds.), *African culture: The rhythms of unity* (pp. 39-70). Trenton, NJ: Africa World Press.

Part V
Conclusion

12

Future Directions for Research on Kinship Care

James P. Gleeson and Creasie Finney Hairston

For as long as there has been a child welfare system, kinship care and child welfare have been inextricably linked. When parents have not been able to care for their children, kin have stepped in, and, when kin have not been available, able, or willing to do so, the child welfare system most often has taken over. What is different today about the relationship between kinship care and the child welfare system is that these types of care are no longer mutually exclusive. Approximately one-third of the children in the legal custody of the child welfare system today are living with relatives in kinship foster care, and this percentage is more likely to increase than decrease. This changing relationship between the child welfare system and the extended families of children who come to the attention of this system is what compels us to pursue a vigorous program of research and to encourage others to pursue it as well.

Although several recent policy initiatives are likely to shorten the average length of time that cases remain in the custody of the child welfare system, there are other forces that make it likely that the use of kinship care as a child welfare service will continue. In Illinois, for example, several initiatives aimed at reducing the number of kinship foster placements have been introduced. The state's permanency initiative mandates shorter time frames for case decisionmaking and encourages concurrent planning, expedited termination of parental rights in cases of egregious harm, and fast-track adoption. Adoption redesign and a court improvement project are eliminating delays and shortening the amount of time to achieve legal permanence. The subsidized guardianship demonstration project provides an additional permanency option for many children in kinship foster care. Also, performance-based contracting, a managed care approach to case assignment and agency and staff accountability have been implemented. However, even in Illinois, where reduction of kinship care placements has been targeted, 51% of the children in out-of-home care are living with relatives. Demographic trends, patterns of poverty in the United States, and the increasingly formidable challenge of recruiting nonrelative foster homes suggest that kinship foster care will continue to be an essential component of the child welfare system's array of services.

Demographic projections indicate that the most pronounced growth in the United States' population will be among persons of color and those who are most financially disadvantaged [Sarri 1996]. Given the consistent finding that poverty is a predictor of child welfare intervention and out-of-home placement [Lindsey 1992; Pelton 1994; Wulczyn 1994] and the increasing overrepresentation of persons of color on child welfare caseloads, particularly in kinship care [Harden et al. 1997], it is likely that the demand for formal kinship care services will remain strong. Also, there is little hope that there will be growth in the number of persons interested in becoming licensed foster parents to care for children not related to them by blood or marriage [James Bell Associates, Inc. & Westat, Inc., n.d.]. In addition, the Personal Responsibility and Work Opportunity Reconciliation Act of 1996, which reformed the welfare system, explicitly encourages states to consider placing children with relatives when out-of-home care is necessary.

Hegar [1999] argues that kinship foster care represents the new placement paradigm for the child welfare system in the United States. Yet, as Gleeson's [Chapter 1] review of the research on kinship care reveals, there is much that we still need to learn about the use of kinship care as a child welfare service. The studies reported in this volume addressed some specific knowledge gaps that Gleeson identified. This research falls into three major categories. The first category of studies examines caseworker practice in facilitating permanency, incorporates caseworker and supervisor perspectives to identify barriers to permanency and conditions that facilitate permanency for children in kinship care, and defines components of best practice [Bonecutter, Chapter 2; Gleeson, Chapter 3; Mason & Gleeson, Chapter 4]. A second category includes studies that examine the experiences and involvement of the children in kinship care [Altshuler, Chapter 5], their mothers [Harris, Chapter 6], and their fathers [O'Donnell, Chapter 7]. Hairston's chapter [8] focuses on parents who have been incarcerated and their children placed in kinship foster care, drawing upon the findings of three studies she conducted and forums that focused on families and the correctional system. A third category of studies examines the experience of providing kinship care and its impact on kinship caregivers, relying on data collected from caregivers in their own homes [Cimmarusti, Chapter 11; Osby, Chapter 9; Petras, Chapter 10].

Each of these studies contributes to the knowledge on kinship care as a child welfare service. Each of these studies has implications for child welfare policy and practice. Perhaps even more importantly, at this early stage of knowledge development, these studies have implications for future research. In this chapter, we discuss these implications, outlining a detailed agenda for research on the use of kinship care as a child welfare service. We have organized this agenda around eight general themes that flow from the research reported and issues examined in this volume. They include the following:

- world views of caregivers, parents, extended family, and children;
- consequences of caregiving;
- parents' roles and functioning;
- children's safety and well-being;
- extended family functioning and systems of support;
- casework services;
- the impact of policy initiatives and alternative service models; and
- methodological concerns.

World Views of Caregivers, Parents, Extended Family, and Children

Several chapters of this book on kinship care research demonstrate the importance of understanding individuals' day-to-day lives from their perspectives as a prerequisite for informing the development of effective public policies and programs. The chapters written by Osby [Chapter 9], Petras [Chapter 10], and Cimmarusti [Chapter 11] demonstrate, in particular, the power of an individual's system of beliefs, values, and general views of the world in day-to-day life. While Osby refers to this as a " world view" and uses it to frame her research, Petras [Chapter 10] and Cimmarusti [Chapter 11] discover it through observations and caregivers' responses to open-ended questions that were secondary to the quantitative aspects of their studies. Osby and Cimmarusti refer to the importance of the "meaning" that kinship caregivers attach to caring for relatives and being involved with the child welfare system. These meanings are created through the person's world view.

We have identified three ways that a world view perspective can contribute to knowledge development about kinship care: (1) by helping us understand similarities and differences in the experiences and perceptions of kinship care across cultures and various members of the kinship network (e.g., children, parents, caregivers, other relatives); (2) in formulating research problems and questions and defining outcomes from the perspectives of children, parents, caregivers, and other relatives; and (3) in selecting or developing measures that are appropriate to specific cultural groups and various members of the kinship network.

Experiences and Perceptions Across Cultures and Members of the Kinship Network

Examining and comparing the world views of the various cultural groups involved with the child welfare system is an important area for future research, in part, because this type of research may help us identify effective ways of working with caregivers and other members of a child's kinship network. This type of research may also help us identify the types of services that could be provided to support informal kinship care arrangements and to prevent unnecessary involvement with the child welfare system. This research could also help us identify what services are necessary to assist families of children who are in the custody of the child welfare system.

Cultural experiences shape not only the way in which individuals view the world, but also how they perceive and react to different situations and how they respond to new roles and circumstances. For example, African American families' use of spirituality and religion as a means of dealing with serious family problems and difficulties and the sense of obligation that caregivers felt toward the children in their care and other kin, major findings of Osby, Petras, and Cimmarusti, are essential elements of an Africentric world view (see, for example, Jackson & Sears [1992]). Similarities between the world views presented in these studies with those found in literature on African American culture are not surprising since belief systems and values are embedded in one's culture.

Given the prevalence of kinship care among African American families and the relevance of an Africentric world view, additional research using a world view framework as a means of appraising African American families' kinship care experiences should be undertaken. We need to examine directly how aspects of an Africentric world view such as a communal orientation, shared responsibility for child rearing, spirituality, and time flexibility influence kinship care under informal and formal caregiving arrangements. We also need to examine the factors that influence kinship caregiving within and across other cultural groups. Research of this nature could provide a better understanding of the forces that are instrumental in families' decision making and behaviors and of the ways families mediate stress and obtain and use support. It may also lend understanding to the ways in which proposed and enacted child welfare policies and programs undermine or support individuals and families in kinship caregiving arrangements.

To date there have been no systematic examinations of the world views of other members of the child's kinship system who participate in child-rearing or are otherwise affected by the kinship care arrangement. This may include persons who provide support to the kinship caregiver or who provide direct care to the child. It may also include the caregiver's biological children, grandchildren, spouse, or others who may feel displaced by the child who has been "taken in" [see Crumbley & Little 1997]. Learning more about the perceptions of these family members would improve our understanding of the potential stresses that impact the kinship care arrangement.

It is also important to explore the world views of parents, whether they are attempting to keep their children with them or working to have their children return to them. A world views perspective would also be helpful in examining the adjustment of parents to their children living permanently with relatives or other caregivers through adoption or transfer of guardianship. What is the meaning that parents attribute to the child welfare system's involvement in their lives? What is their understanding of their relatives' role in rearing their children? What is their understanding of their own roles in the lives of their children in the past, now, and in the future? Understanding the world views of parents will help us devise effective policies, programs, and interventions for engaging parents of children in kinship foster care.

A world view perspective can also help us understand the perceptions and experiences of children in kinship foster care. What is their understanding of the reasons that they are involved with the child welfare system and living with relatives? What is their understanding of their relationships with their parents, their caregiver, and other members of the household and extended family? Do these children feel as if they belong, that they have adults in their lives who have made a permanent commitment to care for them until they reach adulthood? Do they believe that they will be cared for and included as a permanent member of the family? Who is it that these children include in their definition of family? What are the factors that were most helpful and most challenging about the kinship foster care experience?

Formulating Research Problems and Questions and Defining Outcomes

Arguably one of the most important parts of the research process is defining the problem that will be studied. A close second is defining the research questions that will guide the study. Implied in both of these is the desired outcome of a successful policy, program, or intervention. This desired outcome is then operationalized through selection or creation of a criterion or dependent measure. Who defines the research problem, questions, and desired outcomes is a crucial question. A world views perspective can be helpful in formulating research problems and in defining desired outcomes from the perspectives of kinship caregivers, parents, children, and other relatives. This perspective can be helpful in generating research questions that address the major concerns of children and other persons who are most involved in the kinship foster care experience. It is important that research problems, research questions, and outcome indicators are shaped by the perspectives of these persons and not only by the child welfare system and policymakers. In line with current thinking about how to make research more useful and relevant, we take the position that persons who are subjects of the research or whose lives are impacted by the research, including clients and service providers, should be included in all phases of research development and implementation.

Selecting or Developing Measures

Using a world views perspective can be helpful in selecting and developing valid measures that are appropriate to the caregivers, parents, children, and other relatives who are affected by the kinship foster care experience. Cimmarusti [Chapter 11] suggests that the measure of perceived social support used in his study did not accurately reflect the types of support and assistance that caregivers may need from their family, friends, and others. While the measures of caregiver preparation and sense of control that Petras [Chapter 10] used in her study have been used in studies of spousal caregivers and caregivers of the frail elderly, it is not clear that these are valid measures of those constructs for kinship caregivers of children in the custody of the child welfare system. A world views perspective may be helpful in developing measures of preparation for caregiving and sense of control that are specifically relevant to the provision of kinship foster care.

Measures of parental motivation to rear their children may also be informed by using a world views perspective. What are the indicators of this type of motivation from the perspectives of these mothers and fathers? A world views perspective may also be helpful in developing measures of a sense of belonging and permanence from the perspectives of children in kinship foster care. Consequences of kinship care arrangements experienced by other members of the child's kinship network may be more accurately assessed by using a world views perspective to identify the items to be included in measures of this construct.

Consequences of Caregiving

Studies conducted by Osby [Chapter 9], Petras [Chapter 10], and Cimmarusti [Chapter 11] indicate that the costs of caregiving are high. Some caregivers in Osby's study reported that loss of employment was one of the costs of caring for their grandchildren. These caregivers were unable to continue their outside employment while caring for grandchildren who were involved with the child welfare system. Also, both Osby and Cimmarusti report that caregivers' intimate adult relationships often became casualties of their decision to assume responsibility for the care of related children. The caregivers interviewed by Petras displayed moderate levels of depression and those interviewed by Cimmarusti displayed a moderate level of caregiver burden and emotional distress. Cimmarusti's study demonstrates that the degree of emotional distress was associated with the degree of burden and Petras' study revealed a relationship between the behavioral problems of the most challenging child in care and caregiver depression.

We believe that there are two types of studies of the consequences of caregiving that are needed to inform development of programs and policies to support caregivers of children in state custody. These are (1) systematic examinations of the sources of caregiver burden, and (2) research and demonstration projects that test the effectiveness of services designed to reduce caregiver burden.

Sources of Caregiver Burden

We do not know how much of the burden experienced by kinship caregivers comes from caring for children, managing the relationships with the children's parents, involvement with the child welfare system and the courts, and from other sources. Caregivers interviewed both by Osby and Cimmarusti reported that dealing with the child welfare and court systems were some of the most stressful aspects of kinship foster care. Petras points out that there are many sources of stress that caregivers experience beyond the decision to care for the related child or their involvement with the child welfare system. Many of the caregivers she interviewed reported that their families had experienced community violence and losses that were not directly related to the kinship foster care situation. Studies are needed that examine the sources of burden and stress that caregivers experience in order to help develop policies, programs, and interventions that help caregivers deal with these stressors and provide adequately for the care of the children in their homes.

The Effectiveness of Services Designed to Reduce Caregiver Burden

Future studies should test the effectiveness of services and interventions designed to reduce caregiver burden and its negative consequences. Cimmarusti concludes that much of the stress experienced by kinship caregivers could be reduced by competent child welfare practice that includes providing accurate information, ensuring access to services and resources in a timely manner, and being respectful of kinship caregivers. Measures of kinship caregivers' satisfaction with child welfare services should be incorporated into program evaluations and studies that test methods of improving the effectiveness of casework services in kinship foster care.

The studies by Osby, Petras, and Cimmarusti indicate that many caregivers require a higher level of services and supports than had been provided to them by the child welfare system. However, not all caregivers need the same services or the same level of intervention. Petras points out that many caregivers in her study had considerable caregiving experience within and outside of the family. These experienced caregivers probably need a different level and type of support and services than is required by less experienced caregivers. Research can be helpful in identifying the various levels and types of services that caregivers need and testing the effectiveness of accurately matching the services and supports with the individual needs of kinship caregivers.

Not all consequences of caregiving are negative. The caregivers interviewed by Petras reported high levels of satisfaction with caregiving and both Osby and Cimmarusti report the obvious pride that caregivers displayed when talking about the related children in their homes. It is important that research efforts include satisfaction with caregiving, pride in the child, and other positive indicators as criterion measures when kinship foster care services are evaluated. As Petras' study points out, caregiver satisfaction and negative consequences of caregiving, such as depression, are not mutually exclusive. It is important that policies, programs, and interventions be tested in terms of their abilities to maintain or increase positive consequences of caregiving as well as reduce negative consequences.

Parents' Roles and Functioning

The Adoption and Safe Families Act of 1997 and local permanency initiatives mandate shorter time frames for permanency planning and place greater emphasis on adoption and guardianship than reunification. The window of opportunity for parents to regain their parenting roles is shrinking, yet, we still have a great deal to learn about quick and effective ways of helping parents do this. Also, we know very little about the roles that biological parents play in the lives of children who are adopted by relatives or for whom relatives assume guardianship, and what impact parental involvement has on child safety, stability of the living arrangement, and well-being of the child. Consequently, research is needed that (1) examines parents' roles and responsibilities in child rearing prior to, during, and after children's placements in kinship foster care; (2) tests the effectiveness of policies, programs, and interventions in engaging and involving parents in the lives of their children and in overcoming problems that lead to involvement with the child welfare system; and (3) determines the impact of parental involvement on child safety, stability of living arrangement, and child well-being.

Parents' Roles and Responsibilities

Research on parents of children in kinship care is sparse. What we do know comes primarily from caseworkers' reports and case records and focuses on the parents' demographic characteristics, their involvement with the child welfare system, and the reasons for the child welfare system's involvement. We know very little about the roles that parents played in the lives of their children prior to the involvement of the child welfare system and how this relates to later outcomes for children. We also know very little about the actual involvement of mothers and fathers in the lives of their children while the children are living in kinship foster care, since much of this contact is not reported to child welfare caseworkers.

Research on fathers of children in kinship care has been even more scarce than the research on mothers. Though fathers may have been involved in their children's lives prior to placement, and even during placement, they are generally overlooked or not included in child welfare system actions. This is the case even in family oriented services such as kinship care. O'Donnell's study [Chapter 7] documents the absence of information about fathers in kinship care case records and the failure of caseworkers to include fathers in planning regarding their children's care and futures. His work also indicates that caseworkers do not view the absence of fathers' involvement in their work as a deterrent to effective casework practice or children's well-being. Further study is needed to determine, however, why caseworkers, in general, exclude fathers, and how, when, and under what conditions they do involve fathers in meaningful ways. Of special significance is the context for practice that is established by agency policies and expectations specific to father involvement. It is also important to determine how, and under what conditions, fathers are involved in their children's lives despite noninvolvement in child welfare planning and services and how they view and carry out parental roles, obligations, and commitments.

A research focus on fathers, including fathers who were not married to children's mothers and/or not living in the same household with children prior to their placement in relatives' homes, would lend greater understanding about father's real, rather than assumed, connections with their children. This understanding might lead to different programs and services for families and children during separation or following reunion, and to the use of different approaches and guidelines in making decisions about children's best interests. Also, it is important to examine the role of stepfathers and other men, such as uncles, mother's boyfriend, even older brothers, who may be "father substitutes" in the lives of children.

Although mothers are much more visible than fathers in the child welfare system, mothers' relationships with their children in kinship foster care and with their relatives who are providing care are not understood that well. Achievement of broad child welfare goals including the preservation of family ties, family reunification, and prevention of return to care depend on better understanding of mothers' and fathers' roles and functioning, their relationships with their children, and their ability to relate to and use effectively systems of social support, including extended family networks.

Effectiveness of Policies, Programs, and Interventions

As Harris' study [Chapter 6] indicates, parents' abilities to function effectively as parents and to resume care of their children are shaped by several factors including their own personal problems or difficulties and their relationship with their children and relative caregivers. Parental drug addiction, incarceration, and mental illness are among the major factors that have resulted in children's placements with relatives. These are also the factors, along with parental interest and involvement, that child welfare decision makers and relatives alike monitor, looking for improvements and changes, in considering when and if children should be returned home, and in some cases even allowed to maintain relationships with parents. Yet, we know very little about the services offered to parents and the effectiveness of these services in addressing these problems. Research is needed which develops and tests services to parents that help them resolve problems and adequately care for their children. In some cases, a positive outcome of these services may be reunification of the child with the parent. In others, the parent may become a supportive person to the child, although the child may live permanently with a relative through adoption or transfer of guardianship.

It is also important to develop and test methods of engaging mothers and fathers in the assessment, case planning, and decision making process and to identify barriers that inhibit fathers and mothers from entering into partnership with social service providers. Hairston [Chapter 8] identifies a series of important research questions that focus on maintaining contact between the child and parent when the parent is incarcerated, but these questions are relevant to any service systems that are involved with the parents of children in kinship foster care. What assistance is needed from the child welfare system and other service systems to facilitate parent-child contact? What roles do kinship caregivers, other family members, and child welfare caseworkers play in maintaining contact between parents and children. What types of support and assistance could be provided to caregivers and other members of the kinship network that would facilitate regular contact? What types of supports and services do caregivers and other members of the kinship network need to help them explain the parents' incarceration, psychiatric hospitalization, or in-patient substance abuse treatment to children?

Impact of Parental Involvement on Child Safety, Permanency, and Well-Being

Research that has focused primarily on nonrelative foster care indicates that parent-child visitation is a positive predictor of reunification [Fanshel & Shinn 1978] and child well-being [Thorpe 1974, 1980; Weinstein 1960]. While research on kinship care indicates that parent-child contact is more frequent when children are placed with relatives [Berrick et al. 1994], an empirical relationship has not been established between parent-child contact, reunification, and child well-being when the child is living in kinship foster care. This study needs to be conducted. It is also important to examine the impact that parental participation in services and involvement in the assessment, planning, and decision making process has on the child safety, stability of living arrangements, achievement of permanence, and child well-being. In addition, studies are needed that examine the different ways that parents remain involved in the lives of children who live permanently with kinship caregivers through adoption or transfer of guardianship? What is the relationship between this involvement and the child's immediate and long-term well-being?

The relationship between mothers' situations and children's well-being found in Altshuler's study of children's kinship care experiences [Chapter 5], indicates that mothers' functioning also directly affects their children's functioning even during periods of separation. Studies of mothers in different circumstances and situations as they relate to their children and children's caregivers are crucial areas for any comprehensive research agenda on kinship care. Similar studies should be conducted that examine the relationship between fathers' functioning and the well-being of children in kinship foster care.

Results of Harris' study [Chapter 6] indicate that mothers of children who had been placed in kinship foster care received support from their extended families, whether the children were reunified with the mothers or remained in kinship foster care. Future studies should examine the relationship between the quality of extended family support that mothers experience and the achievement of permanency through reunification, adoption, or transfer of guardianship to kinship caregivers. Also, it is important to conduct studies that examine whether the quality of relationship between the mother and extended family is predictive of child well-being and stability of the permanent placement.

Children's Safety and Well-being

The essential purpose of kinship care is to protect and nurture children who have been abused or neglected and to assure their healthy development and well-being. Yet, children's well-being is seldom used as a measure of success in assessing child welfare policies, programs, or practices. Although cost of services, length of stay, and the achievement of legal permanence through adoption, private guardianship, and family reunification are appropriate system success measures, they are not synonymous with children's well-being. Measures that are more sensitive to children's developmental needs and family cultures must be developed and used to appropriately assess the status of individual children and to determine the outcomes of different care arrangements for individual children. These measures should be available for research studies and assessment of trends and patterns; more importantly, they should be a component of basic casework practice. As research measures they can be used to compare outcomes for children over time and at different points or stages of their involvement in the child welfare system. They can also be used to assess the effectiveness of different programs or services for children. We believe that research should be conducted that: (1) assesses the safety of children in kinship foster care; (2) examines children's perspectives on safety, permanence, and well-being; and (3) identifies the factors that contribute to the well-being of children in kinship foster care.

Assessing Child Safety

Assessing the safety of children in kinship foster care has not received much attention by researchers. Although a couple of studies have indicated that rates of subsequent abuse in kinship foster homes are lower than observed in licensed, nonrelative foster care, there are methodological concerns with studies that rely on reports of abuse or neglect as a source of data. Since casework contact has been less frequent for children placed with relatives compared to those placed with nonrelatives, it is not surprising that reports of abuse or neglect are also lower. Studies of the factors that predict safety and risk in kinship care are important and are likely to also be helpful in guiding family assessments and the selection of appropriate relative homes for children. Though only a small percentage of kinship homes may present safety risks to children, research in this area is, nevertheless, important. Longitudinal studies that assess the risk of future harm, intergenerational transmission of pathology, and substance abuse problems, as well as factors that may buffer the effects of maltreatment, parental mental illness, and addiction should also be conducted.

Children's Perspectives on Safety, Permanence, and Well-Being

Research on safety, permanence, and well-being should incorporate children's perspectives. It is essential to learn more from children about their concerns, worries, and interests. It is likewise important to know how they experience care and what practices in care could help alleviate their anxieties and fears.

To date no studies have examined the degree of permanence that is experienced by children in kinship care and whether perceptions of permanence become stronger when children are reunited with parents, adopted, or guardianship is transferred to their kinship caregiver. Do these children experience a sense of belonging? Do they feel like a permanent member of the family? Comparing the experiences of children served by a variety of child welfare programs, including family preservation, non-related foster care, residential and group home care, as well as kinship foster care, may provide better understanding of the benefits and the limitations of kinship foster care from the child's perspective.

Identifying Factors That Contribute to Child Well-Being

It is not enough to compare the well-being of children in kinship foster care to that of children in other types of placements. We need to know what factors contribute to or hinder the well-being of children in kinship foster care. Although children in relative foster care may not experience the same type of trauma as children who are placed with strangers, this assumption has not been empirically tested. There are no doubt separation issues and related concerns. Systematic study is needed to determine what factors lessen the trauma and predict positive outcomes for children who are placed with relatives. For example, to what degree does the prior relationship between the caregiving family and the child predict the degree of trauma experienced by the child, the child's adjustment to living in the home, and the child's overall well-being? What type of assistance do caregivers need from the child welfare system to ease the child's adjustment? What are the components of kinship foster care services that help a child feel safe, accepted as part of a family, loved?

As Altshuler [Chapter 5] demonstrates, children are concerned about their futures and what happens to them. These concerns may intensify when they hear or overhear caseworkers and relative foster parents discussing adoption and other permanency options and when they are confronted with whatever the realities of termination of parental rights will mean for them. Older children are also no doubt cognizant of the health problems that their caregivers have and of what that may mean for them in the future. They are also likely aware of the tension or stress that their parents' behaviors may be creating for family members. Effective practice with children and assurance of their well-being requires much more than a cursory notion of how children experience and manage these situations. In-depth interviews with and observations of children under different conditions can provide guidance for programs, services, and casework practice. Research that systematically examines the quality of care in kinship homes, and research that examines the relationship between parenting styles and practices, commitment to the child, and child safety and well-being is also needed.

It is also important to collect data from a variety of sources when studying the well-being of children, including parents, caregivers, teachers, siblings, and other relatives to examine this construct from a variety of perspectives. The validity of research on child well-being can be improved through triangulation of measures collected from several of these sources.

Extended Family Functioning and Systems of Support

There are no published studies of the functioning of extended families of children in kinship foster care, leaving an obvious gap in our knowledge base. Also, there are few studies of the social support available to kinship caregivers or parents of children in kinship foster care. We recommend that research be conducted that systematically examines (1) the functioning of extended families of children in kinship foster care, and (2) the systems of support for kinship caregivers and parents of children in kinship foster care.

Extended Family Functioning

One would expect that extended families that experience less conflict, more easily resolve conflict, and provide greater support to family members are less likely to come into contact with the child welfare system, and if they do, are involved for shorter periods of time. This hypothesis has not been empirically tested. Harris' [Chapter 6] study suggests that strained relationships between mothers and their mothers were more common in those cases where the child remained in kinship foster care compared to cases in which the child was reunified with the mother. It is not known, however, if strained relationships are causes or results of the child remaining in care. Osby [Chapter 9] describes the anger that some grandparent caregivers expressed regarding their adult children's failure to provide adequate care for the grandchildren. Yet, these caregivers were advocates for their children and did not want the child welfare system to judge them unfairly.

A broader exploration of relationships among members of the extended family would reveal whether conflict and anger are common among most members of the extended family or if it is relatively isolated, with most members of the extended family relating in positive and supportive ways. The validity of this broader view of families, recommended by Bonecutter [Chapter 2] for casework practice, can be tested in research. Is healthy and supportive extended family functioning associated with the achievement of safety, permanence, and well-being for the child? Are interventions that help extended family members resolve conflict and engage in decision making effective in facilitating these outcomes?

Systems of Support

Both Cimmarusti's [Chapter 11] and Osby's studies suggest that there are kinship caregivers who receive very little or no support from family or friends. What supports do caregivers need? Is concrete help caring for the child, such as providing transportation, recreation, respite, or financial support most important, as Cimmarusti suggests? Osby reports that the grandparent caregivers who had more contact with family members and received more help in caring for children, were more satisfied with caregiving than those who received little contact or help. Studies are needed that examine the relationship between these variables more closely. Specifically what types of help are best provided by family and other informal systems of support and what types of help are best provided by child welfare agencies or other social services providers? Research is needed that describes how needs for formal social services vary with difficulty of medical, behavioral, or other problems displayed by the child, the level of functioning of the extended family, and the availability and quality of informal supports.

Research is also needed that examines the social support needs of parents who are attempting to keep their families together and are participating in family preservation services as well as those who are attempting to have their children reunified with them. What types of help are needed to support adoptions by relatives or transfer of guardianship to a relative? What types of support are needed from the child welfare system and other formal social service providers? How does the child welfare system assess the adequacy of informal supports? When should the child welfare system get out of the way and let informal systems work? When should the child welfare system intervene to strengthen informal systems or to create informal systems of support? Are there unintended negative consequences of providing formal services and how can these be avoided? For example, when does the provision of formal social services inappropriately replace informal supports?

How do extended families and other informal systems protect children from subsequent abuse or neglect so the child welfare system can responsibly discontinue its monitoring responsibilities? Research is needed that examines this question for families served in family preservation and kinship foster care programs, for families diverted from the child welfare system through informal kinship care arrangements, and for children who are reunified with parents or are placed permanently with relatives through adoption or transfer of guardianship.

Research is also needed that examines what it takes to sustain a support system over time. Are there short-term interventions that the child welfare system and other formal social service systems can provide that would support the efforts of the extended family and other informal support systems over an extended time period?

Casework Services

The major problems which parents of children in kinship care have and the situations which lead to their children's involvement in the child welfare system and placement with relatives are quite serious. The ability of parents to reunify with their children and be positive forces in their children's lives, the ability of relatives to provide adequate care for children who may have multiple problems, and the ability of extended families to adjust to changes in permanent caregiving arrangements in the family depend not only on their personal and family preferences but also on their use of effective social services. These services must recognize and build on strengths while addressing in comprehensive ways their major problems and difficulties. As Harris' study [Chapter 6] suggests, case monitoring is not enough. Models of intensive casework services that are conceptually sound, culturally relevant, and that involve multiple services and the extended family network must be developed, tested, replicated and evaluated. Research findings and theoretical understandings must undergird the development of these models and the training of staff who will used them.

We recommend that research and demonstration projects be conducted that: (1) test the effectiveness, efficiency, and feasibility of models of casework practice with children, parents, caregivers, and extended families; and (2) develop and test models of service coordination when specialized service needs require the involvement of multiple service providers.

Casework Practice with Children, Parents, Caregivers, and Extended Families

As nearly every chapter in this volume indicates, casework practice in kinship foster care is complex. It is complex because it involves so may people:

the children, the parents, the caregivers, and other extended family members, as well as the child welfare system, other service providers, and the courts. As Bonecutter [Chapter 2] points out, the caregiving arrangements often include several large sibling groups living in one home, or siblings living in several different households within the extended family network. Cimmarusti [Chapter 11], Petras [Chapter 10], and Osby [Chapter 9] describe the burden and the multiple challenges that relative caregivers experience, which caseworkers must address in their work on behalf of children. Petras' study [Chapter 10] indicates that some of the children placed in kinship foster care have serious behavior problems and the caregivers of these children may require ongoing behavioral management consultation from the caseworker. Harris [Chapter 6], O'Donnell [Chapter 7], and Hairston [Chapter 8] advocate for greater involvement of the parents of children in kinship foster care in the case assessment, planning, and decision making process and in services to address the parents' problems. Altshuler [Chapter 5] reminds us that children in kinship foster care need to be heard; that caseworkers need to talk to children, listen to children, and involve them in planning for their future. In addition, there are other members of the child's kinship network who may need to be involved in decision making about the future living arrangements for their child. Bonecutter [Chapter 2] and others [see Gleeson, Chapter 1] recommend convening family group decisionmaking meetings to help extended families ensure the safety, permanent living arrangement, and future well-being of children. As complex and demanding as all of these tasks are, they would be considerably easier if they were not further complicated by the policies, procedures, and idiosyncracies of the child welfare bureaucracy, the court system, and the legal process [Gleeson, Chapter 3; Gleeson & Mason, Chapter 4]. We are certainly asking a great deal of caseworkers when we expect them to address these multiple needs for all of the families on their caseloads.

The components of "best practice" that are recommended by the authors of chapters in this book and others are as yet untested. There are at least four steps in the research process that must be undertaken to develop valid models of 'best practice" in kinship foster care that are effective, efficient, and feasible. First, it is important to develop and test methods of teaching specific components of the "best practice" models to child welfare caseworkers. How can child welfare caseworkers best be taught to implement the components of these practice models? Second, it is important to monitor implementation of these practice models in daily practice, to identify barriers to implementation, and to develop and test supportive interventions at the level of the supervisor, agency, and larger systems to facilitate implementation of components of these practice model. Third, it is essential to test the effectiveness of these practice models and their components in facilitating safety, permanency, and child well-being, reduction of caregiver burden and its consequences, and extended family functioning. Finally, it is necessary to refine the practice models based on the results of the prior three types of studies and then to begin the process over again.

Given the implementation problems that were identified in Bonecutter's [Chapter 2] and Mason and Gleeson's [Chapter 4] studies, it is important to examine the limits of best practice. Is it feasible for child welfare caseworkers carrying full caseloads to conduct family group conferences and to mediate disputes within families and between families and the child welfare system? What is the appropriate caseload for this type of practice and is this feasible given the demands for service and cost containment? What types of services should be provided by special service teams or through contracts with private providers? Under what circumstances should families be referred to others for family group conferences or mediation? To what degree should family meetings and mediation become part of casework practice? Research is needed that compares different models of service delivery and casework practice to help service providers and policymakers answer these questions.

Service Coordination

Some problems experienced by children in kinship foster care, their parents, caregivers, and sometimes others in the family, require specialized services. For example, many kinship caregivers in Petras' [Chapter 10] study reported that they and others living in their household had chronic health problems. In addition, many of these caregivers indicated that members of their family had been victims of violence and these families had suffered many losses. All of the studies reported in this volume mention the high level of parental substance abuse problems that contribute to the placement of children in kinship foster care. Harris' study also identified parental mental illness as a contributor to children remaining in kinship foster care. Serious child behavior problems, health problems experienced by children, caregivers, and other members of the family, substance abuse and mental health problems most often require specialized treatment and services that are beyond the expertise and qualifications of most child welfare caseworkers. Supportive social policies and effective case management are required if families are to receive the specialized services that they need to address these serious problems.

Supportive social policies are needed to ensure that these specialized services are funded. Effective case management is needed to ensure that the needs of children and families are accurately assessed and that these children and families are linked to the specialized services that will meet these needs. Effective case management can facilitate appropriate utilization of services by children, parents, caregivers, and other family members. Research is needed that tests the effectiveness of well implemented case management on the achievement of safety, permanence, and well-being for children, reduction of caregiver burden and its consequences, and extended family functioning.

Although the majority of child welfare caseworkers do not have the expertise or the time to provide treatment for substance abuse or mental health problems, they are in key positions to help families understand the impact that these problems have on the children, the caregiver, other members of the household, and other members of the kinship network. Research and demonstration projects could develop and test models of casework practice that help members of the child's kinship network understand this impact and support treatment efforts. These studies could also examine the relationship between extended family support of treatment efforts, treatment outcomes, and the achievement of permanency, safety, and child well-being.

Effective case management is even more challenging when multiple service providers are involved, and when these service providers are driven by different public policies. Hairston [Chapter 8] describes the dilemmas that emerge when parents are incarcerated and their children are in the custody of the child welfare system. Correctional policies and child welfare policies often conflict or run on parallel tracks. It is the role of the case manager to develop an understanding of these policies, facilitate communication between the two systems, negotiate with representatives of the correctional system and the child welfare system to coordinate efforts and facilitate the achievement of safety, permanence, and well-being for the child. Case managers face similar challenges when parents are mentally ill or addicted to alcohol or other drugs, and are heavily involved in a inpatient and out-patient treatment. Also, when domestic violence threatens the safety of mothers of children involved with the child welfare system, the work of service centers for battered women and child welfare agencies need to be coordinated. Child welfare caseworkers are challenged by the competing priorities of these different systems. The primary goals of these various organizations differ and it is the child welfare case manager who attempts to negotiate a common goal that results in safety, permanence, and well-being for the child. Research and demonstration projects are needed that test coordinated service agreements between child welfare systems and correctional institutions, psychiatric and substance abuse treatment centers, and domestic violence programs.

Impact of Policy Initiatives and Alternative Service Models

We recommend that two types of policy research studies be conducted, and that they be conducted as soon as possible. These studies include systematic examination of the impact of (1) recent policy initiatives, and (2) levels of financial support and services on the safety, permanency, and well-being of children in kinship care.

Assessing the Impact of Policy Initiatives

A recent flurry of public policy initiatives have probably already had significant impact on children who are unable to live with their parents and now live with relatives. However, it is not possible to say with any degree of certainty what this impact has been. The Personal Responsibility and Work Opportunity Reconciliation Act of 1996 eliminated Aid to Families with Dependent Children (AFDC), replacing it with Temporary Assistance to Needy Families (TANF), placing new work requirements and time restrictions on the receipt of financial assistance. Since most states had relied on AFDC as a source of financial support for foster care that is provided by relatives who were not licensed foster parents, it is likely that many children placed in kinship foster care and their families were affected. While work requirements and time limits do not apply to persons caring for dependent relative children, they do apply to those caregivers who receive TANF for their biological children. It is not known how many children and families have been affected by this policy change, and how these families have adjusted to this change. In many cases, the time limits are just becoming effective, so results of these time limits are not yet known. We also do not know what impact these changes are having on informal kinship care and whether more children will be coming to the attention of the child welfare system because kinship caregivers are unable to continue to provide care without the financial support they had previously received. We also do not know if changes from AFDC to TANF affect caregiver burden, extended family support, child safety, or child well-being. These are important considerations and research is needed that examines them closely.

Now is the time to conduct research that examines the impact of the Adoption and Safe Families Act of 1997, permanency initiatives in various states, court improvement projects, subsidized guardianship demonstration projects, concurrent planning, performance-based contracting and other managed care approaches. These federal and state policy initiatives seem to have the potential to reduce caseload size and to be declared an overwhelming success. It is important, however, that success be measured through the eyes of several different interested parties. For the child welfare system, reductions in caseload size and the cost of providing care may be good news. For children is may be good news that more children are reunified with parents, adopted or placed permanently with relatives or others through transfer of guardianship. However, it is also important to examine the safety and well-being of these children in the short and long run. We must be concerned about those children who reenter the custody of the child welfare system because reunification, adoption, or transfer of guardianship was not appropriate or was not adequately supported. We must also be concerned about those children who do not appear again on child welfare caseloads but who are worse off than they were before the child welfare system discharged them from care. Research is needed that addresses these crucial issues.

Research is also needed that examines the well-being of children who are returned to their parents, are adopted by relatives and non relatives, or who exit the custody of the child welfare system through transfer of legal guardianship to a relative or nonrelative caregiver. It is important to examine child well-being and family functioning within each of these permanency options, in relationship to the decision making process that was used to arrive at the particular permanent plan. Both Bonecutter's [Chapter 2] and Gleeson's [Chapter 3] studies indicate that permanency decisions are often made by the child welfare system and other formal social service providers with little involvement of the children and family members who are most affected by the decision. Research is needed that examines whether permanency plans that are achieved through informed family decision making are longer lasting and result in higher levels of child well-being and family functioning and lower levels of caregiver burden than permanency plans that are enacted primarily through decisions by social service professionals.

The shortened time lines for decision making, increased pressure to terminate parental rights, and initiatives that encourage relatives to adopt or take guardianship may have unintended negative effects on caregivers, parents, and other family members. Do these policy initiatives further strain relationships among family members as Cimmarusti's [Chapter 11] study suggests? It is important to measure this type of strain over the course of the child welfare system's involvement. How does this strain vary with discussions of reunification, termination of parental rights, adoption, or transfer of guardianship?

Impact of Different Financial Support and Services for Kinship Foster Care

In Chapter 1, Gleeson cites studies which consistently demonstrate that special service fees and access to specialized services are rare for children placed with kin, yet Petras' [Chapter 10] study is consistent with others that found that a substantial portion of children in kinship care need special services. Research is needed that systematically tests the effects of providing special service fees and specialized services on the achievement of child safety, permanency, and well-being as well as extended family functioning and caregiver burden. Also, research and demonstration projects should be conducted that systematically examine whether children with serious emotional and behavioral problems can be adequately served in kinship foster care if intensive mental health services are provided on an outpatient basis.

Similarly, the impact of providing substantially lower subsidies for kinship homes that are not licensed as foster homes than is provided for licensed foster care needs further study. The impact of licensing itself requires further study. Does meeting licensing standards indicate that a home is of higher quality than a home that does not meet these standards, when quality is measured by improvements in child safety, permanency, and well-being? If better outcomes are achieved in licensed homes, are these due to the quality of the homes or more adequate economic resources because of the foster home subsidy? Research is needed that examines these questions.

Methodological Concerns

Methodologically rigorous research designs, valid and reliable measurement instruments, and appropriate data analysis and interpretation must be used in evaluating program results, benefits, and outcomes. Earlier in this chapter, we discussed the importance of using a world view perspective in formulating research problems and questions and in selecting or developing measures that are appropriate to specific cultural groups and various members of the kinship network. There are three additional substantial, yet common, methodological challenges facing kinship foster care research. These include (1) balancing generalizability and depth; (2) establishing causal relationships; and (3) examining trends over time.

Balancing Generalizability and Depth

Research on kinship care has included: analysis of administrative data collected by child welfare agencies in the normal course of business, surveys that compare kinship foster care and nonrelated foster care; structured interviews with caseworkers, kinship caregivers, and parents; and in-depth qualitative interviews with caregivers and children. One of the benefits of administrative data is that it is collected for all cases that are in the custody of the child welfare system, making it the most representative and generalizable of the four types of studies mentioned. The problem with studies that rely on administrative data is that they are only able to analyze the limited number of variables that are part of the agency information system and they are limited to the way that these variables are measured.

Studies that rely on smaller samples cannot claim to be as representative of the population of children in care but are often able to develop richer descriptions of the phenomenon under study and may explain patterns observed in administrative data. Studies that rely on interviews with caseworkers are able to recruit relatively representative samples, but some limits need to be placed on the amount of time that caseworkers spend in research activities. Several studies in this book analyzed data collected during the "Achieving Permanency for Children in Kinship Foster Care Project" which selected two cases randomly from the caseloads of caseworkers in participating agencies. The problem with this type of study is that it relies totally on caseworkers as sources of information. When children, parents, caregivers, or other family members are interviewed directly, recruitment of a representative sample is considerably more challenging.

Human subjects procedures that protect potential participants from unwanted intrusion, low response rates, and suspicions that potential participants have about research, all present barriers to recruitment of a representative sample. Without some confidence that the sample that is selected is representative, one is unable to determine if the findings are typical, represent persons who are higher functioning or have greater resources, or represents those who are lower functioning and have fewer resources.

Two types of solutions are proposed. Research efforts that engage child welfare practitioners in data collection efforts and provide incentives both to clients and caseworkers are likely to result in higher participation rates and, therefore, more representative samples. In addition to incentives, caseworkers and clients will be more likely to participate in studies if they have some influence on the definition of the research problem, research questions, design of the study, and dissemination of the results.

A second solution also relies on caseworkers. It involves incorporating specific measures in administrative databases [Altshuler & Gleeson 1999]. This is clearly only a partial solution, because increasing the amount of data that caseworkers must collect on all cases increases the already heavy paperwork burden on caseworkers, and may decrease the accuracy of all data collected. Short-term additions to administrative data bases for specific purposes or replacement of current requirements with more appropriate data collection requirements may be considered.

While larger samples that are randomly selected tend to be more representative, more detailed, information rich data can be collected and analyzed with smaller samples. Generalizability of findings of these studies can be improved through replication with different segments of the population. Replications of studies in different states with different policies and different demographics is also important to determine whether findings of the original study will be repeated, transcending differences in the policies, the demographics, or other factors

Establishing Causal Relationships

The ability to determine causal relationships is most important when testing the effectiveness of policies, programs, and practice models in achieving specific case outcomes. While multivariate statistical models are often used to test hypotheses of causal inference, experimental designs do the best job of establishing causality. The subsidized guardianship IV-E waiver demonstration project in Illinois is an example of a study that uses an experimental design, randomly assigning eligible cases to an experimental group which has the opportunity to select subsidized guardianship as a permanency option and a control group that does not have this option [IDCFS 1995]. This is a large scale project with a large sample and substantial financial support. Smaller studies that are much less expensive may be conducted to test the effectiveness of program interventions, training programs for caseworkers, etc. Replication of smaller scale studies to determine if the findings were a fluke of the specific sample or location can be as effective in establishing causal links as large scale studies.

When random assignment to experimental and control groups is not possible, quasi-experimental designs are recommended. For example, one team of caseworkers could be trained to implement family group decision making meetings, comparing the case outcomes they achieve to those achieved for similar cases served by caseworkers not yet trained in the this intervention method. While one cannot be certain that any differences in outcomes are attributable to differences in interventions, replication is helpful here as well. It is highly unlikely that replicated quasi-experiments would consistently demonstrate more favorable results for cases exposed to the experimental intervention unless the intervention contributed to these results. Of course, if findings of replications differ, then causal relationships cannot be assumed.

Examining Trends over Time

Some of the more compelling questions that have not been answered are related to changes that may occur over time for children, parents, caregivers, and other members of the kinship network. For example, how does caregiver burden and caregiver satisfaction vary over time. Does caregiver burden increase while satisfaction decreases? Do both increase or decrease? What factors affect caregiver burden and satisfaction early and later in the caregiving relationship? Measures of child well-being, parental participation and functioning, extended family functioning, and adequacy of social support systems administered over time using longitudinal research designs could be useful in understanding these changes, developing assessment tools that are sensitive to these changes, and developing interventions that are specific to changes that occur over time as well. Longitudinal studies can also be helpful in developing understanding of changes in children's perceptions of belonging, being loved, and feeling safe that occur over time and as changes in case status occur, such as reunification, adoption, or transfer of guardianship.

There are several logistical problems in conducting longitudinal studies. Probably the most difficult problem is loss of subjects, which increases as time passes. It is often difficult to recruit a representative sample for any type of child welfare study. If a representative sample is recruited, but a significant percentage of the sample drop out, cannot be found, or refuse to participate at later data collection points, the sample may no longer be representative. Mechanisms can be put in place to reduce subject loss through follow-up tracking and incentives, but these are expensive undertakings. Also, there is always a question of relevance when longitudinal studies span a long time period. For example, findings from a longitudinal study of children entering kinship foster care ten years ago may teach us a great deal about changes that families in this study experienced over the last ten years, but would these findings be relevant to children entering kinship foster care today?

Conclusion

Although the research has grown considerably since 1990, there is much that we do not know about the use of kinship care as a child welfare service. This chapter describes an extensive agenda for research on kinship care that builds on the findings of studies described in earlier chapters of this book, and addresses many of the knowledge gaps that remain. We describe a research agenda that encourages further examination of the world views of caregivers, parents, extended family members, and children who are involved with the child welfare system and live with kin. We encourage systematic study of the positive and negative consequences of caregiving, the roles and functioning of parents of children in kinship care, the safety and well-being of children in kinship care, and the functioning of extended families and other systems of support. We also encourage research that is instrumental in improving casework services in kinship care and systematically examines the impact of policies and alternative service models that are being applied to kinship care. Finally, we encourage research that improves upon the methodologies employed thus far in the quest to build knowledge about the use of kinship care as a child welfare service.

References

Altshuler, S. J., & Gleeson, J. P. (1999). Completing the evaluation triangle for the next century: What is "child well-being" in family foster care? *Child Welfare, 78* (1), 125-147.

Berrick, J. D., Barth, R. P., & Needell, B. (1994). A comparison of kinship foster homes and foster family homes: Implications for kinship care as family preservation. *Children and Youth Services Review, 16,* 33-63.

Crumbley, J., & Little, R. L. (Eds.). (1997). *Relatives raising children: An overview of kinship care.* Washington, DC: Child Welfare League of America.

Fanshel, D., & Shinn, E. B. (1978). *Children in foster care.* New York: Columbia University Press.

Harden, A. W., Clark, R. L., & Maguire, K. (1997). *Informal and formal kinship care: Volumes 1 and 2.* Washington, DC: U. S. Department of Health and Human Services.

Hegar, R. L. (1999). Kinship foster care: The new child placement paradigm. In R. L. Hegar & M. Scannapieco (Eds.), *Kinship foster care: Practice, policy, and research* (pp. 225-240). New York: Oxford University Press.

Illinois Department of Children and Family Services [IDCFS]. (1995, July 31). *Illinois Title IV-E Waiver Request.* Chicago: Author.

Jackson, A. P., & Sears, S. J. (1992). Implications of an Africentric worldview in reducing stress for African American women. *Journal of Counseling & Development, 71,* 184-190.

James Bell Associates, Inc., & Westat, Inc. (n.d.). *The national survey of current & former foster parents*. Washington, DC: U. S. Department of Health and Human Services, Administration for Children and Families, Administration on Children, Youth, and Families.

Lindsey, D. (1992). Adequacy of income and foster care placement decision: Using an odds ratio approach to examine client variables. *Social Work Research & Abstracts, 28*(3), 29-36.

Pelton, L. H. (1994). The role of material factors in child abuse and neglect. In G. B. Melton & F. D. Barry (Eds.), *Protecting children from abuse and neglect* (pp. 131-181). New York: The Guilford Press.

Sarri, R. C. (1996). An agenda for child and youth well-being. In P. R. Raffoul & C. A. McNeece (Eds.), *Future issues for social work practice* (pp. 141-150). Needham Heights, MA: Allyn & Bacon.

Thorpe, R. (1974). Mum and Mrs. So & So. *Social Work Today, 4,* 691-695.

Thorpe, R. (1980). The experiences of children and parents living apart. In J. Triseliotis (Ed.), *New developments in foster care and adoption* (pp. 85-100). London: Routledge & Kegan Paul.

Weinstein, E.A. (1960). *The self-image of the foster child*. New York: Russell Sage Foundation.

Wulczyn, F. (1994). Status at birth and infant placements in New York City. In R. P. Barth, J. D. Berrick, & N. Gilbert (Eds.), *Child welfare research review: Volume one* (pp. 146-184). New York: Columbia University Press.

About the Editors

James P. Gleeson, Ph.D., is Associate Professor at the Jane Addams College of Social Work, University of Illinois at Chicago, where he teaches in the Child and Family Concentration of the M.S.W. program and in the Ph.D. program. Dr. Gleeson completed his M.S.W. and Ph.D. degrees at the Jane Addams College of Social Work in 1984. He has extensive experience as a child welfare practitioner, administrator, consultant, and researcher. He has been principal investigator for several federal- and state-funded child welfare research, curriculum development, and training projects. Dr. Gleeson has conducted more than 60 workshops and presentations at national and local conferences and has authored or co-authored more then 30 journal articles, book chapters, training manuals, and technical reports. Dr. Gleeson's research and publications focus on kinship care policy and practice, child welfare training, and evaluation of child welfare programs and practice. His articles have been published in *Child Welfare*, the *Journal of Multicultural Social Work*, *Children and Youth Service Review*, *The Clinical Supervisor*, *Administration in Social Work*, the *Journal of Social Work Education*, and *Adult Education Quarterly*. Dr. Gleeson is a reviewer for *Child Welfare* and is a member of the Child Welfare League of America's national task force on the development of best practice standards for kinship care.

Creasie Finney Hairston, Ph.D., was appointed Professor and Dean of the Jane Addams College of Social Work, University of Illinois at Chicago, in 1991. Previously, she served as Associate Dean at the Indiana University School of Social Work and on the faculties of the University of Tennessee, West Virginia University, and the State University of New York at Albany. Dr. Hairston is an active researcher and program consultant and is one of the pioneers in the development of family programs in prisons and jails. She is a member of the National Institute of Justice's national working group on children, families, and the criminal justice system and several state and local groups concerned with children's well-being. She has written extensively on management of nonprofit agencies and policies and services affecting poor children and families and has served as editorial consultant for *Administration in Social Work, Journal of Social Services Research, Journal of Social Work Education*, and *Families in Society*. Dr. Hairston is guest co-editor of a recent special edition of Child Welfare and was keynote speaker at the Child Welfare League of America's Institute on Children of Incarcerated Parents. Her articles appear in publications for general audiences and in leading academic journals, including *Social Work, Affilia, Journal of Social Work Education, Administration in Social Work*, and the *Journal of Sociology and Social Welfare*. Dr. Hairston received her B.S. degree with highest honors from Bluefield State College and her M.S.S.A. and Ph.D. from Case Western Research University.

About the Contributors

Sandra J. Altshuler, Ph.D., is currently on the faculty at the University of Illinois at Urbana-Champaign as Assistant Professor teaching courses in School Social Work, Group Work, and Interventions with Children and Adolescents. Dr. Altshuler's current research focuses on supporting the well-being of children living in foster care. She has been principal investigator for two projects: "Comparing Adolescent Health and Well-Being Across Populations in Care" and "Evaluating the Effectiveness of Teachers-as-Mentors for Students Living in Foster Care." Dr. Altshuler is currently principal investigator for "Aging Out of Care: The Experiences of Older Adolescents in Foster Care." She received her Ph.D. from the Jane Addams College of Social Work, University of Illinois at Chicago, in 1996. Prior to that, she provided clinical social work services to children, adolescents, and their families for more than 10 years in a variety of settings.

Faith Johnson Bonecutter, M.S.W., is Clinical Associate Professor at the Jane Addams College of Social Work, where she teaches courses in social work practice and currently directs the B.S.W. program. She has more than 15 years' experience providing training, consultation, and technical assistance to schools, mental health agencies, public and private social service agencies related to services to low income and minority children and families. Professor Bonecutter was training director for a three-year research and demonstration project on permanency planning for children in kinship care and has been co-principal investigator of the Kinship Care Practice project of the Jane Addams College of Social Work since 1995. She is the primary author of *Achieving Permanency for Children in Kinship Foster Care: A Training Manual* and is co-author of several articles on kinship foster care.

Rocco A. Cimmarusti, Ph.D., is Coordinator of Evaluation, The Family Institute at Northwestern University and Lecturer in the Department of Counseling Psychology, School of Education and Social Policy. Dr. Cimmarusti has more than 20 years of experience as a social worker and family therapist, and more than 14 years of professional experience in the child welfare field. He wrote the family systems training curricula for the family preservation and family reunification initiatives of the Illinois Department of Children and Family Services and has consulted with and training many public and private sector child welfare professionals. For nine years, Dr. Cimmarusti was a family therapy trainer with the Family Systems Program, Institute for Juvenile Research. He has published numerous articles and book chapters on family therapy training and supervision, child welfare, school truancy, clinical assessment, and kinship foster care.

Marian S. Harris, Ph.D., is Assistant Professor at the Jane Addams College of Social Work. She recently completed an NIMH Postdoctoral Fellow in the Mental Health Services Research Training Program at the University of Wisconsin, School of Social Work in Madison. For the past 20 years, Dr. Harris, a licensed clinical social worker and diplomate in clinical social work, has focused her career on children, adolescents, and families. Dr. Harris is Adjunct Assistant Professor and Research Advisor at the Smith College School for Social Work, where she has lectured for the past three years. She is a former lecturer at the University of Chicago, School of Social Service Administration. Her current research includes two studies: "Foster Care Placement and Discharge: Issues of Race" and "Family Structure and Mother-Child Interaction in Early Head Start Families." Dr. Harris received her Ph.D. in 1997 from the Smith College School for Social Work, where she received the Roger R. Miller Dissertation Grant from the

Smith College Alumni Association. Dr. Harris' work on kinship care has been completed in connection with the Jane Addams College of Social Work. As an administrator in one of the demonstration sites, Dr. Harris was involved in the development and implementation of the first phase of the "Achieving Permanency for Children in Kinship Foster Care" project in 1992.

Sally J. Mason, Ph.D., is Assistant Professor of Clinical Social Work in Psychiatry at the Institute for Juvenile Research, University of Illinois at Chicago. Dr. Mason completed the M.S.W. degree at Loyola University of Chicago and her Ph.D. from the Jane Addams College of Social Work. She is principal investigator for "Kin Caregivers for HIV-Affected Children: Identifying Services That Support Permanency" and the evaluator for the "Family Options Project," a federally funded custody planning program for HIV-affected families. She recently completed a community-based assessment of HIV-affected families' social service needs. She has also been co-investigator for two federally funded projects with the Jane Addams College of Social Work: one that studied case planning for children entering state custody as infants and another that is a curriculum development and training grant for exemplary practice in kinship care. Dr. Mason's publications focus on women and HIV and the efforts of mothers with HIV/AIDS to develop permanent plans for their children.

John M. O'Donnell, Ph.D., is Assistant Professor in the School of Social Work at the University of Illinois at Urbana-Champaign and teaches courses in the School's child welfare specialization. He received his Ph.D. from the Jane Addams College of Social Work in 1995. Dr. O'Donnell was the project coordinator for the "Achieving Permanency for Children in Kinship Foster Care" project that was conducted from 1992 through 1995. Dr. O'Donnell has more than 20 years of experience in child welfare, including direct service and administration. One of his primary research interests is engaging members of the biological family in the lives of children in substitute care. This topic includes kinship foster care as well as working with non-custodial fathers and extended family to meet the ongoing needs of children in placement, including the need for permanency.

Olga Osby, Ph.D., is Assistant Professor at the Jane Addams College of Social Work, where she teaches courses on human behavior and the social environment, human diversity, and organizational theory. She received her doctorate from Howard University in Washington, D.C. As a social work practitioner, she concentrated on the needs of families in public housing and her dissertation research studied the world views of caregivers of children living in public housing developments. Her research focuses on educational deficits of children in poverty-stricken environments as well as the parenting strategies, survival techniques, and coping mechanisms of single mother households in violence-prone inner city communities. Dr. Osby has traveled to South Africa and Japan to lecture on the social and educational issues of minority families and children in the United States. In her role as co-investigator of a curriculum development and training project at the Jane Addams College of Social Work, Dr. Osby interviewed grandparents caring for children in state custody.

Donna D. Petras, Ph.D., is Assistant Professor at the Jane Addams College of Social Work, where she completed her Ph.D. in 1998. Dr. Petras has extensive experience in the field of child welfare as a caseworker, supervisor, administrator, teacher, consultant, and author. She served as Chief of the Office of Foster Care, Illinois Department of Children and Family Services, for eight years and is past president of the National Association of State Foster Care Managers. Dr. Petras has played a major role in the development of foster parent training curricula that have been testing nationally and internationally. Her current research interests include the needs of kinship caregivers and the role of the child welfare system in preparation and support of kin caring for children in state custody.